australia

at work

just managing?

australia

at work

just managing?

ACIRRT

australian centre for industrial relations research and training

PRENTICE HALL

Sydney New York London Toronto Tokyo
Singapore Mexico City Rio de Janeiro New Delhi

Acquisitions Editor: Paul Petrulis
Cover design: John Hewitt, Ruff Rider

Printed in Australia by Ligare Pty Ltd, Riverwood

1 2 3 4 5 03 02 01 00 99

ISBN 0 7248 0289 4

Prentice Hall of Australia Pty Ltd, *Sydney*
Prentice Hall, Inc., *Upper Saddle River, New Jersey*
Prentice Hall International, Inc., *London*
Prentice Hall Canada, Inc., *Toronto*
Prentice Hall Hispanoamericana, *SA, Mexico*
Prentice Hall of India Private Ltd, *New Delhi*
Prentice Hall of Japan, Inc., *Tokyo*
Simon & Schuster (Asia) Pte Ltd, *Singapore*
Editora Prentice Hall do Brasil Ltda, *Rio de Janeiro*

 PRENTICE HALL

A division of Simon & Schuster

Foreword

It is unusual to have an institution as an author of a book but our decision to do so is based on our commitment at ACIRRT to collaborative work. While a number of people have either written chapters or sections of the book, others have helped by tracking down references or sources, or by providing administrative support that allowed others to make their contribution. The input of former ACIRRT staff that have moved onto work in other organisations is also recognised. Despite the approach and individual contributions, an undertaking such as this needs a coordinator and 'driving force'. In this case much of the vision, intellectual input and inspiration was provided by Ian Watson, Research Fellow at ACIRRT. The book would never have appeared if not for Ian's devotion and commitment to the project. Other contributors to the book were Betty Arsovska, John Buchanan, Merilyn Bryce, Ron Callus, Shannon O'Keeffe, Kristin van Barneveld and Murray Woodman. To our other fellow workers at ACIRRT go our thanks for their support and role in generating many of the ideas and information that has been used in this book. Finally, we also benefited from valuable feedback and useful materials provided by supporters outside ACIRRT and we would like to thank them for their generosity.

Ron Callus
Director
Australian Centre for Industrial Relations Research and Training
(ACIRRT)

Contents

Foreword... v
Contents vii
Acronyms.. x
List of Figures and Tables... xii
About ACIRRT.. xv
Introduction.. xvii

Chapter 1: The human face of workplace change................................ 1
Labour maket change: Losers and winners...................................... 2
Workplace change and new job pressures 3
   Working longer.. 4
   Working harder.. 5
   The new forms of bargaining.. 6
Why has it all happened? 8

Chapter 2: What's behind the changes? 10
Australia's post-war social settlement... 12
The dismantling of the settlement 15
   Structural weaknesses... 16
   Historical ruptures 17
     A transformed labour market 17
   Shifting political alliances—Labor transformed........................... 20
   Shifting political alliances—the death of McEwenism................. 23
The failure of investment 27
The connection with workplace change... 31
Social protection and the market.. 33

Chapter 3: Bargaining for change 36
Changing the formal system 36
   Moving towards the decentralisation of industrial relations.......... 37
     Enterprise bargaining 37
     The enterprise agreement system 41
   The spread of enterprise bargaining 43
What's enterprise bargaining about?.. 44
   The expectations.. 44
   The issues dealt with in agreements 46
   Assessing agreements 48
   New forms of bargaining... 49
Decentralised formal bargaining—an assessment............................ 51
Other changes at the workplace 52

How has change occurred?... 54
The institutional legacy of reform 57
   Crisis in the unions 57
      Union membership 57
      Unions at the workplace 61
   The impact on the Industrial Relations Commission 63

Chapter 4: Wages: winners and losers.. 64
Wealth, income and earnings inequality—an overview.. 65
   The top of the labour market.. 67
   The bottom of the labour market 69
   Non-market incomes... 69
Earnings inequality—behind the aggregate view... 72
   The aggregate view... 72
   Dispersion within the earnings distribution 74
   Fragmentation in wage fixing institutions 75
   Occupational dispersions 81
A new classification scheme for earnings 84
Segmentation in the labour market... 86
The problem of low paying jobs 90
   A comparative view.. 91
   The implications of being a low paid workers.. 94

Chapter 5: Working longer and harder.. 101
Working longer 103
Working harder 106
The overworked Australian.. 109
   Why are people working longer and harder.. 109
   The industrial relations context... 112
Assessing the changes 115
Responding to workplace change... 117
Goodbye to the standard working week.. 119
Selling the changes in working time arrangements.. 122
   Enterprise agreements and family friendly measures 124

Chapter 6: Job security in a changing labour market... 126
Insecurity—the labour market story... 127
   Unemployment and retrenchments—the backdrop to insecurity................................... 127
      Risks of unemployment.. 129
      Retrenchments—the experience of losing work.. 132
      Regaining employment.. 133
   A changing labour market... 136
      The rise of part-time employment 136
      The growth in precarious employment: casuals and temporaries.................................. 139
   The rise of 'non-employees': outworkers, contractors and agency workers 142
Outsourcing—a closer look 145

Insecurity—the workplace story 147
    Corporate downsizing 147
    Restructuring of workplaces 150
    The links between job insecurity and workplace change—workers' perceptions 153

Chapter 7: Managing work in the future: new directions for policy **156**
The argument in brief 156
How can we respond to these developments? 157
    The globalisation dilemma 157
    Putting workplace 'reform' in context 160
    Getting the macro policy right 161
        Dealing with unemployment 161
        Industry policy 163
        Rethinking the role of fairness 164
A new agenda for policy at work 165
    The providers of labour: from employees to workers 167
    Providers of jobs and employment benefits: augmenting the
        enterprise with portability and pooling arrangements 168
    The framework: from awards and ad hoc income support to
        integration of industrial and social security rights over the life cycle 169
    Wages: revamping the foundations for a new era 173
    Hours: augmenting the full-timer model with work scheduling rights 174
    Employment security: more than a matter of working life policy alone 175
Conclusion 176

References **179**

Index **197**

Acronyms

AA	Affirmative Action
ABB	Asea Brown Boveri
ABS	Australian Bureau of Statistics
ACAC	Australian Conciliation and Arbitration Commission (now called the AIRC)
ACCI	Australian Chamber of Commerce and Industry
ACIRRT	Australian Centre for Industrial Relations Research and Training
ACOSS	Australian Council of Social Services
ACTU	Australian Council of Trade Unions
ADAM	Agreements Data-base And Monitor
AGPS	Australian Government Publishing Service
AIRC	Australian Industrial Relations Commission
AMES	Adult Migrant Education Service
AMWU	Australian Manufacturing Workers Union
ANZSIC	Australian and New Zealand Standard Industrial Classification[1]
APEC	Asia-Pacific Economic Conference
ASCO	Australian Standard Classification of Occupations[2]
ASIC	Australian Standard Industrial Classification[1]
AWA	Australian Workplace Agreement
AWE	Average Weekly Earnings
AWIRS	Australian Workplace Industrial Relations Survey
AWOTE	Average Weekly Ordinary Time Earnings
BCA	Business Council of Australia
BRW	Business Review Weekly
CCH	Commercial Clearing House
CFMEU	Construction, Forestry, Mining and Energy Workers Union
C-O	Consenting-overworked
CPI	Consumer Price Index
CRA	Conzinc Rio Tinto Australia
CSIRO	Commonwealth Scientific and Industrial Research Organisation
DIR	Department of Industrial Relations
DITAC	Department of Industry, Technology and Commerce
DWRSB	Department of Workplace Relations and Small Business
EAC	Employee Assistance Centre
EEO	Equal Employment Opportunity
EFA	Enterprise Flexibility Agreement
EFT	Electronic Funds Transfer
ETM	Elaborately Transformed Manufactures

G8	Group of eight leading industrialised economies— US, UK, Germany, France, Italy, Canada, Japan and Russia
GATT	General Agreement on Tariffs and Trade
GDP	Gross Domestic Product
GMI	Guaranteed Minimum Income
ILO	International Labour Organisation
IR	Industrial Relations
IRA	Industrial Relations Act
LHMWU	Liquor, Hospitality and Miscellaneous Workers' Union
MAC	Motor Assembly Company
MTIA	Metal Trades Industry Association
NAFTA	North American Free Trade Agreement
NESB	Non-English Speaking Background
NLCC	National Labour Consultative Committee
OEA	Office of the Employment Advocate
OECD	Organisation of Economic Cooperation and Development
OHS	Occupational Health and Safety
PAYE	Paye As You Earn
R&D	Research and Development
REP	Restructuring and Efficiency Principle
SEP	Structural Efficiency Principle
SPRC	Social Policy Research Centre
TA	Trades Assistant
TINA	'There is no alternative'
WTO	World Trade Organisation

1   The classification system used for defining industries reported in ABS publications changed in 1993. Between 1983 and 1993 ABS data was reported on the basis of ASIC categories. Since 1994 ANZIC codes have been in use. Strictly speaking industry data reported using the two frameworks is not directly comparable for many industries. This has limited our capacity to consider some industry trends over the entire period considered in this book. For example, some of the data on industry trends in casualisation ends in the early 1990s for this reason. Where-ever possible we refer readers to more recent, though not necessarily directly comparable, information in other publications. For details on how the ASIC and ANZSIC categories align see ABS and NZ Department of Statistics, *Australian and New Zealand Standard Industrial Classification*, [First Edition], ABS Cat No 1292.0/NZ Cat. no. 19 005 0092, 1993 pp. 253–298.

2   The original ASCO was introduced in 1986. A second edition was released in 1996 and made substantial changes to the way in which occupations were classified in ABS publications. Because of this it is important to note that even though the same terms (eg professionals, trades workers) are used in the two editions data reported on the basis of the different edition is not comparable. This severely limits the ability to analyse occupational change. This constraint has meant that some of our consideration of occupational issues ends in the mid 1990s or involves only consideration of issues in the later 1990s. For details on how the old ASCO codes align with the new see ABS and Department of Employment, Education, Training and Youth Affairs, *Australian Standard Classification of Occupations*, Second Edition, Cat. no. 1220.0, 1997, pp. 593–668.

List of figures

2.1	Unemployment rate, 1945–96	18
2.2	Relative changes in Australian commodity exports, 1946–85	25
2.3	Share of manufacturing value added by industry subdivision, 1968–69 and 1989–90	29
3.1	Workplace changes introduced since the 1987 Restructuring and Efficiency Principle, 1989	39
3.2	Common provisions in enterprise agreements, 1994–95 to 1996–97	45
3.3	Non-union bargaining effect in hours, 1997	50
3.4	Non-union bargaining effect in wages by industry, 1997	50
3.5	Types or organisational change that happened at the workplace in the last two years prior to the survey, by sector, 1995	53
3.6	Involvement in decision-making by workers likely to be affected by change, by type of change, mid-1990s	55
3.7	Level of workers' influence over decisions which affected them, by occupation, 1995	56
3.8	Trade union membership by industry, 1990 and 1996	59
3.9	Industrial disputes, 1970–97	60
3.10	Union and delegate presence at the workplace, 1990–95	62
4.1	Wages and profits as components of GDP, 1976–97	73
4.2	Stagnation in earnings, 1984–97	73
4.3	Trends in earnings dispersion in the bottom half of the earnings distribution, 1983–95	77
4.4	Trends in earnings dispersion in the top half of the earnings dispersion, 1983–95	75
4.5	Average annual wage increases in registered enterprise agreements and award wages	78
4.6	Relative changes in salaries and wages, 1984–96	78
4.7	Male workers below benchmarks, selected occupations, 1981 and 1991	81
4.8	Female workers below benchmarks, selected occupations, 1981 and 1991	83
4.9	Growth in self-employment and wage and salary earners 1978–98	84
4.10	Characteristics of the bottom quintile of jobs in the labour market, Australia 1995	88
4.11	Characteristics of the top quintile of jobs in the labour market, Australia 1995	89
4.12	Employment as a proportion of the population related to wage dispersion	91
4.13	Incidence of low-paid employment by industry by country	92
4.14	Real wage growth over the last 10 years for low-, median- and high-paid workers, selected OECD countries	94
4.15	Consumption patterns for 'Harvester Households' (buying their own homes) by level of income, 1988–89	96

5.1	The current distribution of working time: proportions of the labour force working overtime, standard hours, part-time and who are unemployed, 1995	102
5.2	Hours worked for full-time workers, 1978–97	103
5.3	Occupation by hours worked, 1993	104
5.4	Industry by hours worked, 1993	105
5.5	How the overworked have responded to workplace change	118
6.1	Job security and unemployment, 1978–97	128
6.2	Unemployment rate and the incidence of long-term unemployment, 1978–97	129
6.3	Retrenchments and lay-offs, 1986–97	130
6.4	Employment growth, 1978–98	137
6.5	Casual density by industry divisions, 1984 and 1993	139
6.6	Incidence of temporary employment, 1983 and 1994	140
6.7	Main reason for workforce reductions in the year prior to the survey, 1990 and 1995	148

List of tables

3.1	Basis of enterprise agreement pay rises	47
3.2	Some issues rarely included in enterprise agreements	48
3.3	Managers' assessment of effect of agreement, 1995	49
3.4	Reasons workers gave for why they were not given a fair say about workplace change, 1995	57
3.5	Trade union density, 1976–96	58
3.6	Percentage of union delegates reporting how skilled they considered themselves in the negotiation of a workplace or enterprise agreement, 1995	62
4.1	Top Ten BRW Rich List, Australia 1983 and 1998	66
4.2	Average salary packages for computer professionals and managers, Australia 1998	68
4.3	Typical contractor rates for computer professionals, 1998	68
4.4	Mechanisms for regulating wages in 1996	77
4.5	Relative movements in earnings for tradepersons and labourers employed in manufacturing, 1986–95	80
4.6	Different approaches to determining employment-based earnings classified according to formal arrangements and relative level of earnings	85
4.7	Incidence of low-paid employment by occupation, age and sex	93
4.8	Financial difficulties experienced by childcare workers during the last year, Australian Capital Territory 1996	99

5.1   Workers' views of changes related to work intensification in the last 12
            months, 1995   106
5.2   Occupational background of the overworked   116
5.3   Industry location of the overworked   117
5.4   Family-friendly provisions in agreements   125
6.1   Job losses and gains by industry, Australia 1988–98   131
6.2   The distinctiveness of casuals in the workplace, Australia 1995   141
6.3   Corporate downsizing, 1990–95   149
6.4   Main factors associated with job insecurity   153
7.1   Redefining the people involved in working life: a comparison between
            the 'classical wage earner' model and the 'working life' model   166
7.2   Rethinking priorities concerning wages, hours and employment
            security: current and 'working life' policy approaches compared   172

About ACIRRT

The Australian Centre for Industrial Relations Research and Training is based at the University of Sydney. ACIRRT is an independent, multi-disciplinary based organisation committed to making a difference to the Australian workplace through research, training and by sharing its ideas and findings with others. It was established in 1989 as an Australian Research Council Key Centre. It currently has a staff of 19 researchers, trainers and administrators.

The work of the Centre focuses on workplace structures and practices. It pays special attention to analysing workplace experiences in the context of wider labour market and policy developments.

There are a number of distinctive features about our centre. These can be summarised as follows.

(a) We are self-financing and provide services to a diverse range of clients.
ACIRRT provides a wide range of research, information, education and training services on a fee for service basis. We have worked hard to maintain the respect of all parties in industrial relations. To date our clients have been as diverse as the union covering coal miners (ie CFMEU) and the mining company, Rio Tinto. They also include the Reserve Bank of Australia and the Church of England's Brotherhood of St Laurence. We work for governments of all persuasions, State and Federal. We also have overseas clients including the International Labour Organisation (ILO) and Telekom Indonesia.

(b) We combine a concern with analytical rigour with a commitment to maintaining relevance to understanding practical problems.
From our experience practice throws up just as many, if not more interesting, problems for investigation as academic debate. In understanding and suggesting responses to practical problems we use multiple research methods including sample surveys, focus groups and indepth interviews as well as the standard procedures for desk based research. The hallmark of our approach is the workplace and organisational case study that combines these different methods. We also maintain Australia's most comprehensive data base on enterprise agreements - the Agreements Database And Monitor (ADAM). This is a resource for both researchers and practitioners interested in what's happening in enterprise agreements.

(c) Our multi-method approach is based on teamwork
Over the years we have refined our multi-method approach through conducting nearly all our research on a teamwork basis. As contract researchers we find this not only helps meet tight deadlines - it also helps ensure the strengths of different research methods interact in generating new understandings about key workplace and labour market issues.

(d) We believe the diffusion of ideas is just as important as their generation
Too often the findings of research are confined to a small audience of scholars. We publicise the findings of our research through a variety of mechanisms: free seminars, a twice yearly newsletter, commercial conferences, a working paper series and public presentations to groups and organisations. Our education and training activities drawing heavily on our research. Our publication program includes monographs, working papers and a quarterly update on developments in enterprise agreements - the *ADAM Report*. Our most recent service is a quarterly *Industrial Relations Intelligence Report*, produced jointly with Newsletter Information Services - the publishers of *Workforce*.

(e) We foster debate on workplace and labour market issues
New ideas are hard to come by. To help generate them we actively promote critique and debate. Our conferences are forums for interaction between different currents in the debate about work. In our secondment/sponsored research program we deliberately involve people from diverse backgrounds, especially from amongst thoughtful practitioners and policy makers.

How to get in touch with ACIRRT

There are a number of ways to get in touch with ACIRRT:

- ❑ visit our Web site;
- ❑ add your name to our mailing list to our twice yearly newsletter;
- ❑ attend our conferences and seminars;
- ❑ commission a special report or briefing;
- ❑ get us to help your organisation investigate a problem about which you need new insights;
- ❑ subscribe to our working papers and/or quarterly briefing services (ie *ADAM Report* and *Industrial Relations Intelligence Report*);
- ❑ get your organisation to take out a 'Corporate Sponsorship Package'. These can be tailored to your needs to ensure you get access to a range of ACIRRT services as a discounted price.

Contact Details

Address:
    ACIRRT
    Institute Building (H03)
    University of Sydney, NSW, 2006.

Phone: (02) 9351 5626
Fax: (02) 9351 5615

Email: acirrt@econ.usyd.edu.au
Web site: http://www.econ.usyd.edu.au/acirrt/

Introduction

Anyone who has experienced paid work in Australia over the past fifteen years will have noticed dramatic changes have occurred in the organisations where they have been working. This book examines some of these changes and the impact that they are having on peoples' lives. We are interested in explaining why these changes occurred, how they came about and what their consequences have been. In the final chapter we outline our ideas on how things could be managed better in the future.

In exploring these issues we have drawn on nearly ten years of commissioned research undertaken by ACIRRT. ACIRRT (pronounced ay-sert) is an acronym for the Australian Centre for Industrial Relations Research and Training. The Centre is based at the University of Sydney, and earns its way in the world largely through contract research and training. Over the last ten years our research has been far reaching and has dealt with issues like wages, shift work, bargaining arrangements and enterprise agreements, part-time work, new training arrangements, migrants in the labour market, long-term unemployment, mature age workers, the youth labour market, and redundancy practices. Our work has taken us into a range of organisations in industries such as manufacturing, finance, hospitality, construction, mining, public administration and retailing. Throughout this book we draw on this research to illuminate what is happening in the Australian economy and in workplaces. It's important to appreciate that many of the changes we examine have been widespread: there are few workplaces where working arrangements have not been dramatically altered over the last decade and a half.

ACIRRT's approach in making sense of workplace change draws on the experiences and training of researchers with backgrounds in economics, sociology, law, history, education and industrial relations. This multi-disciplinary approach enables us to examine complex phenomena without being locked into a single disciplinary mind-set and the assumptions which go with it. Similarly, many of the materials and data presented in this book have been gathered using a range of research methodologies: surveys, focus groups discussions, in-depth interviews and case studies of organisations and industries. One of our great assets is a solid collection of independent data sets, many of them produced by the Australian Bureau of Statistics (the ABS). In this book we have also made extensive use of the Australian Workplace Industrial Relations Surveys (AWIRS) carried out in 1990 and 1995. Finally, we have been fortunate in drawing on our own extensive database of registered enterprise agreements, known as ADAM (Agreement Database and Monitor).

It's obvious that any book which examines social and economic change will give more attention to some issues and ignore others. The choices will depend in part on the interests of the authors and the framework they use. In our case, we have focused on the period since 1983. We've done this because during these years Australia underwent a major re-regulation of working practices and the arrangements that go with them. The institutions which had traditionally made the rules for regulating workplaces underwent major changes and the legislation which dealt with bargaining between management and workers was also dramatically overhauled. We call this period of change *re-regulation*, not *de-regulation* (Buchanan and Callus 1993). Even at the end of the 1990s, there are just as many rules regulating work as there have always been. What has changed is that the interests and the institutions which had traditionally played a dominant role in making the rules have been sidelined or significantly marginalised.

The so-called 'external' third parties to the management-worker relationship—trade unions and industrial tribunals—have seen their role and influence change over the last decade. Unions have emerged from this period of enterprise level bargaining in a weaker position than they were before. The Federal industrial tribunal—the Australian Industrial Relations Commission—has had its interventionist wings severely clipped, and a rival institution established to oversee the new workplace contracts. Management, on the other hand, has seen its decision-making power in the workplace grow considerably. Most of the workplace changes which have taken place have been at the behest of management: their agenda and their interests have led the way. The new 'rules' at work are largely their rules.

In this book we focus on this shifting power relationship as it has influenced workplace outcomes. We are interested in how the tussle over rule making powers has affected the industrial landscape and the lives of the workforce. In so doing we deliberately use the term 'industrial relations'. Some people now view the term as dated or unfashionable. They think 'industrial relations' reflects a narrow institutionalised view of the relationships that arise out of work and that it places an undue emphasis on the bargaining that takes place between management and unions. We see things differently. At its heart, industrial relations has always been about the 'contested terrain' (Edwards 1979) of working conditions: how much people are paid for their labour, how much and how hard people should work, and the security of their employment. While these are also the core industrial issues over which unions and management have always bargained, they are at the heart of the work relationship between management and all its workers, either as individuals or collectives. How these core matters are determined and the outcomes which flow from this are the central themes of this book.

In concentrating on earnings, hours and job security and the way these are determined we have made the decision not to cover the field of industrial relations exhaustively. There are certainly other important industrial relations issues, such as occupational health and safety, equal employment opportunity, training, best practice, recruitment, strategic management, job design, worker participation or empowerment. We acknowledge the importance of these issues but our decision to concentrate on the 'core' has been based on the constraints of book-length, the desire not to deal superficially with issues, and the fact that many of these issues have received considerable attention by researchers, policy makers and practitioners during the period under study. In a similar vein we have also chosen not to deal with particular groups of workers as separate themes. Throughout the book we focus on the impact of workplace change on women, on migrants, on mature age workers and on the blue-collar workforce; and concerns with equity are at the forefront of our minds. But our book is a thematic study in which the central argument requires us to focus on the historical context, the bargaining process, and the core issues of earnings, hours and job security.

We emphasise these core issues because they play such a central role in people's working lives and feature prominently in the judgments they make about the quality of those lives. While people may choose to trade away some aspects of their working lives for other 'benefits', increasingly people are being asked to compromise more and more of the central aspects of their work life for objectives which are never met. The sacrifices are often significant but the rewards—if they come—are invariably unfairly distributed. Organisations have generally become more efficient and competitive, but amongst the workforce there are very definite winners and losers emerging. For many workers the outcomes of a decade of workplace change have not been fair ones. The notion of fairness, however much it may appear to be 'value laden' or imprecise, lies at the ethical heart of industrial relations. This book seeks to find alternative ways to ensure that fairness in outcomes ranks just as highly as efficiency when it comes to understanding and identifying new approaches to workplace change.

CHAPTER 1

The human face of workplace change

Over the last two decades profound changes have occurred to working life in Australia. Wherever you look—the labour market, the workplace, trade unions or the industrial relations system—changes have been rapid and dramatic. Most people caught up in this change, ordinary people in shops, offices and factories, have carried the costs of change: things like longer hours of work and greater stress, more job insecurity, and stagnant or reduced earnings. Some people have done quite well. Those workers with the right skills or those in favourable labour market niches have ridden the waves of change and won for themselves better wages and conditions. They have, however, been in the minority.

The biggest losers without doubt have been unemployed people. After a quarter of a century of full employment, Australia entered an era of chronic unemployment from the late 1970s onwards. For less skilled workers the labour market became a minefield, as they found themselves scrambling for fewer and fewer job opportunities. The full-time labour market for teenagers collapsed in the 1980s and seems unlikely to revive. There was a time when older male manual workers could look forward to secure employment until their retirement, but after two major recessions, they have swelled the ranks of the long-term unemployed. More generally, blue-collar workers—both men and women—have been the major casualties of rapid economic change in Australia.

The other side of the coin to job shedding in blue-collar occupations has been a dramatic growth in service occupations, but the jobs here have been overwhelmingly part-time or casual. Consequently, the new jobs do not make up for those well-paid full-time jobs which have been lost. Nor do the same people always fit into both kinds of jobs. Older men and women, often from migrant backgrounds, have lost the full-time jobs, while middle-aged women and school students have found new opportunities in the mushrooming part-time job market.

How have these changes affected ordinary workers? What has been their experience of rapid change? Who carries the costs of workplace change? The following sections give a flavour of how workers, in their own words, have experienced recent changes. These experiences have largely been drawn from material collected by ACIRRT and span industries as diverse as coal mining, manufacturing, health, finance and hospitality. Occasionally we supplement these comments with material drawn from other sources. Together they shed light on what it's like to be caught up in workplace change in Australia today.

LABOUR MARKET CHANGE: LOSERS AND WINNERS

There's two measures of labour market success: one is having a job—particularly a secure job—and the other is earning a reasonable income. Over the last 20 years significant changes have occurred in both these areas. Unemployment and job insecurity exemplify the whirlpool of economic change engulfing the workforce, particularly in working-class communities. At the same time, income inequality has continued to grow, particularly during the 1990s. We now face the prospect of 'two nations' emerging within the labour market: an affluent elite for whom globalisation and technological change promise great rewards; and a low-paid service class whose future can be glimpsed in the image of America's working poor.

One way of measuring just how bad unemployment has become during the last quarter century is to look at the fate of school leavers. For those who ventured into the labour market in the 1980s or 1990s, job prospects were pretty grim:

> When I first left school I did a receptionist diploma. It was a ten weeks' course ... Then I was unemployed for ages, over a year. I thought: What is happening? I have a diploma and there is nothing ... Being out of work really upsets you. You sort of start thinking that there's something wrong with you because you can't get a job. One day I decided I would go out and go to every shop and ask them for a job. It took a lot to do that ... I got all dressed up and went out. I kept asking people and they kept saying, 'No, I'm sorry we have enough staff.' *Young school leaver.* (Turner 1983, pp. 231–2)

By way of contrast, here are the recollections of a male worker who left school in the 1950s:

> I applied for this job, you know, I rang up for it and said I'd be there at a certain time. But I didn't turn up. I sort of didn't know what I wanted to do, you know. There was a fellow that used to be at school ... he was years ahead of me ... and he happened to work at this place and he called down. He used to play Aussie Rules football ... and there's a Crown Hotel near us, he used to go there for a drink. It was right near my place so they must have said, 'This kid lives at 23 Smith Street,' where I lived, 'drop in and see him.'
>
> I mean, that's how the jobs were, they chased me, you know. I didn't have to line up and get picked out of one of 200. They chased me after I didn't turn up ... So anyway, I come in, didn't I. *Factory worker.*

The labour market has never treated everyone the same. Indeed, much of Australia's income inequality springs from how the labour market works, the way it parcels out the better paid jobs to some people, and the lower paid jobs to others. When it comes to unemployment, this differential treatment is particularly stark. For older manual workers, and for migrants, being retrenched can lead to quite futile experiences in the labour market:

> I've had interviews about jobs since the sawmill closed but they've got that many younger people with families out of work that they're selecting them before the older people that haven't got a family. As soon as I tell them I'm 50 or 51 years old, 'I'm sorry, there's 30 or 40 ahead of you'. And that's just the way it goes. *Retrenched North Coast timber worker.*
>
> Now I sit at home with my family, my kids. For man, this very hard to sit at home. If I have a full-time job, I have a better life, better everything. I go around every day, me and my wife, but nothing. No jobs here. *Retrenched migrant steelworker, Wollongong.*

As well as labour market 'losers', the last few decades have also seen some 'winners' emerge, particularly women wanting to work part-time and young, highly skilled, flexible workers. Sometimes known as 'gold-collar workers' this latter group of workers has benefited considerably from technological change and economic deregulation. Often found at the cutting edge of computer technology in banking or in publishing, 'gold collar workers' have found high paying jobs which stimulate and challenge them. They often spend extremely long hours at their job, but because they are young, ambitious and very well paid, this kind of commitment is taken for granted. Their loyalty, however, is owed less to their employer than it is to their careers. As a result they are highly mobile, lured by new jobs which offer technical challenges or opportunities for self-development.

The other group of winners spend less hours at work than the average. They are predominantly middle-aged women returning to the workforce after several years of child rearing. The massive growth of part-time work which has opened this avenue for their return to work is something of a mixed blessing for the economy as a whole because the pay and conditions of many part-time jobs are much worse than the full-time jobs which are disappearing elsewhere. For women returning to the workforce, the job market of the 1980s and 1990s has been a time of 'carrot and stick'. The rapid growth of part-time work in service industries has given them more job opportunities than ever before, but stagnant real wages have made the need for a family's second income more urgent. Several focus group informants summed up what part-time work offered them:

> I'd just had a baby and I didn't want to go back full-time, I wanted to spend the time with the kids. That was the best solution, you know, start at 8.30, work until one o'clock and then I had the rest of the day to myself. Take the kids to the park. *Part-time administrative assistant.*

> For eight years I worked from eight to six o'clock and then Friday I knew ... I sat in the same traffic jams ... And now ... I'll have a day off here and a day off there. And if something does come up, I just swap a shift with one of my workmates. *Part-time tourist resort waitress.*

However, part-time work did not always resolve the dilemma of the 'double shift'. Women part-time workers, like their full-time colleagues, still faced the juggling act of working life and family life. Again, a focus group informant:

> If you'd have to do a split shift ... then you had to be back sometimes at six. I used to get up early in the morning, and get all the vegetables ready and put them all in the fridge and then drag them out when I got home. Stick everything in the oven. And in that time between 3.30 and six, when you had to get back to work, you had to have a shower, and you'd have to make sure that you had all the kid's uniforms ironed, ready for the next day. But you survived. Somehow, you were able to organise your day. *Supervisor, leagues club.*

WORKPLACE CHANGE AND NEW JOB PRESSURES

In the 1990s stress appears to have become intimately linked with work. If you are unemployed, then labour market experiences like job searching, undertaking training schemes, and receiving knock-backs can cause immense stress. If you are either under-employed, working casually or working reluctantly part-time, then worrying about living on a low income can produce chronic stress. Finally, even if you're in a 'normal' job, day-to-day stress is never far away. There is the insecurity about whether you will keep your job, the stress that comes from longer hours or from working harder.

These new pressures in the workplace seem to be driven by two main forces: an attempt by organisations to drive their costs down and an attempt by managers to consolidate their power in decision making. The long-term results of these pressures are quite profound. They are leading to a situation where people are increasingly treated as 'human resources'—that is, 'commodities' in the marketplace—rather than as human beings interacting with one another. As one worker phrased it: 'This mob are playing with our lives—we are referred to as human resources—not as workers—this alone is demeaning'.

The second long-term outcome of workplace change is that collective forms of working life—such as being in a union, working cooperatively, having common conditions and entitlements—are being eroded and a more individualistic style of workplace is emerging. Indeed, in many respects, we are witnessing the 'managerialisation' of the workforce, a situation where ordinary workers are expected to behave like managers: to work long unpaid hours, to negotiate salary 'packages', to plan their careers, and to become very competitive with other 'managers'.

How have these changes been experienced? How do people make sense of these new pressures at work? In the following discussion we draw on unpublished focus group materials from a wide range of occupations and industries, as well as some published materials from other authors who have been exploring the world of work.

Working longer

The most obvious way in which cost-cutting has had an impact on the workforce is through people having to work longer hours. As one finance sector worker commented:

> The general manager sets the budget to cut costs and this flows down: if the work is not being done within the available hours then the staff get pressured and are made to feel guilty for not coming in. *Finance sector worker.*

Traditionally, blue-collar workers have always been paid for their overtime and this often puts a ceiling on just how much extra time managers could demand. However, for some groups of workers, this protection is missing. Apprentices, for example, have always been vulnerable: 'The owner felt that he was entitled to make me work a great deal of overtime without paying me'. Increasingly, though, professionals have been exposed to the open-ended time demands because their work is task based:

> With professional hours, there are minimal costs and management will put the personal pressure on to make you work OT for free … Professional hours are focussed on the task rather than the time worked. If focussing on the task opens the way for exploitation then the focus on the task is the problem. *Finance sector worker.*

The reason why white-collar workers are vulnerable to this lengthening of hours is that collective forms of working have always been much weaker in office jobs. Concern about careers fosters individualism and this, in turn, leaves people open to the competitive pressures of being seen to work longer. Management is very adroit at exploiting these kinds of pressures, and so the working week begins to regularly encroach on normal family time:

> Everyone is watching to see when you leave and you can't possibly leave at 6 or 7 (pm) … it is outrageous. Then, it's how early can you get in? *Focus group member.*

The boss told me to take the laptop home but that would just mean more hours. The difficulty is that I am not in the position to refuse the extra work. *Finance sector worker.*

This expansion of standard hours has not been restricted to the private sector. With budget cuts endemic in the public sector, the same kinds of pressures have been applied to nurses, teachers and other public servants. For many workers in blue-collar and pink-collar jobs, the issue around hours has involved longer shifts, such as 12 hour shifts replacing 8 hour shifts. Family life and recreational time have been casualties of this change:

> You don't know whether you're coming or going. You go to work in the dark, you get home in the dark, you just can't do the simple things any more. You get up at 4.30am and you get home at 6.45pm, then you have tea, bath the kids and a little play with the kids, put them to bed and wash up. A talk to the wife, then to bed. You just get nothing else done. *Coal miner.*

For part-time workers, the 'problem of hours' can be shorter shifts, not longer ones. As management tries to squeeze every last drop of productivity out of its workforce, any apparent 'dead time' is eliminated. This is done much more easily with part-timers, whose hours are already variable, than it is with full-timers, whose expectation of a standard day protects them from this whittling-away process.

> The employer is trying to get us on this four hour shift where we don't have a meal and they can send us home after four hours if we're not busy. That's what they want because we're on a six and a half hour shift and no less. And they want to be able to bring us in for two hours here, when it's busy over lunch or whatever, or four hours, and then send you home. And I think they want to up the wage I think $2 an hour on that basis, which is part of this Enterprise Bargaining. But that wouldn't compensate us for losing two hours ... It's not worthwhile going because you might only be there for two to three hours but you might have travelled for an hour to get there. *Part-time waitress, racecourse restaurant.*

This changing pattern of working hours is testimony to a major shift in the power relations of the workplace. Management has been able to either coerce or seduce its workforce to accept these changes because job insecurity is so extreme and the labour market has become so competitive. In earlier decades, when the labour market favoured workers, a very different power relationship prevailed:

> You give the boss what is his due, the boss has to give you your due. I fulfilled my obligations first, never went after money or overtime. When I saw they needed weekend labour I'd say, 'Seeing that you're in strife, I'll give you a day of overtime'. They never gave *me* overtime, I gave it to *them*! *Toolmaker.* (Lowenstein 1997, p. 41)

Compare this with the power relations of the 1990s:

> I don't think we have as much choice now ... the competition is very fierce ... and if you don't perform, you can forget about it ... there's a million waiting for your job. *Focus group member.*

Working harder

As well as longer hours, the other way in which cost-cutting surfaces is through people having to work harder, often called 'work intensification'. Working 'flat out' has often been a feature of some blue-collar industries, where the timetable for shipping out products can be critical: 'When there are trains to be loaded we work long hours, varied hours, weekend work and have no break until the shipment is finished'. (*Coal miner*).

Increasingly, though, this kind of pressure has crept into more and more jobs simply because individual workloads have spiralled upwards:

> I have huge workloads, no time off in lieu, no tea breaks, no adequate training. Some weeks I don't even have time to think and have suffered from anxiety and stress. I actually had to take time off and sought counselling and medication. People never take a day off in lieu. *Finance sector worker.*

The link with cost-cutting is evident for all to see:

> You find that a lot of companies, especially bigger companies are cutting on staff and contractors but the work load is not diminishing, it may even be increasing ... my company ... has gone from about 900 over the last ten years down to about 350 now and sales are supposed to be higher this year than ever so you can just imagine what we are all doing ... *Focus group member.*

The new forms of bargaining

Management has been able to consolidate its power because of changes in the labour market, as well as changes in the industrial relations system. Organisational downsizing, against a backdrop of chronically high unemployment, has fostered extreme job insecurity. This in turn has given management much greater bargaining power.

> Job security is a thing of the past ... that term has been thrown away. *Focus group member.*

> We are getting too old for the market, they don't want us. *Focus group member.*

The new battalions of labour, the part-time and casual workers, find themselves in weak bargaining positions. This is partly because they are in over-supply in the labour market, due to part-time work being so attractive to workers with family or other commitments. It is also because those very commitments can weaken their flexibility in negotiating, and place them on the back foot. As one line manager observed:

> The part-timers came to us and said, 'This rostering is really awful. It's difficult for us. Can we sit down, and, sort of, work around what your needs are and what our needs are so that we can work something out?' And we said, 'Yes, sure. We certainly understand your point, with children and that type of thing. But you've got to understand ours'.

For most workers, enterprise bargaining has been experienced as a weakening in the worker's bargaining position, as a process of trading away conditions for little in return.

> Enterprise bargaining, that is a big joke because you have to keep on producing more ... with enterprise bargaining, you are losing more than you are gaining because you are giving things away ... *Focus group member.*

Similarly, the Accord between the trade union movement and the Labor Government has also been experienced as a defeat, as a failure for workers:

> With the various series of Accords we've had, they (the unions) have virtually done themselves out of a job because they have agreed to economic restructuring ... workers feel that they have been abandoned by the unions as well as by management ... *Focus group member.*

One of the costs to the union movement of the Accord was that their role in fostering wage moderation helped discredit unions in the workplace:

> We wanted to go for a wage rise and they were discouraging us ... a couple of the lads from the factory stood up and said (to the union) 'Go to buggery, we want this!', so we pushed it through and we got the wage rise, but this guy was trying to discourage us.

Unions were also discredited when they assisted management with workplace restructuring. Technological change, job cuts and new workplace ideologies were all lined up against ordinary workers, and looking to the union for help proved a futile hope for many. With a weakened position within the workplace, unions found themselves in the dilemma of losing their members, which in turn further weakened their bargaining power at the workplace level.

> Unions are a toothless tiger ... they've lost a lot of their clout ... they are no longer a force to be reckoned with because there are not enough union members in any particular place. *Focus group member.*

Unions have been slow to adjust to the enormity of labour market change. Geared to the model of the male full-time worker, they have failed to appreciate the possibilities opened up by the advent of large-scale part-time service work. So their loss of full-time members in the blue-collar industries has not been offset by gains in part-time service workers.

> There is no career paths for part-time workers. They are very much an underclass. And they are also viewed as that culturally by full-timers. There's also been, for the union, an element of the old-fashioned working class full employment argument. *Union delegate.*

Changes in the industrial relations system have enabled management to exploit the problems in trade unionism and to detach workers from collective forms of bargaining in favour of more individualistic arrangements. Individual contracts, for example, have become increasingly common. However, the bargaining position of a worker, as an individual, can be a highly variable thing. Management's power to renew contracts can be a potent device for increasing work intensification:

> Basically, you are on a contract and if you want it, you have to work your butt off to renew your contract ... it's very common ... it's happening even in the government now ... they have to go for their own jobs and renew their contract every 12 months. *Focus group member.*

Moving ordinary workers onto 'salaried staff' has become a favourite device amongst large mining corporations in attempting to weaken trade unions. Even for small firms in the service sector, firms not bothered by trade unions, this device can be used to increase work intensification. Turning part-time supervisors into full-time 'managers' can pay big dividends for management, as one woman working at a tourist resort discovered:

> They push that [full-time] on you fairly quickly once you become a supervisor ... they push you to go on salary so they can pay you for 40 hours and you can do 90 ... they expected me to take on all these extra responsibilities of cashier/supervisor. They expected me to train people, in my own time. To write training manuals. *Tourist resort worker.*

WHY HAS IT ALL HAPPENED?

What's behind the changes we've outlined above? Why have cost-cutting and efforts to increase management power come to the fore over the last twenty years? After all, technology has made working life easier than ever before. Why aren't workers basking in the glow of a century of material progress?

We deal with these questions more fully in the next chapter, but we will end this chapter now with an overview of the issues involved. In particular, we wish to stress that there is no inevitability about workplace change and the direction it has taken. These changes reflect specific choices made by people in power, grappling with problems they've defined in a particular way. Define the problems differently and other choices can be made. With other choices, come other consequences.

The main force behind workplace change has been neo-liberalism, a term we use throughout the book to refer to the advocates of market-driven solutions to economic and social problems. In the next chapter we chart the 'neo-liberal project', which is a shorthand way of referring to a steady accretion of power and influence by these advocates of free market solutions, primarily in business, universities, the media and government bureaucracies. 'Globalisation' is their favourite buzzword. Australia, we are told by the neo-liberals, must become internationally competitive. Our economy is bloated with unproductive sectors which must be downsized. We are burdened with too much government, and its influence must be curtailed. When it comes to the workplace, we are told by the neo-liberals, an 'Industrial Relations Club' has captured industrial relations and 'workplace reform' is hampered by constant third party interventions, mainly trade unions and industrial tribunals. Unemployment remains a problem, the neo-liberals argue, because wages are too high to allow the labour market to 'clear'.

Faced with all these problems, and with the kinds of discontent evident in the pages above, the neo-liberal response is to call for more of the same. Workforce 'reform' has not gone far enough. Managers have still not won enough power to allow them to govern. Unions still have too much power. Individualism in the workplace is hampered by outmoded collective institutions, things like awards and collective agreements. So runs the list of neo-liberal complaints.

The perspective which ACIRRT brings to these issues is a very different one. We don't see increased individualism, stronger market forces, increased competition or the dismantling of the state as solutions to problems. We see them as creating new kinds of problems, things like greater material inequality, a divided nation, and greed and futility running unchecked.

Individuality is important, of course, but individuals exist within communities and they have obligations to others beyond themselves. Often those obligations require that people act collectively, and that they establish institutions which foster collectivity and other social values such as fairness, common wellbeing and security. When these institutions begin to hamper the economic activity of the nation, they have to be examined and judgments made about their continuing relevance. But such a process of scrutiny must not lose sight of the original values enshrined in those institutions. 'Fairness' and the 'common good' do not carry use-by dates, and whatever the shape of the economic and social changes which emerge in the coming years, these basic values remain as the benchmark against which change should be judged.

ACIRRT does not want to see a return to the 1950s, when smokestack industries provided our lifeblood. Australia has moved on, and we fully recognise that new and real problems in our economy have arisen. New and creative solutions are required, and this book is a modest endeavour to outline what directions are both desirable and feasible in the coming decade. A fuller discussion of our policy position can be found in Chapter 7. By way of concluding this chapter, we offer an outline of our response.

Where neo-liberals make profit the ultimate benchmark for evaluating economic change, we favour the core values outlined above. The balance sheets of our public companies, and their share market value, are amongst the crudest indicators possible of what makes up the 'social good'. Performance indicators for the economy need to include social destruction as well as wealth creation. The social costs of constant downsizing never make their way into the balance sheets, but someone, somewhere, has to pay.

Where the neo-liberals seek to increase management power, we argue for collaboration, consultation and workplace relationships built on trust. The anti-state and anti-regulation stance of the neo-liberals threatens to destroy a century of social gains, particularly in health, education and community infrastructure. For ACIRRT, the state is essential to ensuring minimal standards and ensuring fairness and equity across the nation. As John Stuart Mill observed last century, under conditions of competition, standards are set by the 'morally least reputable agent'. Ultimately, the state is the only umpire we have.

Finally, where the neo-liberals argue for industrial relations to be based more solidly on market principles, we argue the opposite. Workers are neither 'human resources' nor are they 'commodities' in the labour market. They have rights as *workers*, rights which extend beyond the cash nexus of the wage packet and which take into account the fact that people live in communities which require fairness, trust and cooperation for survival. No workplace is an island, and the social relationships which people foster are always found both inside and outside the workplace.

CHAPTER 2

What's behind the changes?

When people stop to think about why there's been so much economic change in the last 20 years, the word 'globalisation' often springs to mind. This is no accident. For much of that time we have been bombarded by business leaders, politicians and the media with words like: 'Australia is now part of the world economy, and we have to be internationally competitive'. This globalisation argument is, at best, only part of the picture.

In the mid-1980s, when Australia's current account deficit began to rise dramatically, we were told not to spend more than we earn. Imports were roaring ahead of exports. The fact that a major part of the deficit was due to 'invisibles'—things like dividends sent overseas, interest repayments and other costs related to foreign ownership of our resources—was never really debated in the public arena. So it has been during the mid-1990s. The globalisation threat, demonised like a hungry wolf in the forest, is often a convenient excuse for forcing through cost-cutting measures which would have been more strongly resisted in earlier times. Of course, no-one could argue that global competition in product markets has not become intense during the 1990s. But of more ominous foreboding for Australia's economic future is what globalisation has meant for our financial system, particularly the complete absence of any national social control over the direction of investment. The Australian economy's real Achilles' heel is not to be found on the shopfloors of 'unproductive workplaces', but in the boardrooms of banks, large corporations and other centres of financial power. In seeking to explain workplace change, this chapter will unravel some of the threads which make up 'globalisation'.

But, if it's not international competition that's driving workplace change, what is? It may sound boring but, with our diverse backgrounds in industrial relations, economics, history and sociology, we are more inclined to favour a view which sees workplace change being driven by a range of factors, some of them economic and some political. They do not derive from a single source, such as globalisation, but are part of the changing face of Australia's post-war 'social settlement'. By this term we mean the economic, political and cultural arrangements by which a society functions. We will expand on this definition shortly. For the moment, it's important to note that the Australian social settlement began to unravel during the 1970s. Largely because of economic factors, it had become unsustainable. Then, in the 1980s, that settlement came under direct attack from its enemies. Neo-liberalism—an economic credo—gained political feet and begun to make the running. Originally *economic liberalism* provided an ideology for the expansion of the free market. Within this philosophy, markets were regarded as the most efficient mechanism for organising the economic domain. The philosophy of *neo-liberalism* marks the restoration of economic liberalism, but it takes the idea of the supremacy of the market much further. All *areas of social life* are now regarded as candidates for the rule of the market.[1]

By the mid-1980s the Labor Party had become infected with the neo-liberal credo and turned its back on its own history. From being the midwife of Australia's post-war settlement, the Labor Party became an advocate for its euthanasia. In our view, the 1980s saw the launch of a 'neo-liberal project' in which the advocates of free market economics won unprecedented power within the ranks of business and government. Many of the tumultuous changes which flowed from this neo-liberal project—such as 'micro-economic reform', 'downsizing' and financial deregulation—have lately returned to haunt their architects, so dramatic have been the social costs of economic insecurity and community dislocation.

The idea that economic change in Australia is best understood in terms of 'social settlements' is certainly not novel. The leading political commentator of the *Australian* newspaper, Paul Kelly, has suggested that the 1980s was the 'end of certainty' because during that decade the Australian settlement was revealed as 'unsustainable.' The battle lines were then drawn between those who understood this revelation, and those who fought to retain the settlement; in Kelly's words: between the 'reformers' and the 'sentimentalist traditionalists' (1994, p. 2). It is clear where Kelly's sympathies lie and what he thinks Australia's basic problems are. He wants to see more areas of social and economic life opened to free market forces and the role of the state wound back. The problems he sees are: 'poor productivity, reliance upon materials exports, and inadequate national savings to fund investment'. (1994, p. 219).

Where we take issue with commentators like Kelly is in terms of core values and the analysis of the role played by the social settlement in Australian history. Far from viewing it as a creaking impediment to social and economic reform, we see the Australian settlement as a unique experiment in balancing market forces with state intervention and in providing a remarkable degree of social protection to the Australian people for nearly half a century. We also see Australia's key economic problems differently. Without going into detail now, we would emphasise Australia's failure to take the 'high road' to modern and advanced manufacturing and its failure to make investment work effectively, particularly private sector investment. All these problems have economic, social and political roots and one of the goals of this chapter is to explore them in greater detail.

There are two good reasons for using an idea like 'social settlements' to explain change. The first is historical. All current economic arrangements contain an historical residue. For example, manufacturing in Australia *today* is not just the result of contemporary product markets, investment decisions and workforce characteristics. It is overwhelmingly the result of patterns laid down in the *past*, of how manufacturing was developed in this country, particularly during the post-war years. Similarly, within industrial relations, the balance of power between business and labour in the workplace is critical for understanding contemporary outcomes. But that balance is historically determined, with institutions like trade unions, employer associations and industrial tribunals shaping the evolution of the workplace. Outside the institutional setting, the informal day-to-day activities of workers and managers is also historically driven, as the idea of 'custom and practice' illustrates so well.

The second reason is geographical. All too often in the economic and industrial relations debates we find superficial international comparisons. We often hear, for example, that lower wages for less skilled workers will reduce unemployment, and the United States is paraded as the exemplar of this proposition. Similarly, OECD figures on productivity, taxation, profits or costs are regularly used to draw up 'league tables' showing Australia's relative international position. Whatever the particular case, these kinds of international comparisons fail to take account of the unique circumstances of different countries, the complexity of their product, capital and labour markets, the extent of their social welfare provisions, and so forth. It is these very things which social settlements highlight. What's more, when we contemplate particular economic policies, we gain a glimpse of what their potential social impact may be by locating them in the context of a social settlement. *Ultimately, all economic decisions say something about the kind of society we wish to live in, and looking at other national social settlements helps us appreciate this.* The potential social consequences of greater inequality of incomes in Australia, or of more extreme individualism in the workplace, can be glimpsed in the American social settlement. Conversely, the impact of a more extensive welfare state, or of greater attention to social investment, can be glimpsed in the German and Swedish social settlements. Basically, talking about social settlements puts the 'social' back into the 'economic'.

AUSTRALIA'S POST-WAR SOCIAL SETTLEMENT

What we've called a post-war settlement is really just a shorthand phrase to capture the economic and political arrangements which were put in place at the end of the Second World War. In Australia's case, they also carried over some of the arrangements set up at Federation such as the arbitration system. Across the Western world, what made the post-war settlements unique was that they all involved compromises between business and labour which left business with ultimate power over investment decisions but conceded to labour various social benefits, things like a welfare state and a commitment to full employment.

In looking at Australian economic history, commentators have focussed on several unique features: White Australia, protection and compulsory arbitration. For some writers, these are the hallmarks of 'labourism' (Costa and Duffy, in Beilharz 1994, p. 206). For others, like Paul Kelly, they are part of the 'Australian settlement'. The other components which Kelly adds are: 'State paternalism' and 'Imperial benevolence' (Kelly 1994, pp. 1–2). As mentioned earlier, we also use the idea of an Australian 'social settlement' but we look at it differently to Kelly. We focus on the same features, but we give a much greater emphasis to the role of manufacturing in Australian history and we also view 'custom and tradition' as an important component. Notions of fairness and egalitarianism are often glibly dismissed as 'mateship', but we see these as core values within the Australian social settlement, values which have imbued its arbitration system with some of its enduring relevance. Rather than the 'land of the long weekend', we see traditional Australian attitudes to work as a healthy combination of the social and the economic, of the need for economic production to be balanced by the social needs of communities. This tradition is currently under concerted attack, at a practical level by profound changes in how working time is organised, and at an ideological level by a new generation of business people who have elevated 'productivity' to the status of a Holy Grail.

The post-war settlement in Australia was a response to the immediate past—the Great Depression and the war—as well as the continuation of the earlier Federation settlement. As outposts of the Empire, the Australian colonies had been part of the world economy from their earliest days and this history of relying on commodity exports remained central to all subsequent social settlements. Similarly, the state was always important in colonial days, whether as the builder of infrastructure or the regulator of labour markets. At the core of the Federation settlement was White Australia, an ideology which excluded both Australian Aborigines and non-white migrants—particularly those from Asia—from any kind of genuine participation in managing political or economic life.

The Australia social settlement was tied into a particular kind of capitalism—'settler' or 'dominion' capitalism—which left it with a unique legacy.[2] First, the productive core of its economy was largely colonial, but its social superstructure—its highly developed service sector and state institutions—was essentially metropolitan. Secondly, it never developed a dynamic or entrepreneurial domestic business class who could build an industrial economy. Consequently, Australia's industrial development, like that of its rural exports, hinged on the whims and fortunes of overseas interests.

Much of the character of the labour market was shaped at the turn of the century. Factory acts and wage boards had already helped to regulate wages and conditions of work, bringing sweatshop industries like clothing, footwear, furniture and baking under control. With the establishment of Commonwealth Arbitration in 1901, the scene was set for a unique experiment in the regulation of the labour market. The Harvester Judgment of 1907, handed down by Justice Higgins, initiated an important principle of wage determination: that a 'fair and reasonable wage' should be based on *need*. In the Harvester case the 'basic wage' was set at an amount that enabled a 'worker to live as a "human being in a civilized community" and to keep himself and his family in frugal comfort' (Macintyre 1985, p. 55; Quiggin 1996, p. 20).

The basic wage underpinned a minimum wage structure which, together with the concept of earnings margins for skill, became the bedrock of wages determination for much of the century. Even when the 'needs principle' was overtaken by considerations of 'capacity to pay', the Australian wages system remained wedded to the principle of comparative wage justice, the idea that workers should be paid roughly the same amount for doing similar sorts of work. Their wages should not hinge on the profitability or the productivity of particular workplaces or industry sectors. This meant that the basic wage was a guarantee of livelihood; it placed a floor beneath those workers whose weak bargaining position might otherwise have left them exposed to dire poverty. In political terms, the Harvester judgment was also important for the economic role it assigned to the state:

> The duties of the state towards the community, the need to mitigate the effects of the market, the entitlement of all to earn to a living wage, these ideas became embedded in political discourse (Macintyre 1985, p. 56).

It is important to realise that labour market regulation in Australia offered considerable protection to workers against their labour being treated as a commodity. Such regulation also stamped the daily conduct of working life with certain collective social values. Regulation of wages became institutionalised in the Award system—a set of industrial instruments with the force of law, which covered occupations and industries, and prescribed not only wages and conditions of work, but also aspects of vocational training, such as apprenticeships. The award system provided the basis for trade union organising and other collective forms of activity, ranging from pit-top meetings in the coal industry to the televised national hook-ups of striking teachers or nurses.

This unique form of labour market regulation had other important implications for the post-war settlement. The basic wage principle reaffirmed that the labour market was the central institution for providing for the welfare of the working class. In Francis Castles' classic phrase, Australia developed 'the wage earners' welfare state' (1985). Other forms of public welfare provision were marginal or non-existent. When the labour market failed, as it did dramatically during the 1930s, this absence of public welfare was starkly revealed. As Macintyre succinctly phrased it: 'Most Australians experienced the Depression as an elemental force laying waste to the national economy and reducing whole communities to hardship and despair' (1985, p. 66). Consequently, one of the central pillars of the post-war settlement in Australia was remedying this deficiency by providing social welfare payments, particularly sickness benefits and unemployment benefits. Despite universality in entitlement, compared with insurance schemes, these benefits were nevertheless a secondary layer of support, intended to supplement failings in the labour market but not to replace its central role. They formed a 'residual conception of social security', in Ben Chifley's words: 'bridge building to carry the people over those economic gaps which must necessarily occur from time to time' (Macintyre 1985, p. 83). A situation like this left the post-war welfare state highly vulnerable because this kind of welfare worked fine during periods of prosperity and short-term economic downturns, but it could not cope with any long-term decline in the labour market fortunes of any significant section of the population.

Australia's colonial history surfaced in the post-war settlement in two ways: as a perennial tension between manufacturing and rural production, and as a conflict between domestic and international labour markets. Manufacturing in Australia had largely developed behind tariff walls. The basic wage had only been viable because its mentor, the policy of 'New Protectionism', had linked wage regulation with restrictions on import competition. Without such restrictions, wages in the more labour intensive sectors of manufacturing would have been under constant downward pressure, particularly from cheap Asian labour. In the last decades of the nineteenth century, for example, domestic furniture makers marked their products with the label 'Manufactured with European labour'.

The post-war settlement consolidated industry protection. The Second World War had exposed Australia's economic vulnerability and fostered new kinds of industrial self-reliance, particularly in metals manufacturing. In the post-war years, competition from imports was restricted by quotas and tariffs. Together with increased demands for consumer goods and increased sources of skilled labour from migration, this protectionist regime saw manufacturing grow strongly through the 1950s.

As we have just seen, new protectionism had been directed against cheap Asian labour. White Australia was not just a policy to protect the 'unity of race', as Alfred Deakin succinctly phrased it. It was also a form of labour market regulation which was actively championed by the labour movement to keep out 'Asiatics who threatened the standard of living and the unions' strength' (Hagan in Beilharz 1994, p. 37). It was somewhat ironic then that a Labor Party minister, Arthur Calwell, oversaw the erosion of White Australia in the post-war years, when hundreds of thousands of 'non-white' European migrants arrived in Australia to build its post-war industry and infrastructure. While it remained part of official policy until the late 1960s, White Australia was one part of the Federation settlement which was not fully carried over into the post-war settlement. It was not rejected though: the anti-Asian focus remained as sharp as ever, but the 'non-whites' part was modified to make Mediterranean migrants acceptable. However, racism did not quietly disappear: migrant 'wogs' were still expected to 'assimilate' into the Australian mainstream, and they were usually given the hardest, dirtiest and lowest-paid jobs. Those that were highly qualified rarely gained the opportunity to practice those skills, and those who rose through the ranks battled racism and resentment. Consequently, Australian racism remained central to the post-war settlement, buttressing its other elements of protectionism, arbitration and British imperialism, and ensuring that both Aborigines and migrants remained marginalised within society.

The Australian post-war settlement emphasised collective social values, but gave them a particularly strong gender twist. In industrial relations, for example, trade union solidarity and decision making were based solely on male relationships, and the limits placed on wage inequality within the award system were largely designed for male workers. In particular, the 'basic wage' was based on the idea of a male breadwinner, with a wife and children to support. Women's wages—for most of the century—did not provide a living wage. At a cultural level, these collective values were also strongly influenced by gender, with 'mateship', sport and alcohol all combining to marginalise women. Within the political wing of the labour movement, the term 'mate' was endemic. When it came to the public sector, advances towards building collective values were highly uneven. In some areas, like transport and education, public provision was well advanced. In others, like health and housing, private arrangements dominated. Indeed, Australia's level of private home ownership during the post-war decades was amongst the highest in the world.

This pattern in collective social values influenced the extent to which labour was treated as a commodity. Certainly, for white male workers, the award system and a strong trade union presence in workplaces limited just how far management could treat their workers as chattels. Indeed, the phrase 'Jack's as good as his master' was used by foreign observers to comment on the egalitarian flavour of Australian workplaces. But when it came to women and migrants, the labour market treated their labour like a commodity. Like Japan, it was as if the collective protection offered by labour market regulation only applied to the core workforce. Those on the periphery missed out.

THE DISMANTLING OF THE SETTLEMENT

In this book we view the end of the post-war 'golden age' of economic growth not as a rupture between two epochs, but as a period of transition in which an older social settlement breaks up, and newer social settlements begin to form. The significance of the 1980s and early 1990s—the period of radical workplace change—lies in the fact that the *unravelling* of social settlements which began in the 1970s became an active *dismantling*. At the same time that policy makers consciously began to tackle the structural weaknesses of the post-war settlement, so too did various economic groupings mobilise politically to remould the contours of that settlement to reflect their interests. As mentioned earlier, we've chosen the term, the 'neo liberal project' as a shorthand phrase to refer to this process. Every attack on the post-war settlement saw neo-liberal forces promote an agenda which treated labour as a commodity and wound back collective social values. On the other hand, most defences of that settlement were grounded in nostalgia for the 'golden age' of full-employment and economic prosperity, an era when labour's non-commodity status was more secure and community life reinforced collective social values. As we will argue in Chapter 7, we don't want to go down either of these passages. Neo-liberalism is morally bankrupt and economically inefficient and locks Australia's economy into a 'low-road' to the future. Nostalgic romanticism may be superficially appealing, but it does not have a handle on the new realities of work and the labour market.

Structural weaknesses

A large part of the rhetoric of workplace change in the 1980s centred on 'lifting productivity'. Most of the time this meant two things: working harder (work intensification) or 'reforming' particular workplace customs and practices, like working time arrangements and demarcation boundaries. Was the rhetoric of 'productivity' just an excuse then to pursue greater profits in Australian industry? To answer this we need to look at two issues. First, there isn't much doubt that Australian industry faced greater competition during the 1980s, and as a result productivity amongst *individual* firms did become an important issue. Secondly, sitting over the top of this economic reality was another issue, which was largely political. While strategies to cut costs may have been economically inspired, the pursuit of greater management power in the workplace was political. A large part of this political struggle used the language of productivity to justify the choices made, and this process was made much easier by a phalanx of conservative economists who displayed international productivity figures in every forum.

What makes this whole issue even more complicated is the fact that labour productivity in Western economies has indeed been declining during the last 40 years. However, this is an intrinsic feature of advanced economies and a necessary outcome of economic development (Brenner 1998). It is *not* a moral failing in their workforces. To understand this picture we need to look more closely at how economic growth and productivity were tied up with the post-war settlements and how their decline proved to be fatal for those settlements.

All post-war settlements relied on continuing economic growth. As a compromise which left business in control of investment, the post-war settlement could only placate labour if the cake kept growing. Both high wages and the welfare state relied on high levels of economic growth to sustain them. The end of the long boom in the mid-1970s, and the onset of chronically high levels of unemployment, undermined this compromise because it introduced zero-sum calculations into the political arena for the first time. In Australia, Malcolm Fraser popularised Milton Freedman's famous phrase: 'there is no such thing as a free lunch'. The abandonment of Keynesian economics, and its replacement with the mean-spirited ethos of monetarism, began that slow dismantling of the welfare state which became the norm from the late 1970s onwards: growing restrictions on eligibility for benefits, shelving of social reforms, winding back of public housing, health, education and transport.

These changes could be traced to a more severe weakness in Western economies which centred on long-term changes in productivity (Brenner 1998). The 1950s and 1960s witnessed consistently high levels of productivity growth amongst industrialised nations. Productivity and consumption 'stimulated' each other: the reduced unit costs of consumer goods made them accessible to the mass of wage-earners, while this growth of consumer demand in turn stimulated mass production and further increased productivity (Gouverneur 1983, p. 200). However, from the 1970s onward, productivity began to decline. In Australia, labour productivity averaged 2.9 per cent annual growth prior to 1973, 2.2 per cent for the remainder of the decade, and 1 per cent during the 1980s (Johnson 1995,

p. 40).[3] This decline in productivity was partly self-generated. As the markets for consumer goods became saturated, consumption declined and with it, productivity. In Australia, for example, saturation in the whitegoods market was evident by the 1970s (Maddock and Stilwell 1987, p. 263). The services sector, whose steady growth might have offset this decline in household consumption, was unable to restore high levels of productivity because, by its very nature, it was closed to mass production.[4] Moreover, because services commanded relatively high prices, the expansion in this sector drained household expenditure away from the goods sector of the economy. Thus, one of the key characteristics of advanced economies—a growing services sector—was itself compounding the problem of productivity slow-down (Gouverneur 1983, p. 204; Baumol et al. 1989; Wolff 1987).

This long-term decline in labour productivity had profound implications for the post-war settlement. High levels of labour productivity had underpinned that settlement because they had made possible the simultaneous growth in *both* profits and wages. Growing real wages, moreover, increased household consumption and spurred on further economic growth. High labour productivity also made it possible for the state to spend money on welfare services for the community and thereby keep a lid on social discontent. Consequently, the decline in productivity which became evident during the 1970s threw up a major challenge to this 'everyone a winner' compromise.

Historical ruptures

To chart the unwinding of the post-war settlement we must first acknowledge complexity and unevenness. It is not as if some unitary social phenomenon broke down like an old watch. Rather, different elements of the settlement unwound within their own time frames. For example, the linkages between wage determination and the cost of living—a cornerstone of the basic wage ethos—was temporarily abandoned in the 1950s, modified in the 1970s to apply to low income workers only, and then rejected in favour of productivity bargaining during the 1980s. Similarly, at different stages during the post-war period, industry's capacity to pay has been more influential in setting wages at particular times than has considerations of human need (Quiggin 1996, p. 24). By way of contrast, the Award system remained largely intact throughout the post-war period until the 1990s when enterprise bargaining surfaced.

A transformed labour market

The most vulnerable chink in the armour of the post-war settlement was full-employment. When this collapsed during the mid-1970s, the days of that settlement were numbered because full employment had been the bedrock for the maintenance of living standards. When long-term unemployment became a feature of the Australian labour market in the late 1970s, poverty became a real threat growing to numbers of Australian families. This grew directly out of one of the most severe shortcomings of the post-war settlement, its 'residual' concept of welfare in the form of Chifley's 'bridge' spanning temporary periods of economic adversity. Once the temporary gave way to the permanent—as it did during the 1980s with long-term unemployment—Ben Chifley's bridge collapsed, and widespread poverty emerged for the first time since the 1930s. With remorseless consistency, research studies throughout the 1980s and early 1990s pointed to unemployment as the primary cause of widespread poverty[5].

While poverty directly impinged on about one-fifth of Australian households, a much larger proportion of Australian workers felt the impact of unemployment on their living standards. Persistently high levels of unemployment (see Figure 2.1) from the late 1970s onwards exerted a downward pressure on wages. Even when employment grew strongly during the mid-1980s, wages growth failed to recover. This was partly due to the Accord between the Labor Government and the ACTU, but it was also partly due to unemployment dampening down wage claims. The other important way in which unemployment affected people still in jobs was that it strengthened the bargaining position of managers in the workplace because it fostered job insecurity amongst the workforce. Chapter 6 will explore this issue in greater depth.

Figure 2.1 Unemployment rate, 1945 to 1996

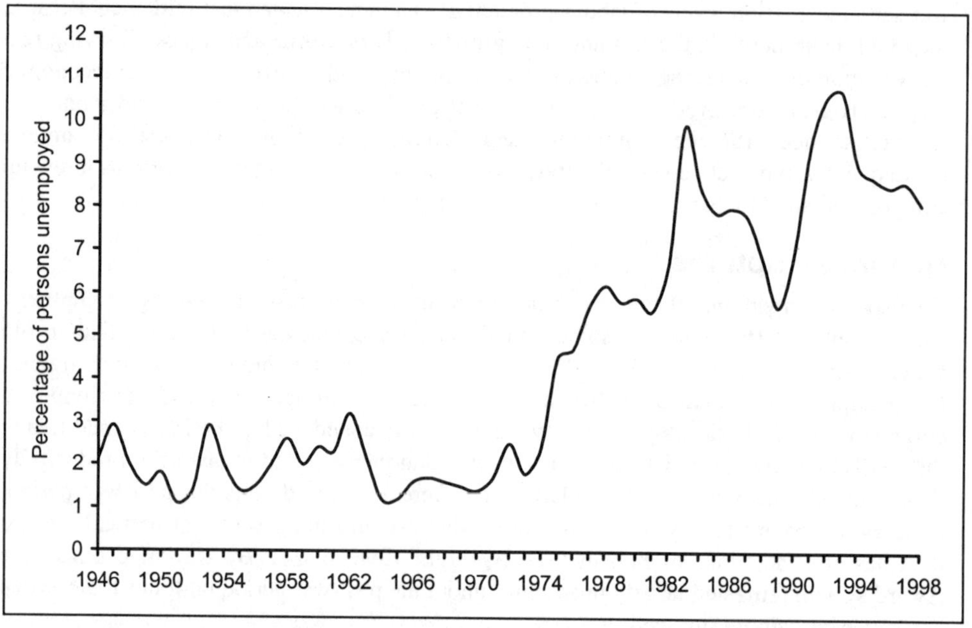

Source: 1945 to 1963, Butlin estimates in Vamplew W.E. (1987) (ed.), 'Australians, Historical Statistics', *Australians, A Historical Library*, Fairfax, Syme & Weldon, Broadway, NSW, vol. 10, p. 152; 1964 to 1998 ABS labour force surveys.

Across the industrialised world, the return of high levels of unemployment signalled the death knell for Keynesian demand management as an economic tool. This had two important consequences. First, the collapse of faith in Keynesianism allowed its old free-market rivals to resurface, with monetarism emerging in the late 1970s, followed in the 1980s by deregulation (particularly in the USA) and privatisation (particularly in the UK). Secondly, policy makers increasingly abandoned state intervention in the macro-economy (apart from juggling interest rates) in favour of intervention in the micro-economy, particularly the workplace. As economist John Quiggin observed:

Although it was not recognised at the time, the abandonment of the full employment objective had the effect of undermining government intervention in general, and hence of laying the basis for micro-economic reform (Quiggin 1996, p. 26).

Consequently, micro-economic 'reform', and its corollary, 'workplace reform', emerged as the key arena for economic struggle during the 1980s. The old struggle—the one which had characterised the long boom—had centred on the distribution of the economy's surplus, but this was now judged an anachronism. In Paul Keating's words, the issue was 'not the distribution of wealth but its creation' (quoted in Beilharz 1994, p. 89). Chapter 4 will chart this process in much greater detail.

The Australian post-war settlement had been based on a particular kind of labour market. It was assumed that Keynesian policies to stimulate consumer demand would soak up excess labour and bring unemployment rapidly down, while policies to contract aggregate demand would reign in inflation, at a small cost in terms of increased unemployment. Fine-tuning this trade-off between unemployment and inflation was the art to the Keynesian science. But the art lost its magic in the mid-1970s with the emergence of *stagflation*—the simultaneous presence of both high inflation and high unemployment. The last budget of the Whitlam government signalled the rejection of Keynesianism by policy makers in Australia. By then inflation was running at 17 per cent and unemployment had risen above 4.5 per cent. To some extent, stagflation was external to the Australian economy and was imported from Australia's trading partners. While the 'oil shock' of 1973 saw inflation explode, it had been steadily increasing during the 1960s for a variety of reasons. However, more significant in eroding the Keynesian full-employment strategy was a profound change in the composition of the Australian workforce, a change which undermined the labour market assumptions of the post-war settlement.

Like the Federation settlement—embodied in the Harvester judgment—the post-war settlement rested on the shoulders of the male breadwinner, usually assumed to be a full-time wage earner. The rapid and systematic ejection of women from their wartime jobs in industry testified to the strength of the ideology that a 'woman's place was in the home'. Yet throughout the 1960s this ideology was defied by reality, as large numbers of women re-entered the labour market or stayed on working after marriage. In 1961 the proportion of women in the paid workforce was 25 per cent; by 1983 it stood at 44 per cent. In the 1960s the second income contributed to rising living standards; by the 1980s, it was essential for simply maintaining living standards.

The significance of this increase in the labour force was twofold. Much of the work women carried out, particularly in the service sector, was part-time. While this often suited women with families, as well as their employers who confronted fluctuations in work flow, the growth of the part-time sector undermined Keynesian assumptions about the workings of the labour market. Increases in consumer demand might no longer lead to a net increase in full-time employment—employers could simply increase the hours of their part-timers or, as increasingly happened during the 1980s, increase their numbers of part-time workers while winding back the number of full-time staff.

Secondly, women's mobility between the paid labour force and their domestic work confounded the traditional link between the labour market and the business cycle. From the 1970s onwards it became evident that during a downturn women left the labour market altogether, reducing the labour force participation rate. During an upturn, women re-entered the labour market. Instead of a stable labour force, with neat movements between unemployment and employment, policy makers confronted a labour market characterised by a highly unstable labour force, with movement in and out of the labour force, as well as movement within it. By the mid-1980s, other non-gender elements were added to this picture: increased casualisation, increased contracting out, and a plethora of labour market programs creating idiosyncratic labour market states. All of these unstable elements combined to produce a large segment of precarious and non-standard forms of employment within the labour market. Predicting how unemployment in a labour market such as this might respond to an increase in aggregate demand was something beyond even the most accomplished Keynesian planner.

It was not simply that managing the economy along Keynesian lines had become so much harder. More significantly, the baton had passed to another group of economists, those in the thrall of the free-market assumptions of the nineteenth century. They provided the shock troops for what we have called the 'neo-liberal project'. For them, and for their corporate and government sponsors, micro-economic 'reform' and raising productivity became the central issues of economic management in the 1980s.

Shifting political alliances—Labor transformed

The political character of the post-war settlement was one in which the Liberals championed the interests of business, the Country Party promoted the interests of farmers, and the Labor Party represented the political wing of the labour movement. All of this was transformed during the 1980s and a new political convergence emerged:

> The fundamental divide in Australian politics in the late 1980s was no longer Labor versus Liberal. Party differences were real and bitter, but the underlying policy direction was the same ... The 1980s saw the Labor-Liberal paradigm being eroded as the major battleground of ideas, though the tensions between the parties still dominated the political debate (Kelly 1994, p. 2).

The reasons for this realignment within the ranks of labour are many and complex. The roots lie in the Whitlam years but the branches grew prolifically during the Hawke-Keating period. Whitlam had begun that process of 'reform' which modernised the Labor Party and made it more acceptable to the middle class, particularly the younger radicals of the 1960s. As Peter Beilharz observed:

> Whitlam marked a significant ideological turn in the development of the Australian Labor Party—away from labourism, away from a close identification with the interests and the more conservative outlook of organised labour, and towards a more open, ambitious and sophisticated West European style of social democracy (Beilharz 1994, p. 87).

This made it much easier for younger, educated clerical and professional workers to embrace the Labor Party as the natural party of 'reform'. In time, middle class technocrats began taking over the institutions of the labour movement, particularly the parliamentary Labor Party and the ACTU (Scott 1991). This takeover played a part in the new style of corporatist Labor politics which emerged during the 1980s, when the Labor Party re-established strong links with the labour movement in the form of the ALP-ACTU Accord.

Finally, Whitlam's failure to prevent economic malaise during the mid-1970s also left the Labor Party with a resolve to become better 'economic managers' the next time round, an intention which left them open to capture by the neo-liberals (also called the 'economic rationalists') who had taken over the Canberra bureaucracy (Kelly 1994, p. 24; Pusey 1991). Paul Keating was particularly vulnerable because of his passion for economic growth and efficiency. They underpinned his particular brand of labourism: contempt for 'old money' and the Balmain 'basket weavers', alongside a romantic gloss on the Labor Legacy and an uncritical awe for the judgments of financial markets.

As Paul Kelly observed, Hawke and Keating imposed a new set of values on the ALP during the 1980s: 'a belief in economic competition, a faith in market forces, a commitment to the internationalisation of the Australian economy, reform sanctioned by a consensus process, and government in collaboration with the ACTU leadership' (1994, p. 20). This collaboration saw the emergence of the Accord, a compact which delivered wage restraint from the trade unions in return for improvements in the social wage, things like Medicare and increased social welfare spending. At the same time that the Labor Party cemented its Accord with the trade unions, its leaders also moved closer to business. For much of the 1980s, important sections of the business establishment favoured the Labor Party over their traditional allies, the Liberal Party. This trend was particularly pronounced in the mid-1980s, when the Hawke Labor Government deregulated the financial system and floated the Australian dollar.

For critics like Kelly, Labor's economic charter during the 1980s was viewed as schizophrenic, as a reforming zeal for deregulating financial markets but a stalled caution about deregulating the labour market. Yet for Kelly, unleashing one without the other was a recipe for failure. As Australia became more integrated into the world economy, so the argument ran, pressures to lower wage costs would become intense. For Kelly then, Labor failed to complete its reform agenda because it left intact key pillars of the Australian settlement—like the arbitration system—and this acted as a deadweight on modernising the economy. The Labor leadership were aware of these kinds of criticisms and Keating regularly championed his unique blend of reform, in which exposing sectors of the economy to international competition nestled side-by-side with protecting the labour market from radical change. The logic of the Labor Government's position was that the Accord with the trade unions delivered certainty in aggregate wage outcomes, and allowed them to promote sustained economic growth without the risk of inflation. And indeed, for most of the mid-1980s Labor delivered that growth and pulled the Australian economy out of the depths of the 1982 recession.

The problem for Labor was that deregulating the financial system unleashed the genie in the bottle and ushered in a current account crisis which profoundly changed the agenda for economic management in Australia. Floating the dollar led to a massive depreciation in the Australian currency, and Australia's foreign debt mushroomed.

Ultimately deregulating the financial system led down the pathway of 'micro-economic reform', that catchphrase for allowing market prices to allocate resources across the economy. As the Treasury Budget Papers observed:

> In many respects the floating of the exchange rate is the pivotal policy decision of the last decade … The greater internationalisation of the Australian economy, the depth and dynamism of its financial markets and the imputation system are already spurring management to improve performance (quoted in Kelly 1994, p. 389).

Paul Kelly saw Labor's embracing of micro-economic reform in 1987 as the final nail in the coffin of Keynesian economics in Australia:

micro-economic reform shifted Labor's traditional focus from the Keynesian orientated demand side of the economy towards the supply side … In its purest form micro-economic reform was a liberation of the supply side, an embrace made far easier for conservative parties than for social democratic parties which were tied to the Keynesian chariot (Kelly 1994, p. 388).

When first elected, the Labor Government had flirted briefly with a Keynesian-style approach to restoring full-employment through a strategy of high growth and public sector spending initiatives (like the Community Employment Program). In a similar vein, the early Accords tried to regulate aggregate wages to underpin high growth without inflation. However, by the mid-1980s the whole scenario began to change because of a collapse in the balance of payments and a rise in Australia's foreign debt. The 'current account crisis' of 1986 saw the Treasurer, Paul Keating, warn that Australia faced becoming 'a third rate economy … a banana republic'. The Accord now became the tool by which to impose real wage cuts, and successive Federal budgets now slashed spending across a raft of social policy areas. In terms of its original conception, the Accord was now dead. Critics like Beilharz have judged it accordingly:

> The Accord would not even deliver wage protection across its various incarnations; rather it reversed the flow of GNP from capital to labour instigated under Whitlam, in the pious hope that capital would invest, guaranteeing economic growth and the revival of full employment. But economic growth occurred in finance and in speculation more than in manufacturing investment. The Accord did not deliver on social policy or on economic policy. As Kelly confirms, it became a kind of holy cow which meant that Labor could actually deregulate finance and wind down protection levels (Beilharz 1994, p. 129).

Once Australia's 'international competitiveness' became the clarion call from all quarters, pressures to deregulate the labour market and transform the workplace moved to centre-stage. The original Accord—a classic Keynesian *macro-economic* tool—was reincarnated as a device for promoting enterprise level bargaining, that is, a *micro-economic* direction in policy.

As we shall see in the next chapter, the issue of 'productivity' became a central component of the wage fixing system from the late 1980s onwards. This took the form of a greater focus on enterprise bargaining. In 1988 Ralph Willis, Labor's industrial relations minister, revealed a strategy for introducing greater labour market flexibility as part of the government's 'micro-economic reform' agenda. The centrepiece was award restructuring, an attempt to:

> remove obsolete classifications, reduce the number of classifications, broadband a range of jobs under a single classification and establish links between training, skills and wages which result in career paths for workers (Willis 1988, p. 12).

By the early 1990s Paul Keating was pushing for even greater levels of enterprise bargaining and criticised the Australian Industrial Relations Commission (AIRC) after it rejected this strategy. As Chapter 3 will show, the AIRC was ultimately dragged into a regulatory system in which both trade unions and the Commission itself were increasingly marginalised.

The profound turnabout in Labor's approach to economic management did not happen in a political vacuum. While the conservative political parties remained impotent onlookers for much of the 1980s, this did not mean that neo-liberal forces were not shaping the course of events. Indeed, profound changes within the ranks of business and the impact of the New Right within economic debates were important components in changing Australia's economic policy climate during the 1980s. It is to these changes we now turn.

Shifting political alliances—the death of McEwenism

As well as these dramatic changes within the ranks of labour, longer-term changes within the ranks of business had been underway since the 1970s, changes which were to have profound implications for industrial relations during the 1980s. One of the most intriguing features of the post-war settlement had been the compromise forged between farmers and manufacturers. In the same way that the Swedish social settlement drew agrarian interests into line with those of the labour movement, so too did post-war rural politics under the Country Party leader, 'Black Jack' McEwen see the promotion of rural exports and the protection of secondary industry go hand in hand. As minister for industry during the long boom, McEwen enthusiastically presided over the maintenance of the tariff wall which sheltered domestic manufacturing. This compromise was forged because McEwen's rural constituency was itself sheltered by a range of protective measures: subsidised farm inputs, cheap rail transport, low interest loans, and trade protection against rival products like margarine (Maddock and Stilwell 1987, p. 258).

This compromise worked successfully while ever rural access to secure British markets was guaranteed, and commodity prices for staples like wool and wheat remained buoyant. By the 1970s, however, these conditions had changed. Britain had joined the Common Market, while competition from synthetic fibres challenged wool's pre-eminence. Its place in the export field shrunk dramatically. In 1960 sales of greasy wool made up 37 per cent of the value of Australian exports, by 1970 the figure was down to 17 per cent, and by 1980 had fallen further to just 7 per cent. Finally, the 'family farm', the centrepiece of Country Party ideology, had begun its slow downhill slide while 'agribusiness' began to increase its presence in the countryside. From the early 1970s to the mid-1980s, 19,000 farmers left agriculture, the farm workforce declined by 32,000, and volume of farm production increased by some 27 per cent (Lawrence 1987, p. 13).

This compromise between rural producers and manufacturers broke down in the 1970s partly because of these changes and partly because of other developments in rural politics. In particular, sections of the rural lobby centred around the National Farmers Federation (NFF) came to reject 'McEwenism' (Kelly 1994, p. 43) at the same time that a powerful new player emerged on the scene: the mining lobby. In terms of economic power, mining's share of export earnings had grown rapidly from the late 1960s onwards. Figure 2.2 shows that until the 1970s mining contributed less than 10 per cent of Australia's export earnings, a period when farm products regularly brought in well over 30 per cent of those earnings. By the 1980s the share of exports held by mining had jumped to nearly 30 per cent and now eclipsed the share held by farm products.

Figure 2.2 Relative changes in Australian commodity exports, 1946 to 1985

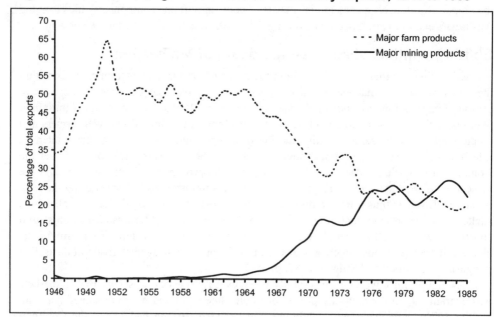

Source: Based on figures in Vamplew W.E. (1987) (ed.), 'Australians, Historical Statistics', *Australians, A Historical Library*, Fairfax, Syme & Weldon, Broadway, NSW, vol. 10, pp. 202–203. *Note*: Farm products comprise wool, wheat and beef. Mining products comprise iron ore, alumina and coal.

Over time, the mining lobby and the NFF wrested control of rural politics away from the heirs of McEwen and embarked on a crusade to destroy the post-war settlement. As exporters this rural lobby began a major onslaught against those elements of the post-war settlement which favoured domestic producers, particularly the centralised wages system and tariff protection. Together with other luminaries of the New Right, this lobby formed the H.R. Nicholls Society to provide a 'rallying point for participants involved in the attempt to transform the industrial system'. The Society gave Charles Copeman, the Chief Executive of mining company, Peko Wallsend, the 'inspiration' he needed to launch a major attack on the unions at his company's Robe River operation and it provided support in those other key struggles of the 1980s: Mudginberri and Dollar Sweets (Kelly, 1992, p. 261).

In the late 1970s the mining industry also snared the allegiance of Paul Keating to their position. Formerly an advocate of industry protection, Keating's years as opposition shadow minister for Minerals and Energy left him primed for the role he would play as Treasurer in the 1980s. In Keating's own words:

> I went to the Mining Industry Council, all around the mining areas of Australia and talked to the business groups. I went down just about every mine in the country, I knew all about it, I knew most of the companies, the personalities. I liked the mining industry because it was a successful, internationally competitive export industry. It wasn't laying down in a sort of rut of tariffs and protection, it was out there doing something' (quoted in Edwards 1996, p. 145).

At an economic level, the increasing influence of mining reinforced Australia's dependence on raw and semi-processed commodity exports, at a time when other comparable countries were re-invigorating their manufacturing sectors. Investment needed for the expansion of high technology in Australia was instead diverted into mining exploration and development. We will return to the implications of this later.

Those elements of the post-war settlement which reflected collective values—things like trade unions, universal welfare provisions, and social infrastructure like public schools, hospitals and transport—became prime targets for 'reform' by neo-liberals. The aim was to 'decollectivise' these areas of social life, and thereby individualise people's social relations in such a way that the market domain might expand. While the New Right mobilised most fervently amongst the mining and farming sectors, the broader neo-liberal project was much more widespread, drawing on support from economists in universities, think-tanks, the media and within government. The same struggle between collective values and market solutions which was fought out in the community and in the media was reproduced within the ranks of the government bureaucracy, with market solutions overwhelmingly gaining the upper hand, particularly through the ascendancy of Treasury and the influence of bodies like the Industry Commission (now incorporated in the Productivity Commission).

As we have seen the arbitration system was a particular focus of scorn for the New Right. In the early 1980s Gerard Henderson coined the phrase 'The Industrial Relations Club' (Kelly 1994, p. 113) and the term quickly entered the language of the New Right as a term of abuse. It symbolised what they saw as a cosy camaraderie between unions and compliant employers, and between bureaucrats, journalists and academics, which stood in the way of market forces. 'Deregulating the labour market' was the centrepiece of the New Right's 'reform' agenda, and arbitration and centralised wage fixing stood solidly in the way.

What was at stake in this neo-liberal project was the comparative wage justice principle, one of the core values of the Australian settlement. In the mid-1980s the Business Council of Australia (BCA), representing Australia's top 80 companies, began to lobby against this principle, publishing its arguments in *Enterprise Based Bargaining Units: A Better Way of Working*. Not only did it argue for a more decentralised wage fixing system, but it targeted the multi-employer unions and awards as major obstacles in deregulating the labour market. As we shall see in Chapter 3, the Labor Government began to embrace a hybrid version of enterprise bargaining in which wage movements were linked to productivity growth within individual firms, rather than being set by economy wide standards. This strategy meant that workers who did the same kind of work in different firms might end up earning very different wages, depending on the profitability of their firm. But Labor baulked at doing away with the AIRC and fully deregulating the bottom of the labour market.

Labor wanted an enterprise bargaining culture, but it still insisted on a role for regulatory bodies like the AIRC and a role for centralised wage fixing mechanisms which would provide 'safety net' wage increases for those outside the bargaining system. These measures were needed to protect workers at the bottom of the labour market, to place a floor under their earnings and prevent the Americanising of their living standards. By contrast, the neo-liberals wanted to make enterprise profitability the only basis for wage fixation. Such a strategy was intended to give full reign to market forces within the labour market.

During the 1980s the Liberal Party had found itself consistently outflanked by Labor when it came to unleashing market forces. Labor went further with financial deregulation than the Liberals ever had. Labor privatised icons like the Commonwealth Bank, an action which would have sent shivers down Menzies' spine. Yet when it came to the labour market, the Labor Party insisted on a role for regulatory bodies like the AIRC, thereby maintaining one of the pillars of the Australian settlement. Labor's concern for low paid workers and its links with the Trade Union movement constrained just how far it could take its free-market urges. However, for the Liberal Party, there were no such constraints. In the early tussles between the 'Wets' and the 'Drys', Liberals like McPhee argued for only moderate change:

> Australians have always wanted consensus. Certain aspects of our society, notably egalitarianism, are deeply entrenched. So we had to modify the system. Get away from indexation but keep the spirit of Higgins [ie. Justice Higgins of Harvester fame] (quoted in Kelly 1994, p. 121).

But for the 'Drys', stamping on Higgins' grave was the only acceptable route into the future. By the late 1980s, the Drys in the Party had decisively won and the industrial relations policy which the Liberals carried into the 1990s was a policy with no place for Higgins. Indeed, unlike the Labor Party's enterprise bargaining system—which nestled awkwardly beside arbitration—the individual contracts system developed by the Liberals threatened the centrality of the arbitration system. The relationship between employer and worker was to become a common law relationship, not an issue for special industrial tribunals. Collective forms of interaction were to be overridden by individualistic arrangements and market forces were to set wages and conditions with minimal uniformity in the system.

In 1996 the Liberal and National Parties came to power, after their own 13 years in the wilderness. A new *Workplace Relations Act*, which sought to implement this strategy for individualised and market-driven industrial relations, was introduced. While some of the sting in their Bill was modified by the presence of the Democrats in the Senate, the core features of the Bill reflected their neo-liberal origins. Australian Workplace Agreements (AWAs)—essentially individual contracts—became the centrepiece of their industrial relations policy. A process of award simplification, aimed at stripping back awards to 20 basic items, was also set in place. It aimed to force unions and workers to renegotiate—at an enterprise level—many of their long-held conditions. Where agreement could not be reached, management prerogative would prevail.

THE FAILURE OF INVESTMENT

We saw earlier that Paul Kelly viewed the Australian economy as hampered by a failure to 'save' and thereby develop the domestic capacity to fund investment. This view is a common one and provides the conventional justification for promoting foreign investment in Australia. It is, however, an extremely crude argument which draws no distinction between productive and non-productive investment, between investment which enhances high-valued added economic activity, and investment which just ships raw materials overseas. This definition of the investment problem also fails to distinguish between property speculation and useful infrastructure development, or between spending on company takeovers and spending on research and development. Yet we would argue strongly that all of these important distinctions in the *character of investment* are far more important than its aggregate level. In the following discussion we will show how the real failure of investment lay not in any shortcoming of the amount of funds available, but in where those funds were channelled and how they were used in the economy. A core part of our argument is that mining activity, far from enhancing Australia's economic fortunes, actually introduced serious distortions into the flow of investment funds throughout the economy. Secondly, the deregulation of the financial system did not lead to economic benefits in terms of useful investment. Rather it simply integrated Australia more tightly into a global system of 'casino capitalism', in which uncontrollable and speculative financial activity became the order of the day (see Martin and Schumann 1997 and Henwood 1997).

An essential part of the compromise between business and labour in all the post-war settlements was that *business control over investment was left intact*. Keynes had wanted to see investment socialised but the architects of the settlement rejected this model. Only in Sweden, with the setting up of 'wage earner funds', were efforts made to encroach on the investment prerogative of business. Overwhelmingly across the Western industrialised world, the state restricted its activities to fostering a favourable environment for investment, and steered clear of directing investment. In return, business was obliged to invest in ways which sustained the other elements of the post-war settlement, particularly the social dividends of economic growth. However, in Australia—like Britain—domestic business failed the challenge.

In Australia, foreign capital had led the expansion of manufacturing during the 1950s and 1960s. Multinational manufacturers slid behind McEwen's tariff wall by setting up local branch plants to service the Australian market. This development has been called 'defensive industrialisation' (Schedvin 1987, p. 22), because it was intended to provide substitutes for imports, rather than exports, into world markets. These high levels of foreign ownership hampered Australia's own exporting potential, since parent companies were loathe to compete with their own subsidiaries. Combined with a small domestic market which restricted economies of scale, these factors held back the expansion of manufacturing industry and by the late 1960s stagnation was evident.

In the next two decades, manufacturing failed to emerge from its malaise. Between 1971 and 1985, manufacturing's share of GDP fell from nearly 25 per cent to just over 17 per cent, while the employment share also fell from 24 per cent to 17 per cent. Australian manufacturing remained backward and inward looking, with import-replacement still

27

dominant. Much of its equipment was outdated and overdue for replacement. Australian manufacturing focused on price competition, rather than competing on design, quality or product innovation. As a government report from the late 1980s conceded:

> a major part of Australian manufacturing is of mature products which are characterised by saturated markets with sales dictated by demand created by population growth and replacement. At this stage of the product cycle, competition tends to be on price (as rival producers compete for shares of largely static markets) and on process innovation aimed at cost cutting (DITAC 1987, p. 36).

When Labor returned to power in 1983, it found a manufacturing industry shattered by the most severe recession since the 1930s. The approach which Labor adopted was a combination of free-market economics and limited industry intervention. As we saw above, the Labor government deregulated the financial sector and floated the dollar. The government also began a program of phased tariff reductions and it introduced industry plans into particular sectors (e.g. motor vehicles, steel and textiles, clothing and footwear). The tariff reductions were intended to modernise Australian manufacturing by exposing it to international competition and forcing it to become export oriented. By the 1990s, the levels of protection in most sectors of manufacturing were at their lowest since the 1920s, yet Australian manufacturing remained in crisis:

> In a sense, Australian manufacturing was caught in a vicious circle by the end of the 1980s: it could not compete with imports because it lacked the productivity gains that would result from large scale production, yet its share of the domestic market was in decline and it could not expand into world markets to a sufficient extent. The result was virtual stagnation relieved only by short run periods of exchange depreciation when Australian manufacturing achieved a temporary boost in international competitiveness (Dyster and Meredith 1990, p. 298).

For many commentators, Australia was basically being 'de-industrialised' during the 1980s. While all advanced economies are characterised by shrinking employment shares within primary and secondary industries, and expanding employment in the services sector, the extent to which manufacturing is allowed to collapse in terms of investment and output remains an economic and political choice. There is nothing inevitable about the 'withering away' of manufacturing. We return to this theme in Chapter 7.

Meanwhile, the growth areas of the economy were mining—which doubled its share of GDP during this period—and services. More importantly, the composition of manufacturing changed little over this time period other than to consolidate Australia's position as a low-value-adding producer. Between 1969 and 1989, the largest areas of manufacturing growth were in the processing of natural resources, things like foodstuffs, paper products and mineral products (Industry Commission 1995, p. 9) (see Figure 2.3). Like their commodity cousins, these products were all price sensitive in international markets and Australia's increasing reliance on these kinds of product markets tied Australia more closely into a labour market which emphasised cost-cutting ahead of skills formation and product innovation. Both in terms of the overall industry structure, and the composition of manufacturing, Australia was taking the 'low road' into the future, not the 'high road'. As we shall see, this had serious implications for the post-war settlement.

By the mid-1990s evidence began to emerge that manufacturing was in 'transition', rather than terminal decline.[6] The export of elaborately transformed manufactures (ETMs) had begun to improve. Whereas in 1984–85, Australia exported $2.6 billion dollars worth of ETMs, by 1994–95 the figure had grown to $12.5 billion. This was a growth rate of 16.2 per cent for each year of the decade, much higher than the 10.7 per cent for simply transformed manufactures for the same period (Clark et al. 1996, p. 115). One commentator wrote of 'a remarkable change in Australian trade performance in elaborately transformed manufactures' (Green 1993, p. 6; also Sheehan et al. 1994). Similarly, during the latter half of the 1980s investment in manufacturing spread into a greater range of industries than had been the case during the early 1980s, when resource-based manufacturing industries had dominated the call on investment capital (Lattimore 1989, pp. 27–28). Despite these improvements, ETMs still constituted only a small proportion of total manufacturing ouput.

Figure 2.3 Share of manufacturing value added by industry subdivision, 1968–69 and 1989–90

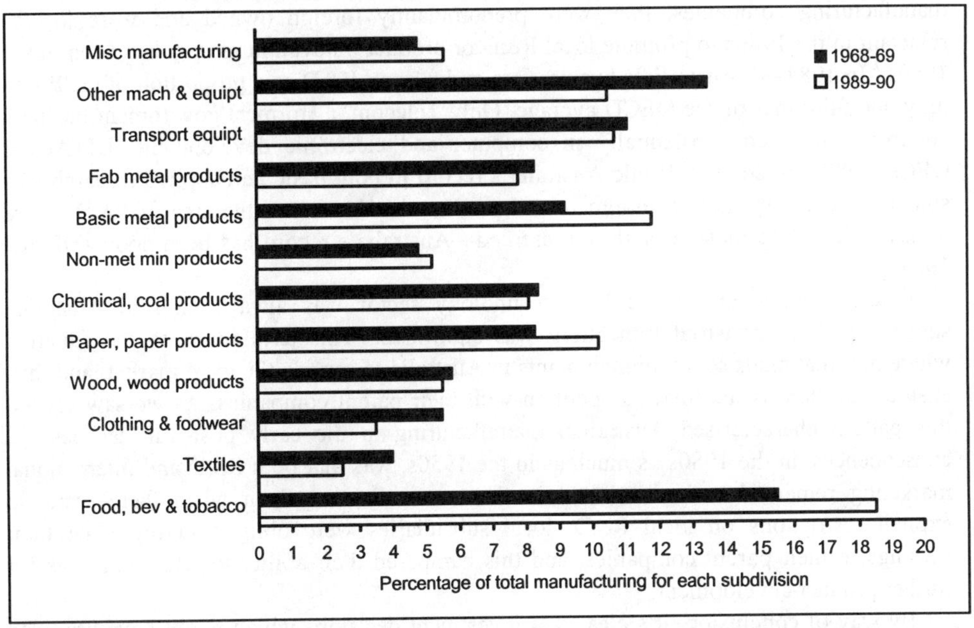

Source: Industry Commission (1995), *Australian Manufacturing Industry and International Trade Data 1968–69 to 1992–93*, Information Paper, p. 9

Why did Australian manufacturing take the low road, particularly when its scientific resources—its universities and the CSIRO—were so well established? Our theme of social settlements helps answer this question. As well as product markets and labour markets, the other important aspect to a social settlement is the ownership and control of production. Australian manufacturing was characterised by a very large number of small producers, and a small number of large producers. In the mid-1980s, for example, of the 23,000 firms in manufacturing, 96 per cent employed less than 100 people and accounted for one-quarter of turnover. On the other hand, the largest 100 firms accounted for 47 per cent of turnover (DITAC 1987, p. 8). While the small firms were efficient at servicing local markets, they lacked the financial resources to undertake research and development (R&D) or to expand into export markets in innovative ways (Study Group on Structural Adjustment 1979, p. 17). As well as capital, poor management also had a role to play. The Karpin Report into Australia's managers found that they rated very poorly for technical and conceptual skills, financial skills and entrepreneurial skills. In manufacturing, managers often took the easy way out and carried on working as they always had. In engineering for example, their history as 'jobbing shops' kept them focused on maintenance, reworking and repairs, rather than producing saleable products (AMWU 1995, p. 18).

Unlike the United States, Australia lacked a well-established venture capital market, and more conventional capital markets were biased towards property and blue chip investments. Only in a few areas like software production—a craft-based, labour intensive form of production—did small Australian companies regularly succeed internationally (and they were often bought out by the big players in the industry). As for the large manufacturing companies, they were predominantly foreign owned and were just as reluctant in the 1980s to promote local R&D or product innovation as they had been in the 1960s.[7] In 1984–85 Australia's business expenditure on R&D as a proportion of GDP was only one-third that of the OECD average. Only Telecom, a (former) government business enterprise, invested substantially in computer and electronic development (DITAC & OECD 1988, pp. 24, 31). While Australia's record in both basic and applied research was sound, 'in experimental development and product development—the area of R&D where industry should be most strongly represented—Australia's record has been poor' (DITAC 1987, p. 36).

Foreign ownership of the high technology sector was always high in Australia, suggesting that 'industrial truncation' was significant. This term refers to the situation where multinationals set up branch plants in Australia to service the local market, and then ensure that there is minimal competition with their parent companies. As we saw earlier, this pattern characterised Australian manufacturing in the early post-war decades. Its consequences, in the 1980s as much as in the 1950s, was that both R&D and international marketing remained underdeveloped in these subsidiaries.[8] Even when there were no explicit restrictions on local R&D, local subsidiaries were obliged to repatriate their earnings to their parent companies, and this hampered their ability to retain earnings for further product development.

By way of conclusion, it's clear that investment decisions which might have provided Australia with both high living standards and greater employment security were squandered during the 1980s. Australia had the *capacity* to take the high road to the future, but control of the economy was not in the hands of those with an interest in this kind of future.

THE CONNECTION WITH WORKPLACE CHANGE

During the 1980s, Australia was increasingly exposed to international competition but there was nothing inevitable about the form closer integration with the world economy took. 'Globalisation' was not an irresistible force of nature, but a catchphrase for a number of related events. The widespread deregulation of national financial markets and the rapid dissemination of communications technologies made international investment flows more volatile then ever before. How severely this volatility affected particular countries was closely tied into the characteristics of their national settlements, particularly product markets, labour markets, and the ownership and control of resources. In the case of Australia, high levels of foreign ownership made the economy particularly sensitive to international capital flows. Moreover, as we have just seen, Australia was vulnerable to increased international competition because it was locked into the price-sensitive 'low road' to the future.

At a time when the world economy was moving to 'more knowledge intensive and less resource intensive patterns of output' Australia remained dependent on exporting primary products and semi-processed products (Sheehan in AMWU 1995, p. 11). Yet increased global competition in primary products has meant the long-run decline in their product prices will continue. The result had been a relative decline in foreign earnings for the Australian economy from mining and farming (Pilat et al. 1993, p. 1). At the same time, the increased liberalisation of international trade in manufactured products has seen Australia's domestic manufacturing sector exposed to severe import competition, particularly from newly industrialising countries (NICs) in Asia. The progressive dismantling of manufacturing protection during the 1980s by the Labor Government increased this import competition. As a result of these changes in the international economy, Australia reached a crossroads:

> This relative decline in real earnings, together with the emergence of large and sustained current account deficits, declining national savings ratios, continued reliance on high levels of foreign investment and a rapid growth in external debt, has brought a seachange in the tenor of economic analysis and policy debate in Australia (Pilat et al. 1993, p. 1).

This sea change has lapped at the doors of Australia's workplaces for a number of reasons. As we saw earlier, the failure of both Keynesianism and Monetarism brought 'micro-economic reform' to centre stage, and workplace change featured prominently in the script. Productivity decline had become a major theme in economic debates from the 1970s onwards. International comparisons were a favourite device in these debates, and Australia's poor ranking was a frequent lament. While these comparisons were often spurious, they added heat to the debates burning in economic policy forums and they fuelled the political onslaught of the neo-liberals. As we saw earlier, this group was largely based around the economic interests of exporters—the miners and the NFF—for whom increased international competitiveness—narrowly defined in cost cutting terms—was paramount.

While labour productivity had indeed been in long-term decline, this was a structural feature of advanced economies. As argued earlier, this was the 'brick wall' which all advanced economies with burgeoning service sectors were bound to hit. But in the productivity debates, this structural limitation was obscured, and productivity decline was treated as a moral failure. By focusing on 'total factor productivity' economists were able to refocus the question of international competition onto a broad review of all factor inputs into production.[9] In pursuit of efficiencies across the board, public sector 'reform' and privatisation joined workplace change as the key elements of the micro-economic reform agenda. Thus the public sector, particularly publicly owned infrastructure, was deemed a drain on productivity because it provided costly inputs (such as electricity) for business activity in the private sector. It was further claimed that as an area of the economy not subject to competitive pressures, the public sector failed to check wages growth, and thereby further increased the cost of inputs for the private sector. Finally, the public sector competed for scarce funds in capital markets, pushing up interest rates for business. This was popularised as the 'crowding out thesis' during the mid-1980s. All of these arguments were used to justify 'small government' onslaughts during the 1980s, both by Federal and State/Territory governments. The fact that the public sector was also the bedrock for the Australian community's general wellbeing was conveniently overlooked in these policy forums.

At a workplace level this pursuit of the productivity holy grail also focused on factor inputs, but it overwhelmingly emphasised 'work practices'; the transformation of the inputs into products. From 1987 onwards the Australian Industrial Relations Commission linked wage increases to productivity and efficiency. This approach was refined for the rest of the decade until 1991 when enterprise bargaining was finally adopted. Chapter 3 explores this transition in greater detail. Two related processes were at work in this transformation of industrial relations. In the first process, attempts were made to break the nexus between the economic conditions of the individual firm and industry-wide and economy-wide standards. In the same way that the factor inputs for the private sector were 'unnecessarily' inflated by the public sector, argued the neo-liberal advocates of 'reform', so too were factor inputs for individual firms inflated by outside standards; things like Award wages and conditions. Interestingly, other factor inputs which were not part of the industrial relations scenario—things like inflated rents, excessive interest charges and monopoly prices for materials inputs—were pursued with far less passion. They were left to await the eventual diffusion of competitive pressures throughout the economy.

When enterprise bargaining finally emerged into the limelight of the industrial relations drama it promised 'benefits all round'. But the single-minded pursuit of a decentralised wages system as the means to reduce 'factor inputs' (particularly wages) revealed that its prime intention was to capture the productivity chimera. Chapter 4 examines in detail the links between workplace change and wage polarisation in the labour market during the 1980s and 1990s.

The second related process was the pursuit of increased productivity within the workplace, predominantly through work intensification—making people work harder and longer. The 'work practices' which raised the ire of the 'reformers' included working time arrangements, 'over-staffing', job demarcation, maintenance procedures and work flows. In Chapter 5 we explore in detail how changes in working time arrangements reflected this onslaught against established custom and practice in the management of time. While many of these workplace issues were implicated in productivity outcomes—and the rhetoric of productivity always accompanied the political struggle—the tussle at the shopfloor level was always more complex. As well as attempting to reduce costs, management initiatives at a workplace level were also aimed at gaining greater control over decision-making. Despite the language of 'consultation' and 'employee empowerment', management sought to consolidate its power in the workplace, particularly against 'outside' influences, such as trade unions. The social model guiding management throughout this process was that of the individual outside the collective. Wherever the collective dimension of workplace life could be individualised, that became the target for workplace change. Performance payments, individual contracts, career pathways—accompanied by longer hours— represented the 'managerialisation' of the worker, the attempt to break a collective into scattered individuals.

Even where management met resistance to changing work practices, work intensification was still pursued through the crude device of workforce reductions. Whether through retrenchments or redundancies, or through failing to replace workers who resigned, management sought to make the remaining workforce carry the workload of their departed colleagues. As Chapter 6 will show, the result was increased job insecurity across the workforce.

Rarely did the rewards of work intensification match the costs. For most workers, the working day did not just consist of transforming inputs into outputs. It also involved relating to one's fellow workers and finding some satisfaction in being at the workplace. Thus attempts to eliminate 'dead time' in the productivity chain also undermined the social relations of the workplace. Workers make boring or difficult work bearable by fostering sociability, particularly humour and other forms of mutual assistance. An agenda for workplace change which undermines these social relations of the workplace is experienced by people as a profound contradiction between the social and economic.

SOCIAL PROTECTION AND THE MARKET

This chapter has set out to explain the political and economic forces behind recent changes in the Australian economy. The next chapter will continue this story, focussing more closely on changes which took place at a workplace level. We've chosen to wrap our story within the twin themes of *social settlements* and the *neo-liberal project* for several important reasons.

First, political activity is integral to economic change, even when economists choose to ignore this. There is no inevitability about economic change, no unstoppable logic in an economic system, but only a series of political choices made by people acting within structures which offer both opportunities and constraints. As suggested earlier, the idea of a social settlement is very useful because it highlights the patterns of choice made by historical actors over the course of many decades. Unlike 'globalisation'—with its aura of inevitability—the idea of a 'social settlement' highlights choices being made under inherited conditions. As we've argued, neo-liberalism has been successful in dismantling a great deal of Australia's post-war settlement because powerful forces combined to form a project to bring it down.

This brings us to our second point. Choices and power are interwoven. We see this in each chapter of this book. In Chapters 3 and 5, which examine workplace bargaining and changes to working time arrangements respectively, we see that management emerged from the process of workplace change with enhanced power; industrial tribunals, unions and workers all emerged with diminished power. In Chapters 4 and 6, which deal with the wages system and with job security in turn, we see that economic power in the labour market determined who became winners and who became losers.

Finally, the issues of choice and power come together in the 'big question': what's good for society? The reasons we reject neo-liberalism is that its prescriptions don't work and that a great deal of social damage is done in the process. The economic historian, Karl Polanyi (1957) explored the emergence of economic liberalism during the nineteenth century and he identified an important tension between what he called the 'self-regulating market system' and the idea of 'social protection'. By social protection he meant adequate labour standards, a stable and sound monetary system, and wise management of natural resources. For Polanyi, when the market was allowed to 'self-regulate', these areas of social protection fell apart and the horrors of nineteenth century laissez-faire capitalism exemplified this process.

Since the emergence of market-based industrial societies, every historical era confronts this same dilemma: how much of the 'social good' will be managed by conscious decision-making processes, and how much will be left to the market to decide? Our own era—the last decade or so—has seen this balance tip towards the market in a way that the last generation would have found inconceivable. In the final chapter of this book we identify new ways of balancing the forces of social protection and the market. The new balance would not involve a return to the post-war settlement, but neither does it mean marching further down the neo-liberal road.

Notes

1 For an excellent account of the emergence of economic liberalism see Polanyi (1957) and for the ideology of neo-liberalism see Rose (1996).

2 For 'settler' capitalism see Peter Beilharz's discussion of Jack Lindsay in Beilharz (1994, p. 3) and for 'dominion capitalism' see Ehrensaft and Armstrong (1978).

3 Productivity has begun to pick up during the 1990s. The most likely reason for this is the increase in work intensification which has been so evident during the late 1980s and early 1990s.

4 As DITAC observed: 'Productivity growth has been significantly higher in manufacturing than in the economy as a whole in Australia and most other countries, largely reflecting the gains from capital and technology inputs' (1987, p. 10).

5 See the extensive work carried out by the Social Policy Research Centre at the University of New South Wales from the early 1980s to the mid-1990s.

6 This was the theme of the AMWU's analysis of manufacturing (AMWU 1995).

7 Foreign ownership accounted for one-third of manufacturing activity (DITAC 1987, p. 8).

8 The DITAC report is equivocal over whether 'industrial truncation' characterises Australia's high technology sector.

9 For a typical analysis see Harris (1996).

CHAPTER 3

Bargaining for change

Continuing micro-economic reform is necessary to shape an economy which can deliver durable improvements in the day to day lives of Australians—more jobs, more work satisfaction, greater growth, fewer people dependent on welfare and capacity to afford adequate assistance for the truly needy. Micro reform serves, very profoundly, human needs. *Bob Hawke, Prime Minister, Statement on Micro-economic Reform, 10th April, 1989.*

This was Bob Hawke's promise nearly a decade ago. The reality, as this book demonstrates, has been profoundly different. In the previous chapter we outlined the economy wide changes that have transformed Australia over the past two decades. In this chapter we look at how workplaces—where workers often spend over a third of the day—have been dramatically restructured in the last decade. We look first at how change was formally introduced through a more decentralised system of enterprise bargaining. We then examine how much change this new system actually brought, as well as changes which have occurred for other reasons. In so doing we look closely at the processes by which changes were introduced and the effect of workplace change on our industrial relations institutions. In looking back at a decade of workplace change, it's clear that management power has been considerably increased as a result of a more decentralised system of enterprise bargaining. Both of the institutions which have traditionally kept management power in check—trade unions and the AIRC—have been marginalised by many of these changes. It's not that workplaces have become deregulated. Rather the *form of regulation has changed*, from a situation where *external regulation*—by outside institutions—was important, to a situation where *internal regulation*—by management's own decision-making power—has become dominant (Buchanan and Callus 1993).

CHANGING THE FORMAL SYSTEM

We saw in the last chapter that in the mid-1980s the Hawke Labor Government hopped on board the neo-liberal bus and began to implement a micro-economic agenda for change. The new agenda represented a shift in policy from the macro to the micro. It was a policy shift that also had the general support of the labour movement, where it was seen as a form of 'strategic unionism'. This involved the acceptance by unions of the importance of economic renewal in the face of the economic crisis. Indeed the future of the union movement was seen to be closely tied to the development and efficiency of the economy and business in particular.

There is an urgent need to develop in Australia a production consciousness and culture, both in industry and in the community ... The creation of wealth is a prerequisite of its distribution. Without in any way diminishing the importance of equitable distribution, the current situation brings into sharp focus the need to develop widespread awareness of the fundamental importance of creating wealth and income (ACTU 1987, p. 154).

Many of the changes and workplace reforms that occurred in Australia in the ensuing years were possible because competitive pressures and the threat of globalisation produced an environment where management, the unions and government agreed, to a degree not seen since the Second World War, that there was now a common objective: economic growth and increased productivity. At the centre of this was the need to change how work was done. But to do this also meant that the parties needed to reassess how *the rules of work* were to be determined. Specifically, this required a change in the roles of those rule-making institutions which regulated work. Australian workplaces were about to be transformed and with them the lives of millions of workers.

Moving towards the decentralisation of industrial relations

Enterprise bargaining

By the mid-1980s it was apparent that workplace change could not occur without also changing the industrial relations rule-making system, particularly around issues like working conditions, work practices and wage determination. Consequently, from about 1987 onward, the Australian industrial relations system began a restructuring that resulted in a profound change in how the rules were made and the terms and conditions under which people worked. In 1987, for the first time, wage rises achieved through the award system became, in part, determined by unions and management at workplaces. Wage rises were granted after the parties had demonstrated to the Australian Industrial Relations Commission (AIRC) that certain levels of restructuring had taken place and cost saving improvements had been achieved. This was known as the Restructuring and Efficiency Principle (REP). The introduction of the REP was the means by which the parties were introduced to formal enterprise bargaining, but within a centralised award-based system. The main aim of the REP was to devolve the responsibility of setting wage levels to the workplace and to move away from wage increases related to primarily macro-economic conditions. Wage increases under the REP were available as a general wage increase, to be topped up by a second tier increase of up to 4 per cent if certain measures were met:

> Increases in rates of pay or improvement in conditions of employment may be justified as a result of measures implemented to improve efficiency in both the public and private sectors.
>
> (i) changes to work practices and changes to management practices must be accepted as an integral part of an exercise conducted in accordance with this principle.
>
> (ii) other initiatives may include action to reduce demarcation barriers, advance multi-skilling, training and retraining, and broad banding (Australian Conciliation and Arbitration Commission, Print G6800, p. 14).

The National Labour Consultative Council (NLCC), a tripartite body, reported that there were difficulties in the implementation of the REP principle because of its novelty (NLCC 1988, p. 19). They suggested a raft of problems had emerged, including indifference, ambivalence, rigid approaches, industrial action, management dragging its feet and inconsistent applications of the principle. The Council found that relatively few agreements involved far-reaching change, and that a 'trade-off mentality' was evident.

While the fragmented structure of the system was a factor, blame was principally placed at the feet of the negotiating parties.

According to some commentators the main difficulties in implementing enterprise bargaining were the attitudes and resources of the parties—they were poorly equipped to carry out enterprise negotiations. In some cases where bargaining was spread over many small firms, unions did not have the resources to sustain bargaining. In other areas employer associations effectively blocked enterprise bargaining (McDonald & Rimmer 1988, p. 484).

In short, the award system was quite flexible in adapting to the special requirements of second tier bargaining but it still posed a problem for negotiating over restructuring and efficiency at a workplace level. Despite these restrictions, a national workplace survey carried out in 1990 (AWIRS—the Australian Workplace Industrial Relations Survey), noted that change was still evident from the REP. Figure 3.1 shows that a significant change in awards was evident, with only 14 per cent of all workplaces (with 20 or more employees) not having introduced at least one change. The most common changes introduced were alteration to award classifications (39 per cent), changes to work practices (39 per cent), and the introduction of payment by EFT (40 per cent). It was evident that workplace change was more likely to occur in large workplaces and in the public sector. It was also more likely to occur in union-active bargaining workplaces, a pattern that was to persist as bargaining continued to decentralise.

In the August 1988 National Wage Case the AIRC stated that the Structural Efficiency Principle (SEP) would be the 'key element' in a new system of wage fixation. This was intended to provide incentive to the parties to review their awards and facilitate reform. The principle aimed at improving what is called 'functional flexibility', that is increasing the range of tasks done by the workforce. In the words of the commission:

> It is not intended that this principle will be applied in a negative cost-cutting manner or to formalise illusory, short-term benefits. Its purpose is to facilitate the type of fundamental review essential to ensure that existing award structures are relevant to modern competitive environments of industry and are in the best interests of both management and workers (Australian Industrial Relations Commission, Print H4000, pp. 5–6).

The 1988 decision only required that the parties promise to adopt the principle. This was extended a year later in the 1989 National Wage Case which continued the principle and provided for two wage increases of 3 per cent. The changes envisaged by the commission included:

❑ establishing skill-related career paths;
❑ eliminating impediments to multi-skilling and broadening the range of tasks which a worker may be required to perform;
❑ creating appropriate relativities between different categories of workers within the award and at enterprise level; and
❑ ensuring that working patterns and arrangements enhance flexibility and meet the competitive requirements of the industry.

Figure 3.1 Workplace changes introduced since the 1987 Restructuring and Efficiency Principle, 1989

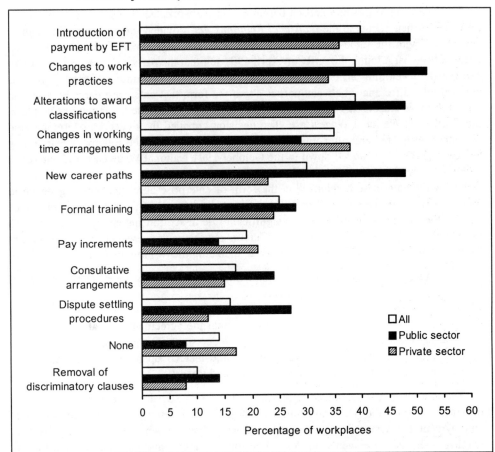

Source: Callus, R. et al. (1991), *Industrial Relations at Work, The Australian Workplace Industrial Relations Survey,* Commonwealth Department of Industrial Relations, AGPS, Canberra, p. 198.
Population: Australian workplaces with at least 20 employees. Figures are weighted and are based on responses from 2004 workplaces.
Note: Some workplaces had several changes.

The Structural Efficiency Principle faced similar problems to the REP as the parties struggled to come to terms with the new bargaining arrangements. The NLCC noted a number of difficulties with the introduction of the principle, which were due to a misunderstanding of the SEP's purpose, a feeling of indifference to the objectives, resistance to the removal of demarcations, and a combination of rigid and narrow approaches to trade-offs (NLCC 1988, p. 20).

Progression towards the SEP principle by the parties was notably slow. The reasons for this were various and included issues such as minimum rates and competency; the linking of industry and enterprise bargaining; suspicion from management and workers; the scope and complexity of issues; and the lack of union preparation for award restructuring. (McDonald and Rimmer 1989, p. 126).

The transition to institutionalised bargaining at the workplace level was not without its problems. Amendments to the *Industrial Relations Act* provided for a system of enterprise agreements with the same legal standing as awards. But after almost four years of formal decentralised bargaining, the AIRC in April 1991 felt that the parties were still not ready or capable of developing arrangements to bargain fully at a decentralised level. This was coupled with differences between parties about the form that enterprise bargaining should take. For these reasons the AIRC refused to provide an enterprise bargaining principle in the April 1991 National Wage Case. The decision appalled the Federal Government and offended the ACTU and after much negotiating and posturing, the Enterprise Bargaining Principle (EBP) was handed down in the October 1991 National Wage case and enterprise bargaining was formally encouraged.

So, while enterprise bargaining in the form of enterprise agreement making began in 1991, at this stage the system was still heavily under the eye of the external umpire—the AIRC. The Commission still played a significant role in scrutinising enterprise agreements that were now possible under the Act. Certain requirements were placed on the parties before an enterprise agreement was approved, including the two requirements listed below.

❑ Wage increases must be 'based on the actual implementation of efficiency measures designed to effect real gains in productivity'.
❑ An agreement must have a fixed term. All wage increases within that term must be specified in the agreement. An exception is that the agreement may allow for further increases consistent with National Wage Case decisions. The parties, therefore, have a choice between the 'closed' agreement or one that is 'open' to the extent that the national wage increases *may* apply (Hancock and Isaac 1992).

The enterprise bargaining principle marked the first step in what was to be an ever decreasing role for the AIRC and National Wage Cases in setting wages and conditions of employment for a significant proportion of Australian workers. But the early days of making enterprise agreements still left a key role for unions and the Commission. Indeed, in the first generation of enterprise agreements the negotiations took place between managers from head office and full-time union officials in over 70 per cent of workplaces which signed agreements. There was, therefore, little evidence that bargaining was taking place at individual workplaces, or at more decentralised levels (DIR 1996, p. 66).

The Labor Government, however, was committed to widening the scope of enterprise bargaining and was keen to further decentralise Australian industrial relations. Five weeks after being returned to office in 1993, the Prime Minister, Paul Keating, described the model of industrial relations to which the government was working, a model that saw a significant decline in the role of the award system:

It is a model which places primary emphasis on bargaining at the workplace level within a framework of minimum standards provided by arbitral tribunals.

It is a model under which compulsorily arbitrated awards and arbitrated wage increases would be there only as a safety net.

This safety net would not be intended to prescribe the actual conditions of work of most employees, but only to catch those unable to make workplace arrangements with their employers. Over time the safety net would inevitably become simpler. We would have fewer awards, with fewer clauses. For most employees and most businesses, wages and conditions of work would be determined by agreements worked out by the employer, the employees and their union. These agreements would predominantly be based on improving the productive performance of enterprises, because both employers and employees are coming to understand that only productivity improvements can guarantee sustainable real wage increases (Paul Keating, cited in Hancock and Rawson, 1993).

As it turned out, it was left to the Coalition Liberal–National Government to complete the Keating vision with the *Workplace Relations Act* of 1996. The Act, through the 20 allowable matters provision, effectively stripped awards to core issues. Other non-allowable matters were either dropped, or left to the parties to negotiate through enterprise bargaining, or where there was no agreement, the option remained for management to determine the outcome unilaterally.

In 1993 the system of industrial relations underwent a further historic change. Collective forms of non-union bargaining—known as Enterprise Flexibility Agreements (EFAs)—were implemented through an amendment to the *Industrial Relations Act*. While never attracting a great deal of interest by employers, the opening up of collective bargaining to workers not represented by unions was a dramatic break with the past. For the first time, changing minimum wages and conditions of workers did not require the active involvement of 'registered organisations'. The formal system had decentralised and the nature of representation, for the purposes of bargaining, had been modified in a fundamental way.

The enterprise agreement system

At one level the new system of enterprise agreements formalised and extended what had been occurring for a long time in some workplaces. There had always been local or workplace level negotiations in Australia, particularly at well unionised and union-active workplaces. This was so even when the system in general was based on a centralised award system that regulated the minimum wages and conditions of nearly 90 per cent of workers. But whenever bargaining actually took place at the enterprise or workplace level, it occurred in the shadow of the award system, usually in the form of over-award bargaining. In 1994, not long after the commencement of formal decentralised bargaining, workplace surveys found that there was bargaining taking place outside formal registered agreements through the use of informal agreements and individual contracts. Overall 11 per cent of workplaces had an informal agreement (Short, Preston and Peetz 1993). In addition, workplace specific work practices grew out of local rules or custom and practice, and these were often the outcome of some bargaining between local union delegates or employees and local managers.

So while the informal system in Australia had always played an important role in certain parts of the economy, it had no legal basis or standing. *The new enterprise bargaining system was significant because it formalised what had been taking part in segments of the economy. But, more than this, it extended and institutionalised decentralised bargaining to parts of the economy that were not experienced with this form of collective bargaining.* All of a sudden the parties in medium and larger enterprises who lived by the award, and had never formally negotiated, found themselves at the bargaining table.

The changes to the industrial relations system intensified following the election of the Liberal–National Coalition Government in 1996 and the subsequent passage of the *Workplace Relations Act 1996.* Once again the system of rule-making was altered. Rule-making via agreements could now be 'negotiated' directly between individuals and their employers. Collective bargaining was no longer the only method of industrial relations rule-making in Australia, a new federal bargaining stream known as Australian Workplace Agreements (AWAs) had come into being. A critical feature of the AWA stream was that it was not under the jurisdiction of the AIRC but was administered by—and AWAs were approved by—a separate authority, the Office of the Employment Advocate (OEA). In short, the powers of the AIRC to oversee bargaining in Australia had become restricted to collective union and non-union (certified) bargaining.

The *Workplace Relations Act* also restricted the powers of the AIRC in other ways, most notably by limiting its role in intervening in industrial disputes. One of the prime reasons for establishing an arbitration system in Australia in 1904 had been the need to have an effective and appropriate method of settling and preventing industrial disputes. The sidelining of the traditional industrial relations umpire in disputes was most dramatically apparent in 1997 with the Hunter Valley Number One dispute, and again in 1998 with the waterfront dispute between Patricks and the Maritime Union of Australia.

THE UMPIRE SIDELINED

The sidelining of the AIRC from effectively intervening to resolve industrial disputes was dramatically demonstrated during 1997 and early 1998. It took place over the dispute between the coal mining giant Rio Tinto and its workforce at the Hunter Valley Number 1 Coal Mine. Justice Boulton decided to terminate the bargaining period in this dispute and institute arbitration (an enforced settlement of the dispute). Under the Federal *Workplace Relations Act 1996* the industrial parties in a dispute are left to 'slog it out' during a bargaining period, and the AIRC is restrained from arbitrating the dispute.

In the case of the Hunter Valley dispute, Justice Boulton determined that industrial action threatened the welfare of the economy and ordered that the parties move to arbitration. Rio Tinto appealed the decision, and the Full Bench of the AIRC overturned Justice Boulton's decision, restoring the bargaining period and ruling out arbitration.

Source: Derived from CCH, *Australian Industrial Law News*, 23 February 1998, p. 9.

The spread of enterprise bargaining

After nearly a decade of enterprise agreement-making in Australia, the regulatory system remains complicated. ACIRRT's estimate of the extent of collective registered agreements is that approximately 30 to 40 per cent of employees have at least some of their working conditions regulated by an enterprise agreement. Awards remain the main regulatory form for approximately 35 to 40 per cent of employees. A further 30 to 35 per cent of the employed workforce are award-free and agreement-free, working exclusively under a contract of employment. In 1998, after just 18 months, AWAs cover only about 20,000 employees or less than one-quarter of 1 per cent of the workforce.

Complicating the matter is the fact that certified collective agreements, where they do operate, generally do not completely replace awards. Instead, they are being used primarily by larger organisations to change some aspects of the award, or to deal with matters on which the award is silent. By 1998 only about 7 per cent of collective agreements completely replaced awards (ADAM 1998). While the newest form of agreement-making—the individual based Australian Workplace Agreements—do replace awards completely, this form of agreement-making is still relatively underdeveloped.

The pattern of agreement-making has not been uniform across the economy. Despite various attempts by successive governments to interest small employers in this form of regulation it has largely been ignored by the vast majority of organisations with less than 100 employees. Successive surveys of small business have found that the award system is not seen as a problem for small employers and most do not see their awards as barriers to change (Callus, Kitay & Sutcliffe 1992). In the second AWIRS, carried out in 1995, it emerged that 76 per cent of small commercial business managers felt that the award system had worked well for their workplace in the past.

The uptake of agreements has also been uneven in terms of industry profile, with less than a third of medium to large workplaces (those with 20 or more employees) in the accommodation and restaurant, property and business services and health and community services industries having an agreement. In contrast, over 70 per cent of workplaces in electricity, gas and water and communication services indicated they had an agreement.

Collective-based enterprise bargaining in Australia has therefore remained confined to the highly unionised sectors of the economy and amongst larger enterprises (ACIRRT 1996a). Bargaining is particularly prominent at public sector workplaces, where about one-half have enterprise agreements.

Even workplaces with agreements often exclude some employees from coverage. The Federal Department of Industrial Relation's 1995 annual report on enterprise bargaining found that in workplaces with Federal agreements, the proportion of employees excluded had increased. White-collar employees were far more likely to be excluded from an agreement than their blue-collar colleagues. The result is that it is not uncommon for a number of different forms of regulation to exist at the same workplace, depending on the occupational profile of the workforce and the industry in which it operates.

What's enterprise bargaining about?

The expectations

To what extent has enterprise bargaining been about achieving workplace change? After all, it was workplace change which critics of the award system felt was difficult or impossible to achieve under a highly centralised system. In this section we examine changes that have been introduced through enterprise bargaining.

It is perhaps true to say that in the early days of enterprise bargaining there was a somewhat unrealistic expectation of what the new system could achieve. Fuelled by governments eager to see enterprise bargaining succeed, unions seeking to justify a leap into the unknown and consultants wanting to build lucrative HRM markets, organisations devoted enormous energy and resources to negotiating and settling agreements. A reading of a cross-section of first generation agreements gives us some indication of the promises which agreements seemed to offer. This reading shows that agreements were viewed as the primary vehicle for change in organisations and the process of agreement-making was itself an integral part of the culture-shift which many organisations hoped to see. Negotiating an agreement, it was believed by many, would produce a new spirit of cooperation and common purpose. In this brave new world of negotiations, the traditional adversarial system which had been a feature of the 'old award system' would be replaced with one that made decisions based on the business needs of organisations and its workers. Indeed, agreements hoped to bring about a cultural change, as much as changes in wages and conditions of work.

Inevitably early agreements set out in some detail their purpose or vision. In many agreements there was a sense of working together to achieve mutually beneficial outcomes. The boxed text below offers an interesting example.

Looking back from the vantage point of the late 1990s, it's clear that a lot of the early agreements set out an ambitious agenda for change. It was an agenda that many organisations soon realised could not be easily implemented. The early generation of agreements did deal with a range of issues which awards had never considered, but these agreements were, in retrospect, largely statements of hope. Many of these agreements never did, and perhaps could not, deliver the attitudinal change that was reflected in the words and sentiment that appear in the boxed text. There was much hype surrounding agreement-making but, in time, innovation and provisions which would transform workplaces into 'best practice' or 'cutting edge' organisations became more difficult to find. Ultimately there was one major issue that most agreements were addressing and delivering—changes to working time arrangements in exchange for wage increases.

Of more than 4,700 agreements examined by ACIRRT up to July 1998, 79 per cent dealt with changing working time arrangements. Generally these provisions concerned the number of hours to be worked each week, increasing the span of ordinary hours and other flexibilities such as averaging of hours worked over a month, quarter or year. Figure 3.2 shows that no other issue was as likely to be found in agreements as flexible hours clauses. Chapter 5 discusses these issues in greater depth and shows that recent workplace restructuring and enterprise bargaining now mean most people are working longer and harder than at any other time since the mid-1960s.

WORKING TOGETHER

The company and the union recognise that this agreement represents a further opportunity to maintain and build upon the Company's market share and profitability by providing products of high quality, excellent customer service and well trained and motivated employees.

The objectives of this agreement are... :

❑ To ensure the efficiency and prosperity of the business for the benefit of the Company's employees, customers, shareholders and the community.

❑ Develop and maintain the most productive and harmonious working relationships possible.

Both the Company and the Union recognise that an important factor to achieving these objectives is to develop a working environment in which all employees are involved in decisions that affect them, care about their jobs and each other, have the opportunity to achieve their full potential, take pride in themselves and their contributions, and benefit from the successes of their efforts.

Source: Derived from Fast Food Agreement, 1994.

Figure 3.2 Common provisions in enterprise agreements, 1994–95 to 1996–97

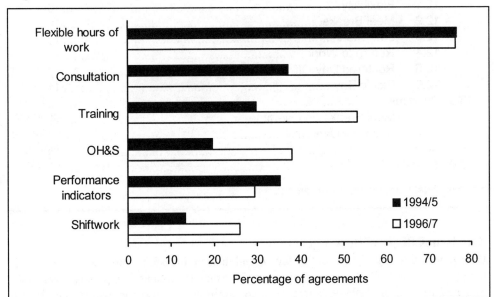

Source: ADAM Database, July 1998.

AN EARLY ENTERPRISE AGREEMENT

Table of Contents

1.0 Application 1
2.0 Duration 1
3.0 Statement of Intent 1
4.0 Classification and Wage Rates 3
5.0 No Extra Claims 4
6.0 Consultative Committee 4
7.0 Equal Opportunity and Non-Discrimination 6
8.0 Induction 6
9.0 Work Clothes 7
10.0 Paint Shop 7
11.0 Tool Kits 8
    11.1   Minimum Tool Kit Requirements 8
    11.2   Electrical Workshop 8
    11.3   Tradesmen and Apprentices 8
    11.4   Mechanical Workshop 9
12.0 Hours of Work 10
    12.1   Flexibility 10
    12.2   Meal Breaks 10
    12.3   Late Starts 10
    12.4   Return to Work 11
    12.5   Rostered Day Off 11
    12.6   Picnic Day 11
13.0 Overtime 12
    13.1   Meal Breaks on Overtime 12
    13.2   Saturday Overtime 12
14.0 Clockcards 13
15.0 Timesheets 13

Source: Metal manufacturing agreement.

The issues dealt with in agreements

Over time issues came in and out of favour and in some industries some issues were more popular than others. Performance indicators, for example, became less popular over time. Some 37 per cent of 1994–95 agreements contained such provisions, whilst only 28 per cent of more recent 1996–97 agreements dealt with this issue. Overall, agreements have become less detailed over the years, possibly because managers and union officials have become more realistic about the role of agreements in the change process.

Provisions for wage rises were a feature of nearly all agreements. Details of wage rise provisions are dealt with in greater detail in Chapter 5. While most agreements continued to be linked to awards, the matter most commonly included in agreements has been wages. *This perhaps remains one of the most significant legacies of the decentralisation of bargaining. Essentially agreement-based wage rises broke with the traditional method of wage determination in Australia. More importantly, the criteria for providing wage increases had fundamentally altered with decentralised bargaining.* Wage increases granted through awards had always been based on concepts such as changes to the value of work, general economic conditions or the concept of comparative wage justice. As expected, the decentralisation of wage bargaining through enterprise agreements significantly altered the criteria by which wage increases would be granted to workers. Achieved or expected productivity gains were to be the new dominant means of acquiring wage increases through the enterprise bargaining system. Data presented in the 1995 Department of Industrial Relations (DIR) annual enterprise bargaining report indicated just how dramatic the new nexus between wage increase and productivity gains had become (see Table 3.1).

Table 3.1 Basis of enterprise agreement pay rises

Basis of wage rise	Percentage of all workplaces with an agreement
Expected productivity gains	39
Achieved productivity gains	28
Changes in skills level	17
Other	16
Achievement of specific targets	14
Increases in prices or CPI	14
Industry-wide pay increase	13
Individual performance or appraisal	12
Increase in award or safety net	10
Economic conditions	9
More hours or workplace flexibility	7
Greater financial performance	4
Customer service	2

Source: Department of Industrial Relations (1996), *Annual report 1995:Enterprise Bargaining in Australia*, AGPS, Canberra, p. 138.
Population: All workplaces with an agreement.

What enterprise bargaining has not delivered, to date, is a transformation of the bargaining agenda. Wages and hours remain the staple items in agreements, and the innovations which would fuel the cultural transformation of enterprises—provisions such as gain sharing, worker empowerment, team working, career paths, performance-based pay systems, or family-friendly clauses—have not been realised (see Table 3.2). (There is, of course, no legal requirement that the types of issues listed in Table 3.2 be negotiated through an enterprise agreement.) It's possible that many of the changes listed in Table 3.2 have been introduced at a workplace level without any bargaining taking place. Their absence from enterprise agreements does not mean their absence from the workplace. Even so, their relative absence is evidence of a relatively narrow agenda for bargaining.

Table 3.2 Some issues rarely included in enterprise agreements

Provision	Percentage of agreements
Earnings	
Wages annualised	8
Allowances absorbed	6
Individual performance/piecework payments	6
Gainshare/profit share scheme	5
Bonus payments	4
Leave loading absorbed	4
Management systems	
Teamwork	11
Quality assurance	3
Just In Time (JIT)	0
Family friendly/EEO provisions	
EEO/AA clauses	7
Work from home provision	1
Unlimited sick leave	1

Source: ADAM Database, 1998.

Assessing agreements

The most important changes taking place in Australian workplaces have happened on an informal basis, and most innovations have generally occurred without any bargaining or consultation with workers (an issue we will consider later in this chapter). Even where there has been a widening of the bargaining agenda in some agreements, these need to be kept in perspective. Case studies have consistently shown a gap between the words and the practices. Implementation of clauses have often proved difficult and problematic, especially in the area of training initiatives and the development of performance indicators and performance management systems.

It is hardly surprising, given their increasing power and their greater control over the industrial relations agenda, that managers have expressed satisfaction with the new system and the results achieved from enterprise bargaining. In 1995 some 77 per cent of managers who had an agreement in place at their workplace since 1994 indicated that they were satisfied with the agreement (DIR 1996, p. 134). A further 10 per cent indicated that it was too early to say. Specifically, the benefits from agreement-making derived from the focus on efficiency concerns, particularly hours. Not surprisingly then, managers expressed satisfaction with improvements in labour productivity at their workplaces (see Table 3.3).

It would seem, at this level, that agreements had delivered the goods for managers in a significant proportion of workplaces.

Table 3.3 Managers' assessment of effect of agreement, 1995

	Percentage of workplaces				
	Increased a lot	Increased a little	No change	Decreased a little	Decreased a lot
Labour productivity	17	45	38	0	0
Workplace profitability	11	38	44	6	1
Quality of product or service	12	41	47	1	0
Skills level of employees	13	32	50	6	0

Source: Department of Industrial Relations (1996), *Annual report 1995: Enterprise Bargaining in Australia*, AGPS, Canberra, pp. 129–133.
Note: Based on agreements registered in 1994 only.

If enterprise bargaining has provided the mechanism for managers to win the flexibilities they have sought—for example, through changing working time arrangements—then the time, effort and resources expended has been worthwhile for them. The price to managers has been modest in terms of wage increases or more costly 'employee focussed' provisions. Unions, on the other hand, have been largely unsuccessful under enterprise bargaining in widening the bargaining agenda, or in significantly improving working conditions or opportunities for their members.

New forms of bargaining

One of the anticipated outcomes of a decentralised bargaining system is the emergence of a union / non-union differential in bargaining outcomes. Under the award system the benefits of award changes went to both union and non-union members covered by the award. This is no longer the case with agreements. For the first time since 1993, when non-union collective bargaining was allowed, there is a discernible difference in the outcomes of agreements negotiated by unions and those negotiated collectively by workers without union involvement. Figure 3.3 shows that workers under non-union agreements have had to become more flexible in the hours they work and Figure 3.4 shows—across all industries—that they have also received lower wage increases than workers whose agreements have been negotiated by a union.[1]

The differences here are dramatic. Overall, 85 per cent of non-union agreements deal with some aspect of working time entitlements. This is compared with just over 70 per cent of union agreements. Even more dramatic are the differences in the incidence of particular types of working time clauses:

❑ standard hours longer than 38 are more common in non-union (24 per cent) compared to union agreements (7 per cent);
❑ averaging of hours over a week, month or year is more common in non-union (38 per cent) compared to union agreements (17 per cent);
❑ overtime paid at a single rate is present in 14 per cent of non-union agreements and virtually absent (1 per cent) in union agreements.

Figure 3.3 Non-union bargaining effect in hours, 1997

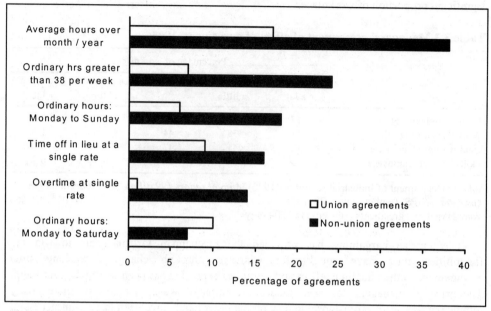

Source: ADAM Database 1997.

Figure 3.4 Non-union bargaining effect in wages by industry, 1997

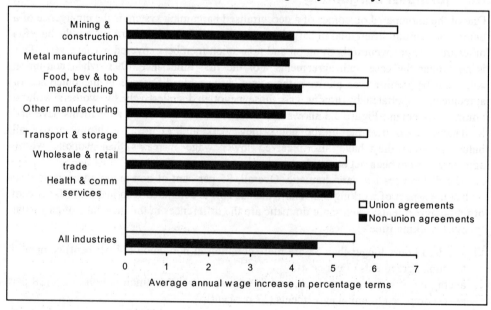

Source: ADAM Database 1997.

The decentralisation of bargaining—especially when it has involved collective bargaining without union involvement—has produced differential outcomes that dramatically reflect the power imbalances of the parties involved in bargaining. Award provisions were a 'common good' available to union and non-union workers alike, but enterprise bargaining has now led to differential outcomes. While this was always one of the attractions of a decentralised system—that it should be made more appropriate to the parties—it was never made clear by its advocates that different outcomes would reflect *power relations*, rather than the different enterprise and worker *needs* which agreements were intended to address.

Decentralised formal bargaining—an assessment

The formal system of enterprise bargaining did more than just formalise and extend what had been a part of informal industrial relations practice in some organisations, it dramatically altered the system of rule-making. Enterprise bargaining is different from the system of award-making in a number of crucial ways.

First, as we have seen, enterprise bargaining explicitly linked the provision of wage increases to changes in work arrangements. Although the concept of productivity bargaining had been discussed in the 1960s and in the 1980s, it was never a central part of wage determination. Initially the linking of wage increases to productivity improvement, or productivity enhancing provisions, was clearly laid down in principles established by the AIRC. While it is no longer a formal requirement for the registration of an agreement, over time this link has been accepted as part of the bargaining process. When managers agreed to wage increases, they increasingly demanded that these be based on achieved or expected productivity benefits.

Second, the system of enterprise agreements significantly changed the focus of bargaining towards the enterprise or workplace. Awards were essentially multi-employer or industry wide and while pattern bargaining has been a feature of a number of enterprise bargaining rounds, particularly in the construction industry, the nature of the regulatory environment had changed. Agreements have been generally more enterprise or even workplace specific than awards. Agreements have been used, mainly by employers, to strategically alter a number of key award provisions, particularly around working time arrangements, and to deal with matters on which the award was silent.

Third, agreements by definition represent the outcome of a negotiated settlement between the parties. There is no role for the traditional system of arbitrated settlements in an enterprise-agreement-based system. On the other hand, awards could be imposed by the AIRC when the parties could not agree.

Finally, the agreement-based system that has evolved has fundamentally altered one of the tenets of industrial regulation in Australia: that the rules should be collectively negotiated by *registered organisations* of workers (unions) and employers. The first generation of laws that provided for enterprise bargaining recognised this feature of our system and preserved the central role of unions in rule-making. Over time, the laws changed, initially by allowing for non-union collective bargaining (with certain rights for unions to intervene or be notified), and then, in 1996, to allow individual bargaining and agreement-making directly between workers and managers. A central feature of the formal system of industrial relations was fundamentally changed with the 1996 legislation. No longer was rule-making necessarily based on negotiations between managers and collectives of workers or unions. Collective bargaining was no longer enshrined by industrial laws as the only method of industrial regulation.

The institutionalisation of enterprise bargaining ensured that the regulation of industrial relations moved from a system of *external regulation*, via awards, to one of *internal regulation*, whereby workers and management determined their own rules and conditions. Such a system of rule-making had been long seen, by its proponents, to be to the mutual advantage of both workers and managers. These advocates believed that under enterprise bargaining the flexibilities which awards had (allegedly) impeded could be introduced unfettered by external rules determined or overseen by the Industrial Relations Commission. Change which was seen as impossible, or at least very difficult to introduce in the award system, was now possible under an enterprise agreement regime. In practice, however, internal regulation rarely amounted to a *collaborative* mode of operation, but predominantly reflected the ability of management to influence the agenda for bargaining and the outcomes.

Other changes at the workplace

While the system of enterprise bargaining has had a dramatic impact on changing working hours and how workers receive wage rises, many other changes which have occurred at workplaces have not been due to the enterprise bargaining system. Indeed, the level and pace of change during the 1980s and 1990s has been breathtaking. The most dramatic change affecting workplaces has been the scale of 'downsizing'. By the mid-1990s over half of all workplaces had undergone some form of downsizing. We return to this issue in greater detail in Chapter 6.

Looking at workplaces with 20 or more employees, the AWIRS data showed that in both 1990 and 1995 significant organisational change had affected nearly all workplaces (81 per cent) in the years prior to the survey. Significant changes have been occurring at workplaces for nearly a decade. Overall, the most common change was the reorganisation of workplace structure (51 per cent), where organisations altered the vertical structure of their organisations, often accompanied by downsizing. This change was followed closely by new office technology (47 per cent) and changes to the work of non-managerial workers (43 per cent) (see Figure 3.5). The public sector led the private sector in most areas of organisational change, except for the introduction of new plant, machinery or equipment.

Figure 3.5 Types of organisational change that happened at the workplace in the last two years prior to the survey, by sector, 1995

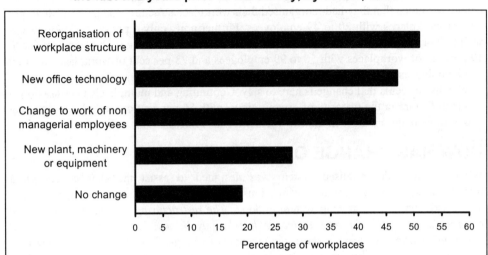

Source: AWIRS 1995, General Management Questionnaire.
Note: Rows add to more than 100 per cent because multiple responses were accepted.
Population: All workplaces with 20 or more employees (sample size 2001 workplaces).

THE EXPERIENCE OF CHANGE— SOME RESERVATIONS

Scepticism about the value of workplace change was evident amongst a large number of focus group participants who worked in the finance sector. During discussions they reflected candidly on the effects of workplace change in their organisation. Although many accepted change as inevitable, there were reservations about the rate of change and the benefits that were supposed to be achieved. Some of the comments included:

'I feel like there is a culture of change just for the sake of change'.

'I've been through so many restructures but my job has stayed exactly the same, the only change is that every time I end up reporting to a different manager'.

'It would be nice to have a change that meant we didn't lose so many jobs and the service to clients improved'.

'We need a period of stability, so we can concentrate on what we are doing, rather than changing all the time without any time to reflect on the benefits of the changes'.

Source: Responses from finance sector focus group conducted by ACIRRT during 1997.

Larger workplaces were also more likely to have undergone some form of workplace change than smaller workplaces. For example, 83 per cent or workplaces with 500 or more employees noted that they had reorganised their workplace structure, compared with 46 per cent of workplaces with 20 to 49 employees. Furthermore, only 4 per cent of workplaces with 500 or more employees reported that there had been no change. This compared with 19 per cent of workplaces with 50 to 99 employees and 23 per cent of workplaces with 20 to 49 employees.

Finally, it seems that change is here to stay. Continuing and multiple changes are now a common feature in the majority of organisations, with 56 per cent of workplaces reporting two or more major changes in the two years prior to AWIRS 1995.

HOW HAS CHANGE OCCURRED?

While the new decentralised system was designed to assist the change process, a remarkably small proportion of organisations which had introduced the changes outlined above used the new bargaining system to do so. *The restructuring that has been a feature of organisational life for over a decade has largely been achieved outside the formal industrial relations system. In short, the majority of changes have been implemented with little involvement, either through bargaining or consultation in the decision-making process, by the workers most affected by the changes.* Many of the changes have occurred without either formal or informal bargaining.

Just as the formal bargaining agenda has been dominated by management, on other matters management has been the initiator of change. However, the decentralisation of industrial relations did not, generally speaking, allow *change itself* to become the subject of bargaining at the workplace or enterprise level. More than ever before, the 1990s have witnessed massive changes and these changes have, overwhelmingly, been introduced by management without the input from external third parties such as unions and the AIRC. Furthermore, despite the almost universal mantra of management schools and texts about the importance of 'involving employees' in the change process, management has largely acted unilaterally in terms of introducing change.

AWIRS 1995 asked managers about the extent of worker involvement in the decision-making process and found that workers had very little role in the process of organisational change. At only 20 per cent of workplaces where there had been a significant change that would affect workers, had workers either *made the decision,* or had a *significant input* into the change decision. At a further 29 per cent of workplaces workers were *consulted* about the changes. In the majority of workplaces undergoing change, workers effectively had *no role* in the decision-making process. They were simply informed that change was about to occur. Amazingly, at 10 per cent of workplaces workers were not even informed of the change—it just happened. Figure 3.6 summarises this picture and shows the involvement of workers by the type of change that occurred at their workplaces.

Figure 3.6 Involvement in decision-making by workers likely to be affected by change, by type of change, mid-1990s

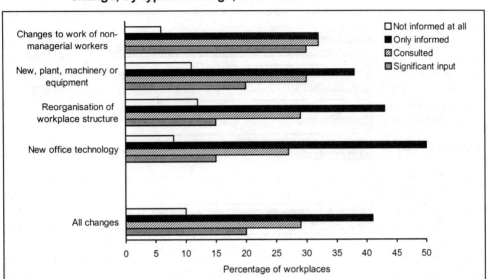

Source: AWIRS 1995, General Management Questionnaire.
Note: 'Not relevant' responses were excluded from this table.
Population: Workplaces with 20 or more employees where managers reported at least one organisational change happened in the two years prior to the survey. Figures are weighted and based on responses from 1618 workplaces.

These findings are also reflected in workers' views on the extent of their influence over the decision-making process. A clear majority of workers thought that they had little or no influence over the decisions which affected them (58 per cent) while a small proportion of workers thought that they had a lot of influence (13 per cent). Figure 3.7 provides an occupational breakdown for this issue of worker influence and highlights that managers and administrators were more likely to indicate that workers had a lot of influence over management and decisions while occupational groups like labourers, plant and machine operators and sales and personal service workers felt that they had much less influence. The AWIRS data also shows that the lack of influence was felt mostly by the younger workers and by casuals. Interestingly, union membership and language background made little difference to the level of influence of workers.

Figure 3.7 Level of workers' influence over decisions which affected them, by occupation,1995

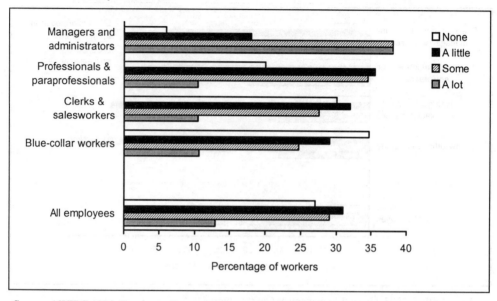

Source: AWIRS 1995, Employee Survey.
Population: All employees at workplace with 20 or more employees.

The workforce appears to be evenly split between those who believe they have been given a chance to have a fair say about the major changes affecting their workplace, and those who felt they lacked such an opportunity. This confirms data collected since the late 1980s which shows a lack of widespread consultative practices by Australian managers (Callus et al. 1991, Chapter 9; M. Short et al. 1994). The reasons why so many workers feel that they have not been given a fair chance to have a say are summarised in Table 3.4. Not surprisingly, given the discussion above, the most common reason was that the decision had been made by management.

The 1990s have seen massive changes at workplaces as a result of increased competition, new technology and an economic climate which gave management the confidence and incentive to make these changes. These were changes that in earlier times management had never seriously considered. Because of the ideological ascendancy of the neo-liberal project, a remarkable consensus between business, governments and trade unions allowed a radical restructuring of industrial relations to take place with minimal opposition. Neo-liberal critics of the Australian settlement have always blamed management's failure to fundamentally change workplaces on the power and influence of institutions, particularly trade unions and the AIRC. What the critics overlooked, of course, was that the limitations which the system had traditionally placed on management power were there because certain kinds of workplace change were not in the interests of the community or the workforce. However, by the 1990s, under the impact of the 'globalisation imperative', community and workforce interests had been well and truly overtaken by share market interests and a preoccupation with the 'bottom line'.

Table 3.4 Reason workers gave for why they were not given a fair say about workplace change

Reasons employees gave	Percentage of employees
Decisions made by management	56
Decisions made outside the workplace	48
Managers do not consult	40
Discussions only between management and the union	13
Part-time or casual employees and thus not involved	13
Could not attend meetings	5
Other / Don't know	5

Source: Department of Industrial Relations (1996), *Annual report 1995: Enterprise Bargaining in Australia*, AGPS, Canberra, p. 87, Table 3.4.
Population: All employees working at locations with 20 or more employees, covered by an agreement made since early 1994 who indicated that they did not believe they had a fair chance to have a say about workplace changes in the previous 12 months.

THE INSTITUTIONAL LEGACY OF REFORM

Crisis in the unions

Union membership

We saw in Chapter 2 that the New Right mobilised against trade unions very effectively during the 1980s. A number of decisive victories in the courts exposed the vulnerability of trade unions to heavy financial damages in commercial cases. In particular, the secondary boycotts legislation proved effective at undermining traditional union strategies of mutual support.

For the unions it was bad enough to come under concerted assault from the Right. At the same time, however, their own policies limited their ability to effectively challenge the neo-liberal project. The ACTU-Labor Government Accord had been formulated to give the unions a greater say in macro-economic policy, but in practice it largely became a formula for wage reductions. Apart from Medicare, few of the other components of the social wage were delivered. On the ground, trade unionists became steadily disillusioned with a system which imposed wage cuts and offered little in return. Trade unionists voted with their feet, and trade union membership fell steadily during the 1980s and 1990s (see Table 3.5). Over the period 1982 to 1996, the fall in union density (the percentage of employees in a union) was dramatic. It dropped by over one-third, and the most severe falls were in the late 1980s and during the 1990s. Some of this reflected industry restructuring, particularly the decline in blue-collar industries which had traditionally maintained high levels of trade union membership, as well as restructuring in the well-unionised public sector.[2] But an important component of the decline in trade unionism in Australia during the 1980s was a fall in the willingness of workers to belong to trade unions. As researcher David Peetz concluded, propensity for union membership fell steadily between 1976 and 1988, with much sharper declines in the period after 1986 (Peetz 1990).[3]

Table 3.5 Trade union density, 1976 to 1996

Percentage of employees belonging to a union

Year	Union density
1976	51.0
1982	48.3
1986	45.6
1988	41.6
1990	40.5
1992	39.6
1994	35.0
1995	33.3
1996	31.1

Source: David Peetz, Deunionisation and Union Establishment: the Impact of Workplace Change, HRM Strategies and Workplace Unionism, *Labour and Industry*, vol. 8, no. 1, Aug 1997, p. 22. Based on ABS *Trade Union Members*, Cat. 6325.0.

In theory, the emergence of enterprise bargaining during the early 1990s should have made trade unions extremely relevant at a workplace level. Decentralised bargaining was seen by the ACTU hierarchy as one way of reviving the membership losses of the union movement. As Bill Kelty, ACTU Secretary, explained in 1991:

> The new wage bargaining strategy is a strategy designed to create more interesting and financially rewarding jobs, by stimulating greater worker involvement in all aspects of the way their industry and workplace operates, thereby driving enterprise reform and pushing up productivity levels. Workers will be able to see for themselves how wages are improved, and see the benefits that unions deliver (ACTU 1991, p. 1).

A decentralised bargaining system, it was believed, would reinvigorate the union movement because the members would see the results on the ground—at the workplace level. In addition, unions could use the decentralised system to widen the bargaining agenda at the enterprise level and open up negotiations over such matters as training, career development and family-friendly policies. The ACTU hoped that this would make unions relevant to workers, who had become alienated from the centralised and macro-economic deal-making which had prevailed during the Accord period. While some union officials expressed scepticism and doubt about the move towards decentralisation, the role of the ACTU in determining the industrial relations reform agenda under a Labour Government ensured that these doubters were quickly silenced.

Figure 3.8 Trade union membership by industry, 1990 and 1996

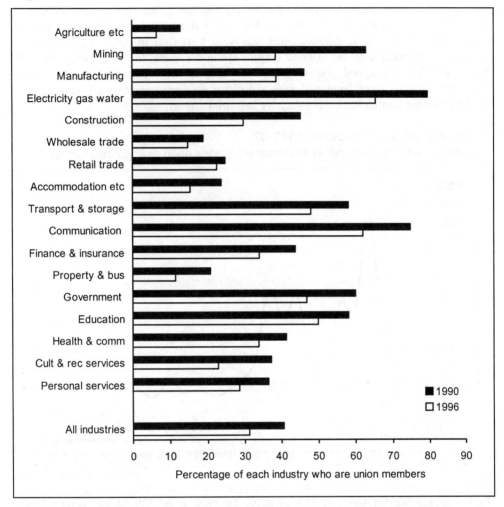

Source: Compiled from ABS (1996b), *Trade Union Members*, August 1996, Cat. no. 6325.0.

The results of enterprise bargaining for trade unions were, however, very different. The union movement has emerged worse off. The decentralisation of bargaining, and the fact that many important changes during this period were simply introduced without significant union involvement, left many unions even further marginalised. Far from slowing the decline in union membership, workplace change during the 1990s appears to have compounded the problem. As Figure 3.8 shows, in just six years, trade union membership fell by nearly 10 per cent and this drop was reflected across all industries. The blue-collar industries with traditionally high levels of union membership suffered very severe declines. In occupational terms, membership amongst white-collar workers fell just 2 per cent between 1988 and 1994, but amongst blue-collar workers the fall was nearly 10 per cent.

As well as wage restraint, there is little doubt that a centralised wage fixing system and the existence of the Accord between the ACTU and the Labor Government dampened down industrial disputes in Australia. As Figure 3.9 shows, industrial disputes dropped dramatically during the mid-1980s, once the Accord was set in place. This decline in militancy continued into the 1990s, despite the move back towards workplace-level bargaining. The weakened position of unions and, in more recent years, the hostile legislative climate, have combined with a difficult economic environment to erode the ability of unions to undertake more decisive industrial action.

Figure 3.9 Industrial disputes, 1970–97
Number of working days lost in industrial stoppages each year (in thousands)

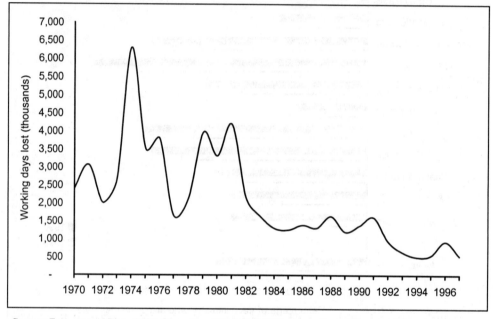

Source: For years 1970 to 1984, Vamplew, W. (ed) (1987), *Australians: Historical Statistics*, Fairfax, Syme & Weldon Associates, Sydney, p. 165. For 1985 to 1997 ABS (1998c), *Industrial Disputes*, Cat. no. 6321.0

Why did ordinary workers feel disillusioned with trade unions during the 1990s? A partial answer to this question can be found in some opinion poll data commissioned by the NSW Labor Council and produced by ACIRRT and Newspoll. Two polls were conducted, the first in 1996 and the second in 1997. Both paint an equally gloomy picture for trade unions. While few respondents—about one-quarter—would agree that 'Australia would be better off without trade unions', more than half felt unions didn't look after their members and over half didn't want to be a in a union. This occurred, moreover, during a period when respondents increasingly felt that the power of managers was greater than that of the unions.

At the forefront of respondents' minds were the traditional trade union issues of job security and wages and conditions. Amongst trade union members in particular, these two issues were way ahead of other concerns (such as OH&S, training, career development, balancing work and family responsibilities, and workplace stress). In a sense, after a decade of rapid change with constant 'downsizing' and a decade of stagnant wages, trade union members wanted their unions to get 'back to basics'.

In the 1997 poll, trade unionists were more inclined to rate their union's performance over the preceding 12 months as negative, rather than positive. Moreover, in the heartland of union membership, amongst blue-collar workers, there were growing signs of disenchantment. Comparing the 1997 poll with that held in 1996, about 12 per cent fewer blue-collar workers responded that they would rather be in a union. The one glimmer of hope for trade unions was that part-time workers and young people were considerably more inclined to feel positive about union performance. These are, however, the groups of workers who often prove hardest to organise into active unionists.

Unions at the workplace

The move towards enterprise bargaining placed enormous strains on the union movement and this was reflected at a workplace level. According to AWIRS 1995, union presence at the workplace declined markedly between 1990 and 1995, as can be seen in Figure 3.10. The number of workplaces with no union presence at all increased from 20 per cent to 26 per cent over the five year period.

This increase in union-free workplaces was most apparent in the private sector, where the proportion increased from 28 per cent of workplaces in 1990 to 36 per cent in 1995. This rise in the number of union-free workplaces appears to be related to whether unionised workplaces had a delegate present at the workplace. For example, those workplaces with union members, but without the presence of a union delegate, decreased by 7 per cent from 1990 to 1995, while those workplaces who had both union members and delegates remained the same.

The union movement also suffered because it largely underestimated the resources that would be required to actively bargain in the decentralised system. Early agreements were mainly negotiated by full-time officials, reflecting the lack of delegate structures in many workplaces. Even where delegates were present, their lack of bargaining skills became a problem, as is evident in Table 3.6.

Another major challenge for the union movement was the move from union-only agreements to non-union collective agreements, and then to individually negotiated AWAs. With these new regulatory options, situations have arisen where some employers, such as CRA and Patrick, have sought to de-unionise their workforce. This is a feature of Australian management which has rarely surfaced in industrial relations this century. The deliberate attempt by management to change the employment relationship of workers who traditionally had been highly unionised represents a more activist management strategy which the new regulatory environment accommodates. In the following quote by Terry Ludeke, former Vice President of the AIRC and consultant to the legal firm advising the employer at Weipa (Comalco Australia), we find an explanation for this strategy which understates its profound ideological significance. Rather, Ludeke emphasises the 'choice' offered workers between employment under a collective agreement or under an individual contract:

> Union resentment has taken the form of allegations that Comalco and CRA have deliberately
> mounted a campaign to rid the sites of union influence, but while this claim has attracted the

61

headlines, it simply misses the point. The decline in union influence has been incidental to the wholesale movement of workers to staff membership. In the Weipa Case the AIRC found that there was widespread acceptance and support among the workers for the staff contract system. The Comalco people prefer staff employment and the problem for unions is how to come to terms with this fact and how to deal with a far more complex situation: the growing irrelevance of unions to several thousand people who once took union membership for granted (Ludeke 1996, p. 6).

Figure 3.10 Union and delegate presence at the workplace, 1990–95

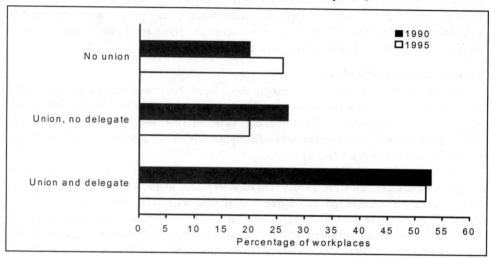

Source: AWIRS 1995.
Population: All workplaces with 20 or more employees. Figures are weighted and based on responses from 2004 workplaces in 1990 and 2001 workplaces in 1995.

Table 3.6 Percentage of union delegates reporting how skilled they considered themselves in the negotiation of a workplace or enterprise agreement, 1995

Level of skill	Percentage of delegates
Excellent skills	9
Good skills	41
Skills aren't really good enough	22
No skills	26
Not applicable	3

Source: Department of Industrial Relations (1996), *Annual report 1995:Enterprise Bargaining in Australia*, AGPS, Canberra, p. 283.
Population: All workplaces with 20 or more employees which have some kind of collective agreement and union delegates for the largest union on site.

The impact on the Industrial Relations Commission

The other major institutional casualty of the process of decentralising Australia's industrial relations system has been the AIRC itself. The successive reforms have led to a major downgrading of the role and function of the AIRC, a fact starkly reflected in the decrease in the budget allocated to the Commission in 1998–99 (see the Commonwealth Budget Papers). The Commission's role in enterprise bargaining is to effectively rubber stamp the agreements, while being almost completely sidelined with respect to the registration of AWAs (except if the Office of the Employment Advocate is undecided if the agreement passes the 'no disadvantage test'). At the same time, legislative changes have also reduced the ability of the Commission to resolve disputes between the parties. Increasingly the civil courts are playing a greater role in resolving industrial disputes. This was dramatically revealed in the 1998 national waterfront dispute between the MUA and Patrick, with the matter being heard initially in the Federal Court and finally the High Court of Australia— everywhere but in the AIRC.

The Commission still retains a central role in unfair dismissal cases, in award test cases that parties may bring before it, and in safety net adjustments for workers who are still under Federal awards and who are not covered by an enterprise agreement. The legislative requirement that Federal awards can only deal with '20 Allowable' matters has further marginalised awards and the AIRC in the regulatory system.

* * *

As it now stands in mid-1998, the formal system of industrial relations has been dramatically reshaped. For employers, the outcomes have included a degree of flexibility in labour use that is unprecedented. *Our system is no less regulated than it was at the beginning of the century, but the form of regulation has dramatically changed. We have moved from a system based on a high degree of external and centralised regulation to a system of internal and decentralised regulation.* The marginalisation of external bodies, such as the AIRC and the unions, is perhaps most dramatically illustrated by the data presented earlier showing the extent of change that has been introduced in organisations, much of it unchallenged and not even discussed. The following chapters analyse the impact of this change on workers by examining the issues of wages, working time arrangements and work effort, and job security.

Notes

1   The industry profile of the non–union and union agreement samples were very similar. Differences in outcomes therefore cannot be explained by reference to an industry bias.

2   Research by David Peetz suggests about half of the decline in union density for the period 1976 to 1988 could be attributed to restructuring (Peetz 1990).

3   It's worth noting that Peetz's own analysis discounts the impact of the Accord and wage restraint in explaining declining union density (Peetz 1990).

CHAPTER 4

Wages: winners and losers

We have seen in the last chapter that wage determination has always been central to industrial relations in Australia. It's been at the core of the award system, and has also emerged as the central element in enterprise bargaining. In this chapter we explore the issue of wage determination over the last decade and argue that a major fragmentation has occurred in the wage-fixing system and that the polarisation of incomes in Australia has also grown during that period.

One of the most enduring aspects of Australia's industrial relations system during the 20th century has been the concept of 'comparative wage justice', the idea that workers should be paid roughly the same amount for doing similar sorts of work. Behind this idea was the view that workers' wages should not hinge on the profitability or the productivity of particular workplaces or industry sectors, but should be based on meeting basic human needs (hence, a 'living wage'). This principle has had important social implications. For a start, it implied that employers should pay a reasonable minimum wage, a wage high enough to guarantee a person's livelihood. It thus placed a floor beneath those workers whose weak bargaining position might otherwise have left them exposed to poverty. For examples of the 'working poor' we need only look to the United States, where the minimum wage was raised to just $5.15 an hour in September 1997. In Australia, on the other hand, comparative wage justice and the notion of a living wage—as embodied in the industrial arbitration system and in the Accord—has prevented the emergence of a working poor. More than this, comparative wage justice has also been a testament to the elevation of fairness and collective values over competitiveness and individualism.

Historically this principle has always been uneven in its application. Male blue-collar workers with strong bargaining positions, such as coal miners or construction workers, have achieved very good wage outcomes while other semi-skilled workers in weaker positions—such as female service workers in hospitality—have fared relatively badly. Nevertheless, the operations of the arbitration system, particularly its national wage cases and its award system, have worked to 'even out' wage outcomes. Sometimes this happened through 'flow-ons' to other awards from pace-setting metal industry awards; at other times it happened through national wage case hearings granting flat dollar wage increases which boosted the relative earnings of those at the bottom of the labour market. Whatever the case, the overall effect has been to keep occupational earnings in Australia relatively compressed, compared to countries such as the United States or Britain.

In the mid-1990s this pattern has begun to change, and Australia finds itself heading down a different wages track, one where workplace profitability is becoming more influential in determining wage outcomes. As we saw in the last chapter, the movement to enterprise-based bargaining in the early 1990s, followed by the imposition of individual contracts in the mid-1990s, has seriously weakened the principle of comparative wage justice. Awards have been steadily eroded to the point where they no longer form the bedrock of wage determination. While the conditions of many awards have been incorporated into enterprise agreements, the concept of the award itself has been redefined as a 'safety net', as crumbs from the table for those workers with weak bargaining power. The attack on awards has not only come from the new emphasis on enterprise bargaining, but also from the award simplification process, referred to as 'award stripping'. After July 1998, awards are to be reduced to just 20 allowable matters. While in theory, wages and hours are still protected by these stripped-down awards, in practice the award-stripping process will severely weaken the bargaining protections traditionally offered by awards. Many other important conditions have also been eliminated.

Workers who still depend on the award system for their basic standard of living have found the late 1990s to be an inhospitable time. Two 'living wage' cases, held by the AIRC in 1997 and 1998, have reinforced their vulnerability. In the first case, they were denied their $20 a week claim and received only a $10 'safety net' adjustment. In the second case, their $20 a week claim was again rejected and they received between $10 and $14 a week. During this period, workers under enterprise agreements have received annual wage increases of between 4 and 6 per cent, while those with strong bargaining power have received annual increases as high as 15 per cent. As the 1990s comes to an end, a major fragmentation has emerged within Australia's wage-fixing system and a growing inequality in earnings has become evident.

At the end of the 1990s it is time to assess just where Australia's wage-fixing system is heading, particularly as calls for labour market 'deregulation' continue to sound in the citadels of financial power and in the other centres of the neo-liberal project. If moves to further dismantle the award system are successful, what then becomes of Australia's tradition of fairness in wage fixation and what does this mean for social inequality in Australia?

WEALTH, INCOME AND EARNINGS INEQUALITY— AN OVERVIEW

The 1980s was certainly a decade of growing inequality. If we look at wealth—the assets people own or control—the 'decade of greed' lived up to its name. Asset-price inflation during the late 1980s afflicted both commercial and residential properties, particularly in the inner cities, and handed windfall profits to many affluent Australians. Share market trading was also caught up in a speculative boom, handing enormous profits to the lucky and the astute. Kerry Packer sold the Nine Network to Alan Bond in 1987 for $1050 million, then bought it back in 1990 for just $200 million (Barry 1993, pp. 244, 390).

During the 1980s, the richest 10 Australians increased their assets fivefold in real terms, whilst the richest 100 increased their wealth about three-fold. At the same time, the concentration of wealth increased substantially: the richest ten Australians increased their share of the top 100 wealth holders' assets from 25 per cent to 48 per cent (Eaton and Stilwell 1992, p. 142–4). Table 4.1 demonstrates the changes which took place between 1983—when Labor came to power—and 1998.

Table 4.1 Top Ten BRW Rich List, Australia 1983 and 1998

1983		1998	
Top Ten	Worth $m	Top Ten	Worth $m
Murdoch family	250	Kerry Packer	5,200
Fairfax family	175	Frank Lowy	2,100
Smorgon family	150	Richard Pratt	1,800
J & R Ingham	150	David Hains	1,200
Kerry Packer	100	Smorgon family	1,000
Robert Holmes a' Court	100	Harry Triguboff	950
J D Kahlbetzer	100	J & T Fairfax	860
Reid Family	100	Myer family	840
Richard Pratt	70	B Liberman family	750
John Roberts	60	Kerry Stokes	700
Total top ten	1,255	Total top ten	15,400

Source: Business Review Weekly, 1983 and 1998.

Workers on wages and salaries were certainly affected by these changes in wealth distribution. Property inflation made it harder for them to become home owners, whilst the orgy of speculative share trading was at the expense of productive investment in rebuilding manufacturing or opening new industries. But apart from a house and car, the average wage and salary earner just does not feature in discussions of *wealth* distribution. Of greater significance to their standard of living is the distribution of *income*, particularly the distribution of *earnings*. How did these fare during the 1980s and early 1990s?

Between 1982 and 1994, the average Australian took a $67 a week decline in real market income, while the top 10 per cent of earners gained an increase in real market incomes of about $100 per week (Harding 1997, p. 8). Throughout the 1980s this kind of inequality in earnings was increasing. It was partly tied into changes in industrial relations and partly related to changes in the labour market, particularly the persistence of high levels of unemployment and the growth in part-time and casual work (Harding 1997, p. 19). Amongst male full-time wage and salary earners, there was a decline of nearly 6 per cent in the proportion who earned between 75 and 125 per cent of median earnings. The great majority (two-thirds) of these men moved downwards into an earnings situation that was below 75 per cent of median earnings. (Harding 1997, p. 3).

According to economists like Bob Gregory, these changes amounted to a 'disappearing middle' and are best explained by important developments in the labour market (1993). Basically there has been a steady decline in full-time manufacturing jobs, which have traditionally been highly unionised and relatively well paid, and a corresponding rise in part-time and casual jobs in the service sector, which have generally been less well unionised and more poorly paid. This view has been challenged by researchers like McGuire (1993), who suggest that increased earnings dispersion had less to do with changes in the industry composition of employment, and more to do with declining earnings within these service industries (1993, p. 6). Whatever the case, there is little doubt that during the 1980s the 'pool' of middle-level earnings in the economy began to shrink.

This phenomenon was discussed at length during the early 1990s and comparisons were drawn with the situation in the United States, where wage polarisation had grown rapidly during the 1980s. In that case, there was little doubt that there had been significant increases in the absolute numbers of low-paid workers moving through the labour market. But what about in Australia? Does the disappearing middle mean that there are more low-wage jobs emerging in the economy? Or does it mean that there are now more new jobs at the top end of the earnings distribution (see Belchamber 1996)? To understand income inequality in Australia during the 1980s and early 1990s, we need to take a closer look at the earnings situation at the top and bottom of the labour market during this period.

The top of the labour market

Certainly, the top end of town did very well under the Labor Government. A regular lament from the ACTU leadership was that executive salary increases went largely unconstrained, whilst wage and salary earners were buckling under the strictures of the Accord. Amongst chief executives, for example, the more notorious high earners included:

❑ Frank Lowy   Westfield $5.6m annual earnings
❑ George Trumbull   AMP $2.4m annual earnings
❑ John Prescott   BHP $2.3m annual earnings
❑ Leon Davis   Rio Tinto $1.8m annual earnings

Source: *Australian Financial Review*, October 11–12 1997, p. 29.

Often these kinds of salaries derived from share ownership in the employing company. Intended as a 'performance incentive', the provision of shares and share options to chief executives also lead to windfall gains when mutual societies or public utilities were privatised. As well as his $2.4 million annual salary, George Trumbull gained $7 million dollars the day AMP was floated on the Stock Exchange.

Even outside corporate boardrooms, high income earners did quite well. Amongst full-time workers, there was a 1.4 per cent increase in the proportion of men earning more than one and a half times median earnings and a 4.8 per cent increase for women. Changes in technology helped spur these changes at the top of the labour market. A new category of worker emerged on the crest of the information technology revolution: 'gold-collar workers'. Described by *Time* magazine as young people with creativity, computer literacy and portable skills, gold-collar workers have found themselves in high demand in the United States over the last decade (23 March 1998, pp. 54–57). A similar pattern has been evident in Australia over the last five years. The Skilled Vacancy Index maintained by the Department of Employment, Education, Training and Youth Affairs has consistently shown very strong growth in demand for computing occupations. Not surprisingly, salaries for computer professionals have reached high levels, even for staff with limited experience. A survey by a large recruitment agency—which came up with the earnings shown in Table 4.2—found that few of the staff recruited had more than two years experience with the particular software they were implementing (*Australian*, 26 May 1998, p. 38).

Table 4.2 Average salary packages for computer professionals and managers, Australia 1998

Occupation	Total annual salary package ($)
Analyst/Programmers	60,000
Consultants	65,000
Business Analyst	78,000
Senior Consultant	88,000
Project Manager	135,000
Senior Manager	170,000

Source: Greythorn recruitment agency, published in *Australian*, 26 May 1998, p. 38. Reproduced with permission.

Table 4.3 Typical contractor rates for computer professionals, 1998

Position	Average $ per hour 1998
Multimedia specialist	103.33
Telecommunications specialist	96.67
Systems manager	88.33
Database administrator	85.20
Systems analyst	83.38
WAN network specialist	81.67
Project leader	81.33
LAN network specialist	80.00
Year 2000 programmer	67.67
Analyst programmer	52.61

Source: Cullen Egan Dell, cited in *Australian*, 9 June 1998, p. 42. Reproduced with permission.

One of the key themes in our book is that traditional modes of work have been breaking down over the last two decades. As Chapter 5 will show, managers and professionals are now working longer hours than ever before, while Chapter 6 will show that non-standard forms of employment have proliferated throughout the economy. In an interesting twist to the 'gold-collar' story, these various themes converge in the persona of the computer professional. Technological change has created an unquenchable thirst in the economy for these kinds of workers, large proportions of whom work as contractors and earn very high hourly rates of pay (see Table 4.3). Yet, at the same time, such workers are now expected to work weekends as a normal part of their duties. A recent survey of 300 companies by Cullen Egan Dell found that:

Employers' demands for IT maintenance during weekends are coupled with their determination to increase contracting numbers and reduce the size of inhouse IT teams ... 'While most businesses are not necessarily physically open, they are open electronically and that requires IT support' (quoted in *Australian*, 9 June 1998, p. 42).

The rewards for such trade-offs are considerable—an extra 53 per cent in pay for weekend work. As the survey company's managing director commented:

'All the wages are extremely high ... A Java programmer is earning the equivalent of a company director. It's incredible, but the market is determining these rates of pay' (quoted in *Australian*, 9 June 1998, p. 42).

The bottom of the labour market

What about low-income earners, how did they fare during the 1980s and 1990s? The answer clearly depends on where one places boundaries. Ann Harding's research showed that the bottom 10 per cent of earners did experience increases in real market incomes between 1982 and 1994. It was a small amount—about $11 a week—but it was an increase, compared with the decrease which the middle earners faced. On the other hand, Jeff Borland has shown that between 1975 and 1995, the bottom 10 per cent of earners suffered a 9.4 per cent decrease in their real earnings. The rival figures are compatible, however, since most of this decline took place in the period 1975 to 1981. Other research which suggests growing earnings dispersions places different boundaries around the earnings groups. McGuire, for example, looks at the situation of those earning less than 75 per cent of median earnings, and he finds an increase in their presence of nearly 4 per cent over the period 1983–85 to 1990–92 (McGuire 1993, Table 1). Similar results for the period 1985 to 1994 have been presented by Latham (1998, p. 89). Basically, the effective cut-off point for these analyses is at the 37th percentile of earnings, whereas the Harding and Borland findings work with the 10th percentile. Clearly, where one places the boundaries—both in time and in earnings cut-offs—makes a large difference to the conclusions drawn.

Non-market incomes

It is clear that market incomes became more unequal during the 1980s as earnings at the top of the labour market soared whilst those at the bottom stagnated. But did standards of living drop at the bottom of the labour market? To answer this question we need to look at non-market incomes, those cash transfers brought about by government benefits and taxation policies. During the 1980s government pensions, benefits and family payments, considerably improved the living standards of households at the bottom of the income distribution. For example, during the 1982–94 period, the share of these transfers received by the top 20 per cent of households halved to only 4.6 per cent while the share gained by the bottom half of households rose by 7 percentage points to total 77 per cent of cash transfers (Harding 1997, p. 11–12). During a decade when average weekly earnings actually declined in real terms, cash transfers which were targeted at the lowest income households increased by significant amounts. For example, sole parent pensioners gained a real increase of about 14 per cent; family payments increased by about 70 per cent; and rent assistance more than doubled (Harding 1997, Table 6, p. 11).

Furthermore, as far as low-income earners are concerned, the Australian income tax system did become more progressive during the 1980s. Most taxpayers, those in the middle of the income distribution, continued to pay about the same proportion of income tax (Harding 1997, p. 13). Tax rates for those in the bottom decile fell from around 20 per cent to 15 per cent (McGuire 1993, p. 4). However, those taxpayers at the very top, earning above two and half times median earnings, also gained a substantial tax cut. In the eyes of some researchers, this weakening in the progressivity of the tax system at the top was offset by two major tax broadening measures introduced during the 1980s which targeted high income earners: fringe benefits tax and capital gains tax (Harding 1997, p. 13). However, what this viewpoint overlooks is the windfall gains provided to high income earners by dividend imputation (the ending of full-taxation on individual share earnings where the company has paid tax). In 1995–96 alone, the dividend imputation system provided shareholders with $3.1 billion dollars in tax credits.

Whether government transfer payments were adequate to social needs, and whether the tighter targeting of social welfare which the Labor Government pioneered was desirable, are certainly contentious issues in terms of social policy debates. *But from the point of view of industrial relations policy, the changes flowing from government welfare interventions did have the effect of significantly diminishing the levels of income inequality which were being generated in the labour market.* This raises an important policy issue around the relationship between labour-market generated inequality and government intervention. McGuire, for example, has argued:

> If earnings dispersion continues to increase, it may be necessary to continually increase the progressivity of the tax/transfer system just to offset the changes in the pre-tax distribution of earnings (1993, p. 14).

Yet for other commentators, such a scenario amounts to a policy of expanded subsidisation of low-wage firms. These commentators argue that decent wages should be paid throughout the economy and if firms cannot pay such wages, they should be allowed to perish. To do otherwise is to invite the expansion of low wage sectors throughout the economy. We return to this theme in Chapter 7.

THEY GET WHAT?!—A JOURNALIST EXPLORES THE LABOUR MARKET

Nikki Barrowclough, a journalist with the *Sydney Morning Herald's Good Weekend* magazine, set out to explore the changing nature of work, the perception of worth, and the new brutalism of the workplace. She found a picture of insecurity and a massively fragmenting labour market, and concluded that 'increasingly, it seems the workforce is made up of separate worlds in which people lead lives that are completely foreign to each other'.

Occupation	Weekly earnings $
Losers	
Actors - battlers	96-212
Strip-o-gram performers	300-400
Dancers and choreographers	342
Waiters/waitresses	346-500
Farmhands	360
Hairdressers (4 yr apprentice)	384
Dishwashers	390
Strappers in racing stable	393
In the middle	
Stevedores (wharfies)	526-700
Bus drivers	577-673
Ministers of religion	663
Science graduates (with PhD)	730
Police officers	929-1,095
Winners	
Futures traders	480-5,760
Actors - top names in regular films	1,923-5,769
Commercial television journalists	2,307 upwards
Medical specialists	2,421 upwards
Marketing directors	2,500-4,423
Computer professionals	up to 10,260
Stockbrokers	2,880-19,230
Lawyers	4,808-13,462
Top fund managers	5,769-9,615

Source: Nikki Barrowclough (1998), 'They get what?!', *Sydney Morning Herald, Good Weekend*, 6 June, pp.16–20.

EARNINGS INEQUALITY—
BEHIND THE AGGREGATE VIEW

We now need to look more closely at what was happening in the labour market during the 1980s and early 1990s. How did wage and salary earners fare? What was the impact of the Accord? What was happening at an occupational and industry level? What kinds of wage fixing institutions were in place by the mid-1990s and what was their impact?

The aggregate view

One of the most basic indicators of earnings are how much of society's output goes to labour and how much goes to capital, that is, the split between wages and profits. Figure 4.1 shows that wages and profits tracked each other quite closely until the early 1980s. After the Accord between the ACTU and the Labor Government the profit share began to pull ahead of the wage share, a pattern which has persisted ever since. This was justified at the time as a measure to restore investment in the economy after the recession of the early 1980s. In time, it came to be recognised that this deliberate shift of resources from labour to capital was a mistake. Large scale productive investment failed to eventuate, and the speculative frenzy of the late 1980s ended in an even deeper recession in 1991 than had ushered in the 1980s. For example, the banks wrote off bad debts in 1992 which were the equivalent of 2 to 3 per cent of gross domestic product (Apps 1992, pp. 53–56). From the point of view of unemployment, the late 1990s are still carrying the burden of the 1991 recession.

Average weekly earnings are consistent with this picture. As Figure 4.2 shows, real earnings fell significantly during the 1980s, as the Accord reigned in wage increases while the economy moved into overdrive. Since the end of the Accord, wages growth has become strong again, with some of the fastest growth occurring during the last two years.

The aggregate picture is only ever a picture of averages, and the trends here can hide as much as they reveal. Behind this simple line are a myriad of other lines: trends for occupations or industries, trends for different wage-fixing institutions, and trends within the earnings distribution. When all of these are taken into account, the wages picture which emerges is much more complex. It does, however, form a discernible landscape, one of growing earnings dispersion within the workforce where fragmentation in the wage-fixing system is becoming widespread.

Figure 4.1 Wages and profits as components of GDP, 1976–97

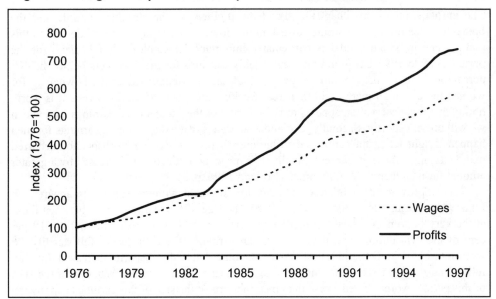

Source: Compiled from ABS (1998a), *Australian Economic Indicators*, Cat. no. 1350.0.
Note: Each year in the graph indicates the financial year ending in that year. Wages are defined as 'Wages salaries and supplements' and profits as 'Gross operating surplus of private trading enterprises'.

Figure 4.2 Stagnation in earnings, 1984-97

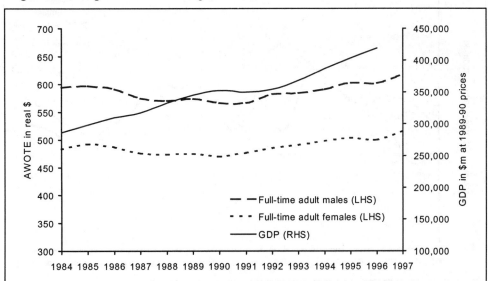

Source: Compiled from ABS (1978-1998), *Labour Force Australia*, Cat. no. 6203.0
Note: AWOTE means average weekly ordinary time earnings.

Dispersion within the earnings distribution

The introduction to this chapter outlined the problem of the shrinking middle and the breakout at the top of the earnings distribution. However, there is a more subtle side to this picture, one in which gender is particularly important. Research by Jeff Borland for the period 1975 to 1995 has found that real weekly earnings for male workers below the 40th percentile (that is, the bottom 40 per cent of the distribution) decreased, whereas for women there was an increase in their real weekly earnings at all decile levels. It is worth noting that this observation appears to be accurate for the occupational earnings data which we will present shortly. Secondly, Borland also argues that a dispersion in earnings for men happened right across the earnings distribution, whereas for women the dispersion occurred mainly amongst the high earners. Finally, this dispersion of earnings increased by a greater amount for men than it did for women (Borland 1996, p. 3).

This improvement in relative earnings for low-paid women workers is apparent in Figure 4.3. During the 1980s and early 1990s the size of the 'earnings gap' between those at the very bottom of the labour market (the first decile, which means the bottom 10 per cent of the distribution) and those on median earnings (the fifth decile) fell steadily for women throughout the period. For men, on the other hand, this disparity increased initially, fell during the 1991 recession, then rose again during the mid-1990s. Whereas at the start of this period, women fared worse than men in terms of the size of this earnings gap, by the end of this period men fared worse.

Figure 4.3 Trends in earnings dispersion in the bottom half of the earnings distribution, Australia 1983–95

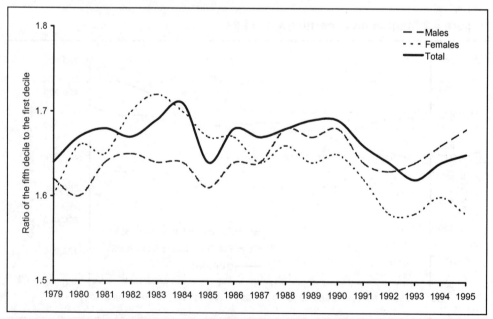

Source: Compiled from OECD (1996), *Employment Outlook*, OECD, Paris, July, p. 61.

At the top end of the labour market, inequality has been increasing. Figure 4.4 shows the size of the earnings gap between those on median earnings and those in the ninth decile. While the ratio between these two deciles has jumped around during the 1980s, the situation which has emerged by the mid-1990s is one where earnings inequality is considerably greater. However, as Figure 4.4 demonstrates clearly, this is almost entirely due to male earnings at the top end becoming much more unequal during the 1990s. By contrast, the inequality amongst high earning women has remained relatively static over this period.

Figure 4.4 Trends in earnings dispersion in the top half of the earnings dispersion, Australia 1983–95

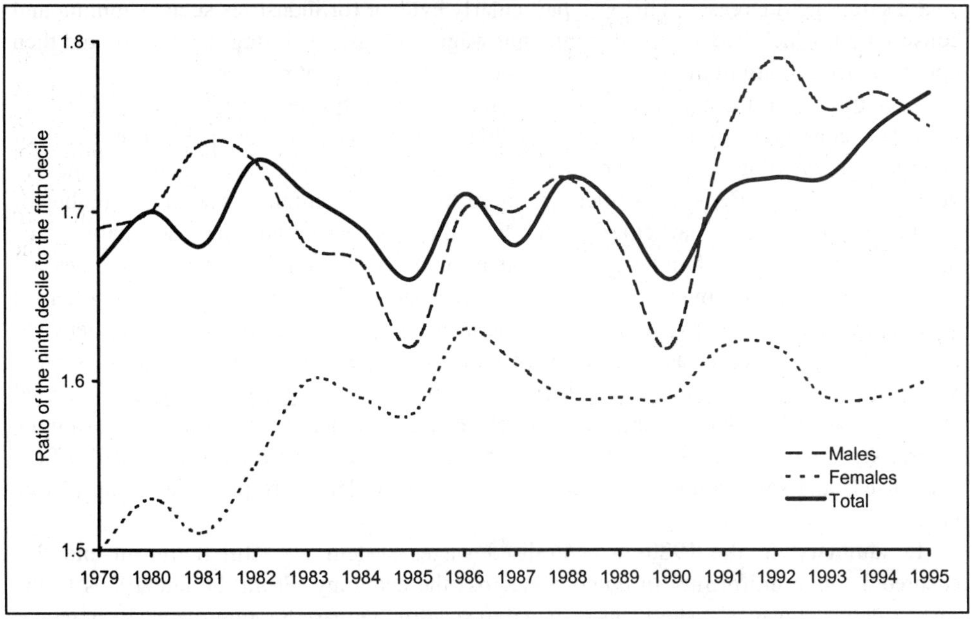

Source: Compiled from OECD (1996), *Employment Outlook*, OECD, Paris, July, p. 61.

Fragmentation in wage fixing institutions

As noted in the last chapter, wage fixation in Australia was relatively standardised until the late 1980s. The award system and national wage cases determined what most people in the non-managerial workforce earned. Wage increases were usually the result of labour market pressures exerted by small groups of workers in key industry sectors. For example, skill shortages might lead to the wage increases in the form of over-award payments, or multi-employer agreements. Increases like these could then be used to justify wage increases in key Federal awards. The most important awards were the metal industry award, the transport workers' award, the construction industry award and the storemen and packers' award. Increases would then flow through to other awards with wage relativities linked to these awards. Under this system wages were primarily determined by occupation (Buchanan and Watson 1997, pp. 20–21). For women gender differences that were entrenched in the arbitration system worked in addition to occupation to determine wage rates.

As we've seen in the last two chapters, the neo-liberal project has sought to shift Australia's wage-fixing system away from principles like comparative wage justice and out of the hands of centralised institutions. In their place, the neo-liberals have sought to make productivity improvements at a workplace level the sole determinant of wage increases. There was strong support from employer groups for wage increases won at particular enterprises to be isolated, so that large increases would not flow on to workers at other workplaces. During the 1990s we've seen those workers covered by collective agreements use their market power to increase their wages, and possibly make up for losses in real wages under the Accord, while those outside the bargaining stream have been restricted to award safety net increases. This was particularly evident for industries such as mining and construction, which had accepted significant wage concessions during the Accord and then under enterprise bargaining received claims of up to 15 per cent per year.

This transition from a centralised to a more decentralised wages system has had important consequences for women, particularly those who are low-paid. The effect of enterprise bargaining is to make industry location more important when it comes to determining wages. Because women are more highly concentrated in a small number of 'feminised industries', particularly service industries like retail and hospitality, this increasing importance of industry means that gender differentials in wage outcomes are more likely to increase over time. Where the old system of centralised wage fixing tended to limit the dispersion between industries, the new system of enterprise bargaining tends to accentuate that increase, as well as increasing the dispersion within industries as well. While the new system is intended to leave a minimum wage in place, in practice the actual outcomes can mean large reductions in earnings for vulnerable workers. For example, enterprise bargaining allows for penalty rates, shift rates and overtime to be traded off (or annualised) and some agreements specify that no extra claims are possible for up to five years.

In summary, in the 1980s a centralised wages system was still dominant and this ensured a rough uniformity in outcomes across the economy. From the late 1980s to the early 1990s, the wages system was changed to steadily increase the importance of practices happening at a workplace level. By the mid-1990s, the wages system had fragmented and a decentralised system with an enterprise focus, and a more individualistic approach, had emerged. Enterprise-based bargaining had become widespread, and individual contracts amongst the non-managerial workforce had become a possibility. The Howard Government has also assisted this push towards greater individualism in wage fixing by implementing its system of Australian Workplace Agreements (AWAs). These contracts allow negotiations over wages (and conditions) to take place exclusively between an employer and their worker without any trade union consultation.

By the late 1990s, the workforce is split three ways: those covered by awards, those by enterprise agreements, and those by individual contracts. Table 4.4 summarises the wages situation for each of these categories of worker.

Table 4.4 Mechanisms for regulating wages in 1996

Form of labour market regulation	Employees %	Estimated average annual wage increase %
Awards only	35-40	1.3
Awards and Registered Enterprise Agreements	30-40	4-6
Enterprise Agreements only	5-10	4-6
Individual Contracts	30-35	0-8

Sources: Note that these estimates have been obtained by splicing together information obtained from a number of sources. The last ABS estimate of award coverage was provided in ABS (1990), *Award Coverage*, Australia, Cat. no.6315.0 in 1990. We have assumed that the secular decline in award coverage that has been evident for some time and which accelerated between 1985 and 1990, has continued. This would put award coverage at around 75 per cent of employees. Estimates for employee coverage of registered enterprise agreements has been obtained from the Commonwealth Department of Industrial Relations (1996), *Enterprise Bargaining in Australia: Annual Report 1995*, AGPS, Canberra by combining data from pp. 23, 143, 148. The proportion reliant on awards is obtained from an estimate of those who received a safety net adjustment in 1995 reported in the same DIR report at p. 147 combined with the residual of those estimated to be covered by awards. Those covered by individual contracts is by definition of the residual of all of the above. Estimates of average annual wage increases have been derived from the following sources: ABS (1997c), *Award Rates of Pay Indexes*, Cat. no. 6312.0, ADAM for enterprise agreements, Cullen, Egan Dell for estimates of executive remuneration for the upper range and ADAM No. 8 pp. 18–19 for non-managerial individual contracts.

Clearly, those workers only on awards have fared badly in terms of wage increases, gaining average annual wage increases of about 1.3 per cent. By contrast, those on enterprise agreements have fared much better, with average annual wage increases of between 4 to 6 per cent. Figure 4.5 illustrates how this gap between award wages and wages based on bargaining has widened during the 1990s.

To place these changes in a wider context, consider Figure 4.6. This shows that from 1985 to 1991, and again from 1992 to 1996, award wage increases remained consistently below the consumer price index (CPI). By way of contrast, executive salary increases were higher than the CPI for the whole period, 1984 to 1996. More importantly, from the point of view of the non-managerial workforce, award wage increases have remained consistently lower than average weekly ordinary time earnings (AWOTE), with the gap at its greatest from the mid-1990s onwards. In 1995, for example, the gap between award wage increases and AWOTE increases was over 3 per cent.

Figure 4.5 Average annual wage increases in registered enterprise agreements and award wages

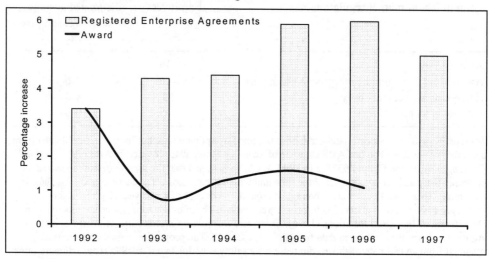

Source: ACIRRT (1997a), *ADAM Database*, November, and Ross, I. (1997), 'Reasons for Decision of Vice President Ross', *Safety Net Review—Wages*, Australian Industrial Relations Commission, Sydney, April, p. 51.

Figure 4.6 Relative changes in salaries and wages, 1984–96

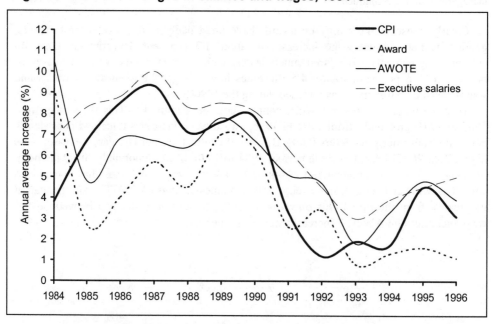

Source: Derived from Ross, I. (1997), 'Reasons for Decision of Vice President Ross', *Safety Net Review—Wages*, Australian Industrial Relations Commission, Sydney, April, p. 51.

It's important to realise that within the realm of enterprise agreements, there's also been a growing dispersion of wage increases. In the March quarter of 1998 the average annualised wage increase from enterprise agreements per worker was 4.2 per cent, down slightly from 4.4 per cent in the December 1997 quarter. However, only 9 per cent of workers actually received this average increase. There were some who received as much as 15 per cent, while others only got 0.7 per cent. Over the period 1993 to 1998, workers in the top quartile of the distribution consistently gained at least 5 per cent a year, but for workers in the bottom quartile, the increases have only been in the order of 2 to 3 per cent (Gittins 1998, p. 37).

There's been an industry aspect to this story, with enterprise agreements in construction and mining consistently offering higher average annual increases than other industries, and with agreements in private services, such as hospitality and retail, offering the lowest. It goes without saying that men are predominant in construction and mining, whilst women predominate in private services. Clearly, under enterprise bargaining, industry location has become a major factor influencing wage outcomes. The uniformity offered by the award system has therefore broken down at two important levels: the workplace and the industry sector. Comparative wage justice—which attempted to nullify these two sources of earnings inequality—has begun to sink beneath the waves of decentralised wage fixing which has spread through the economy during the 1990s.

Not only do industries differ in what they pay under enterprise agreements. They also differ in terms of what workers have to trade away to gain their wage increases. For example, two agreements which provided similarly low wage increases of about 2 per cent average per year—one in metal manufacturing and one in hospitality—had very different conditions attached. As the boxed text shows, the manufacturing agreement retained rostered days off and penalty payments, as well as a significant commitment to training. By contrast, the hospitality agreement reduced penalty payments, allowed for averaging of hours and introduced 12-hour shifts.

The metal manufacturing industry is worth a closer look because it provides an interesting case study of the impact of enterprise bargaining on earnings dispersions within occupations. During the 1980s wage relativities remained almost constant. In 1983, for example, process workers under the Metal Industry Award earned 82 per cent of the fitter's rate, a proportion that remained virtually unchanged in 1991. In the 1990s, however, this situation began to change as a growing disparity in earnings between those on agreements and those reliant on safety net increases began to emerge. Since 1991 the cumulative growth in wages for the former has been in the range of 27 to 31 per cent, whilst the cumulative outcome for the latter has only been in the order of 8 per cent in total. In the decade from 1986 to 1995, male trades workers improved their wages by about 56 per cent (in nominal terms), but this outcome favoured the more highly paid workers. Those in the lowest quartile gained only a 49 per cent increase, whilst for those in the top quartile the increase was 66 per cent. A similar pattern was evident amongst both male and female labourers, with the starkest differences occurring amongst the women. This suggests that as the wages system has decentralised, wages have not risen as quickly for the male unskilled as compared to the male skilled (see Table 4.5).

Table 4.5 Relative movements in earnings for tradespersons and labourers employed in manufacturing, 1986–95

Occupation	Mean - Ordinary Time	Quartile Mean - Ordinary Time Hourly Rate (estimates)	
		1st Quartile	4th Quartile
Male Tradespersons earnings	$ 14.99	$ 11.44	$ 18.89
Percentage change since 1986	56%	49%	66%
Male Labourer earnings	$ 12.94	$ 10.07	$ 16.21
Percentage change since 1986	52%	45%	58%
Female Labourer earnings	$ 11.00	$ 9.07	$ 13.80
Percentage change since 1986	56%	43%	69%

Source: J. Buchanan and I. Watson (1997), 'The Living Wage and the Working Poor' in M. Bittman (ed), *Poverty in Australia: Dimensions and Policies*, SPRC Reports and Proceedings, No. 135, May, p. 27.

WHAT YOU HAVE TO DO TO EARN A 2 PER CENT PAY INCREASE—A TALE OF TWO AGREEMENTS

Metal manufacturing

❑ Wage increases noted are supplemented by a recognition of skill levels and a reclassification process.
❑ A productivity incentive payment system is also incorporated into the agreement.
❑ Hours of work are to be 76 per fortnight with one RDO every two weeks.
❑ There is some flexibility if there is agreement with the majority of workers.
❑ Internal training programs will be provided to allow training of workers beyond the needs required for their immediate jobs.

Hospitality

❑ A new classification structure and rotation through different areas of the company breaks down traditional occupation demarcations.
❑ Normal hours of work are 38 averaged over a 4-week cycle. Workers may work 12-hour and broken shifts.
❑ Loadings are reduced for new workers, and for some groups all days of the week are regarded as normal working days.
❑ There is a recognition of the role of the union.

Source: Derived from CCH/ACIRRT 1998, p. 9

Occupational dispersions

We saw earlier that women fared better than men when it came to aggregate real earnings during the 1980s. But what about within occupations, did this pattern hold up? The general answer is yes, but with some interesting variations. Figures 4.7 and 4.8 show the proportion of workers below a particular benchmark for a number of selected occupations during 1981, and then again for 1991. (The benchmark chosen for the higher earning professionals and paraprofessionals is median earnings; for the other occupations the benchmark is the 20th percentile.) With the exception of police and nurses, most male occupational groups went backwards during that decade, and the more severe losers were at the top end of the labour market. For example, amongst school teachers the proportion below median earnings more than doubled, from 4 per cent to 10 per cent. At the bottom of the male blue-collar labour market, the situation for occupational groups remained fairly static, whilst amongst pink-collar workers, the deterioration was more pronounced, as is evident for sales assistants and food-tradespersons (such as chefs).

Figure 4.7 Male workers below benchmarks, selected occupations, 1981 and 1991

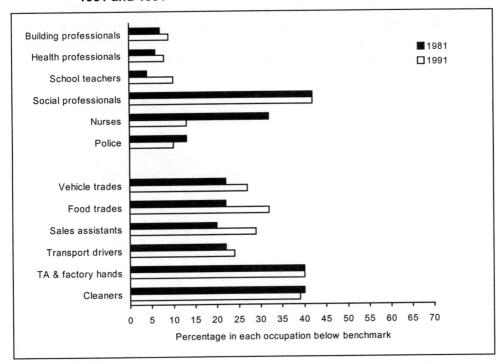

Source: Unpublished data from 1981 Census Household Sample File and 1991 Census Person Sample File.
Note: Benchmarks for professionals and paraprofessionals are median earnings, for the rest the 20th percentile has been used. Earnings have been fixed at 1991 dollars for both time periods.

Amongst women, on the other hand, nearly all occupational groups showed improvement. At the bottom of the blue-collar labour market, there was little change, but in the pink-collar jobs where the men fared badly, women did much better. In the food trades, for example, the proportion of women below the 20th percentile dropped from 47 per cent to 38 per cent, at a time when the male proportions increased from 22 per cent to 32 per cent. Similarly, amongst female shop assistants the situation barely changed, whilst for men there was a very large deterioration. Like their male colleagues, female nurses fared well over this decade, with the proportion earning below the median nearly halving. Amongst health professionals men and women fared much the same, though in both cases it was a backwards step. On the other hand, amongst school teachers and social professional there was a very sharp gender difference. There was only a marginal change for women teachers compared to men's dramatic deterioration, and for social professionals there was a significant improvement for women compared with the static position for men.

How might we explain this picture? To begin with, the choice of time boundaries is quite significant to this story. The endpoint—1991—largely precedes the spread of enterprise bargaining, and thus this pattern is pretty much the product of the centralised wages system which prevailed during most of the 1980s. The stability in earnings dispersions for men at the bottom of the labour market, and the improvement in the relative situation of most women, is probably one of the few great legacies of the ACTU-Labor Government Accord. While it failed to deliver on most of its promises, the Accord does nevertheless appear to have kept occupational earnings inequalities more tightly constrained than would have been the case in a more decentralised system.

Figure 4.8 Female workers below benchmarks, selected occupations, 1981 and 1991

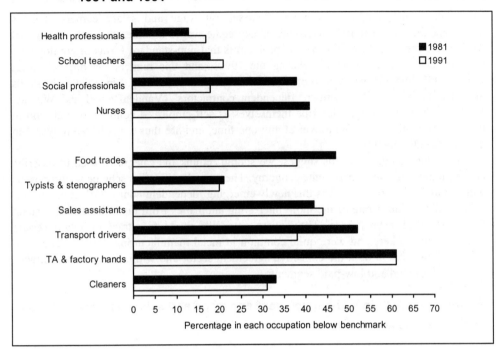

Source: Unpublished data from 1981 Census Household Sample File and 1991 Census Person Sample File.
Note: Benchmarks for professionals and paraprofessionals are median earnings, for the rest the 20th percentile has been used. Earnings have been fixed at 1991 dollars for both time periods.

Clearly, the award system and the process of centralised wage fixing provided by the Accord played a major role in dampening down wage and salary inequality within the non-managerial workforce. A comparative study of earnings dispersions by the OECD found dispersions greatest in the United States and Britain, both of which had highly decentralised wages systems (McGuire 1993, p. 13). Summing up the role of the wages system in keeping a lid on earnings inequality, McGuire quotes Gregory and Daly:

> All the results ... support the commonly expressed view that Australian labour market institutions, relative to those of the US, have been a force for reducing the dispersion of relative earnings and increasing relative earnings for those employed full-time at the bottom of the earnings distribution (cited in McGuire 1993, p. 13).

A NEW CLASSIFICATION SCHEME FOR EARNINGS

Up to this point our discussion has focussed on wage and salary earners. This is understandable, since most discussions of aggregate wages assumes that non-managerial workers are the object of interest. The problem is that non-standard forms of employment have increased in the economy during the 1990s, and this renders the old categories somewhat deficient if we want to measure what everyone is earning. Since the early 1990s there has been a rapid growth in 'dependent contractors' (VandenHeuvel and Wooden 1994), workers who might describe themselves as self-employed contractors, but who in reality only work for one employer at any one time, and are thus actually 'employees' in disguise (see Figure 4.9).

Important changes like this suggest we should rethink the categories used to describe how earnings are determined in the economy. The new classification scheme we propose is outlined in Table 4.6. As well as this newly emerging 'dependent contractor' situation, this scheme also captures one of the more interesting anomalies from the older award system: the payment of over-awards. These were payments made to attract or retain certain categories of workers and were quite common in metal manufacturing. Finally, Table 4.6 also illustrates that in both the collective agreement sector and within individual contracts, there are high-paid and low-paid segments.

Figure 4.9 Growth in self-employment and wage and salary earners, 1978–93

Employment numbers, indexed to February 1978

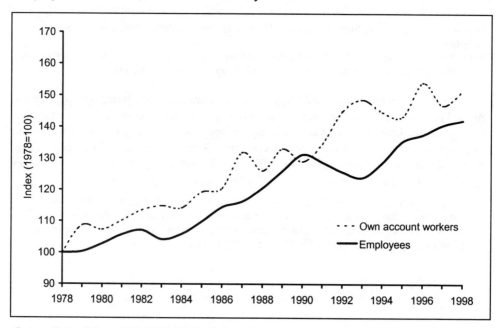

Source: Derived from ABS (1978-1998), *Labour Force Australia*, Cat. no. 6203.0.

Table 4.6 Different approaches to determining employment-based earnings classified according to formal arrangements and relative level of earnings

			Basis of Earnings		
			Contract of Service		Contract for Service
		Award	Collective Agreements	Individual Contract	
Relative level of work-related earnings	High	1. Over-awards	3. Certified Agreements (high wage)	5. Executive-professional contracts	7.Independent contractors
	Low	2. Safety Net Adjustment	4. Certified Agreements (including non-union) (low wage)	6. Minimalist individual contracts	8. Dependent contractors

The labour market characteristics of each cell are as follows.

1. Those workers on over-awards are semi-skilled and trade workers found mainly in small to medium sized metal manufacturing, wholesale trade and cultural recreation services. Workplaces with no union members are also more likely to pay over-awards.
2. The safety net adjustment segment covers low-skilled workers primarily working as machine operators, labourers and cleaners in the textiles, clothing and footwear sector, and in other manufacturing sectors. It also includes a variety of clerical workers across a range of industry groups.
3. The high wage collective agreements have been concentrated in mining, construction and parts of metal manufacturing. Parts of the public sector are also covered.
4. The low wage agreements that have delivered less than average annual wage increases have mostly covered workers in retail trade, insurance and recreational and personal services.
5. High paying executive individual contracts cover managerial and professional occupations in finance and communications and SES officers in the public sector.
6. Information on low-pay individual contracts are difficult to obtain, though evidence from the earlier Victorian and Western Australian agreement suggest that they were prominent in the private services sector in low-skill occupations.
7. Independent contractors have traditionally been prominent in industries such as construction and road transport. In more recent times, they have emerged in finance, property and business services—especially in managerial and quasi-professional occupations.

8. Dependent contractors have been the area of fastest growth in the 1990s. They have been particularly prominent in construction and more specialised sectors, such as smash repairs. Much of this growth has been spurred by employers promoting this form of employment to avoid paying PAYE tax.

SEGMENTATION IN THE LABOUR MARKET

Most of the analysis of inequality using income data works with percentile distributions, and this can be very useful for comparing the situation of low-income individuals or families with those on the median income. The studies by Borland, Harding and Gregory discussed earlier all work with this approach. However, if we want to focus on the mechanisms within the labour market which generate earnings inequality, we have to move beyond this approach. Not only do we need to examine the wage fixing institutions (such as the growing earning divide between awards and enterprise agreements discussed above), but we also have to examine patterns of segmentation in the labour market. Occupation and industry are the major structural determinants of such segmentation, whilst gender, age and ethnicity are the major demographic factors involved. It's still useful, of course, to look at percentile distributions, but our approach is to apply this distributional analysis to *jobs*, not people. Looking more closely at jobs—defined as the intersection between occupation and industry—reveals very strong associations between low pay and other factors. These include labour market factors like union density in the workplace, amount of bargaining in the workplace, credentials held by workers, as well as demographic factors like gender and country of birth (non-English speaking background—NESB—status). A close perusal of Figures 4.10 and 4.11 illustrates this pattern very clearly.

In the bottom quintile (Figure 4.10) we have three broad areas of low-paying jobs: private sector service jobs, mainly in hospitality and retail (with earnings in the range $395 to $490 per week); public sector labouring jobs (in the range $420 to $475); and labouring jobs in factories (in the range $430 to $485). In retailing we find high levels of union coverage, but very little bargaining, suggesting a relatively weak union presence on the job. This is confirmed by the manufacturing picture, where high levels of unionisation have been matched by high levels of bargaining. Gender, however, remains influential within this scenario, with workers in TCF—predominantly women—missing out on the levels of bargaining that have occurred in the metals industry. In the case of hospitality, union activism in the workplace is stronger than in retailing, but the proportion of unionised workers is lower. Consequently, the level of bargaining is also lower. Finally, the very high levels of casualisation in hospitality (from 48 through to 59 per cent) also contribute to the poor bargaining position of workers in those jobs. By way of contrast, similar levels of part-time work, and similar proportions of women workers, are found in the public sector service jobs (mainly cleaning jobs) but casualisation is nowhere near as common as in hospitality. The proportion of bargaining workplaces is still low, but union coverage remains high.

Looking at this picture overall, we can draw several conclusions. Segmentation along gender, industry and occupational lines largely determines the level of wages in any particular job, but this segmentation is offset to some degree by forms of *labour market protection*. Protection takes the form of union coverage (particularly active union involvement in the workplace), full-time job status, and public sector employment conditions. For some low-paid workers, such as in manufacturing, protection can be enhanced by bargaining, since union strength can determine outcomes. For other low-paid workers, remaining under historic award conditions may provide better protection than entering into bargaining when one's position is a weak one. This weakness may be due to high levels of casualisation or low levels of union protection. Hospitality workers exemplify this situation.

By way of contrast, jobs in the top quintile (Figure 4.11) need little in the way of structural protection, since occupational and industry characteristics are themselves so influential. Business services and finance, for example, are at the cutting edge of high paying private sector employment (with earnings in the range $900 to $1125 per week). In the case of business services, there has been little bargaining and union coverage is very poor, but these don't count for much in this industry. Interestingly, the finance industry departs from this picture, since union coverage is much higher and bargaining has been much greater. Even so, the similar demographic profile—mainly highly educated males— suggests the earnings outcomes across both industries for all of these professionals and managers hinges much more on the characteristics of the jobs and the personal characteristics of the incumbents, than it does on the bargaining climate or union coverage in their workplaces.

The same is not true for the public sector professionals and managers. Their earnings (in the range $850 to $1050) appear to be sensitive to workplace characteristics and the way in which bargaining has unfolded. These jobs are to some extent renumerated according to the possession of educational qualifications, but the traditional uniformity of conditions within this sector suggests that workplace characteristics are influential. In education, for example, high levels of unionisation and considerable bargaining are evident and both of these have influenced earnings outcomes. It is interesting to note how public sector employment protects against casualisation, at both the top and bottom of the earnings quintile. Labourers in health (mainly cleaners) have high levels of part-time employment (46 per cent) and low levels of casualisation (10 per cent). A similar pattern applies for professionals in education (32 per cent part-time and just 4 per cent casual).

Figure 4.10 Characteristics of the bottom quintile of jobs in the labour market, Australia, 1995

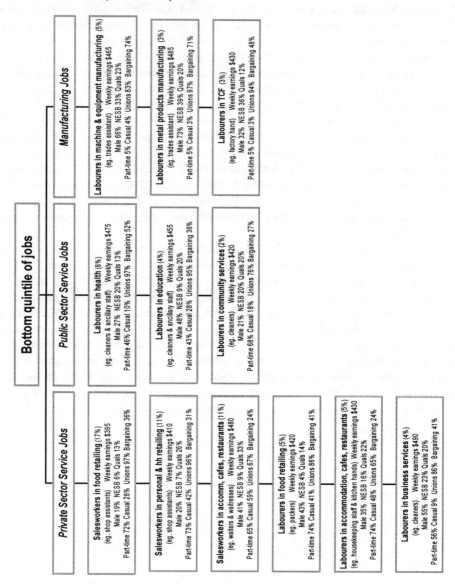

Source: Derived from unpublished AWIRS 1995 employee survey data.

Population: Employees in workplaces with 20 or more employees.

Note: The definition of a job is the intersection between ASCO Major groups and ASIC categories. Percentages in brackets after each job indicates what contribution that job makes to the total number of jobs in the earnings quintile. Earnings are average weekly earnings including overtime. Qualifications refers to post-school credentials. Bargaining refers to proportion of workplaces with enterprise agreements in place. Unions refers to union density in the workplace.

Figure 4.11 Characteristics of the top quintile of jobs in the labour market, Australia, 1995

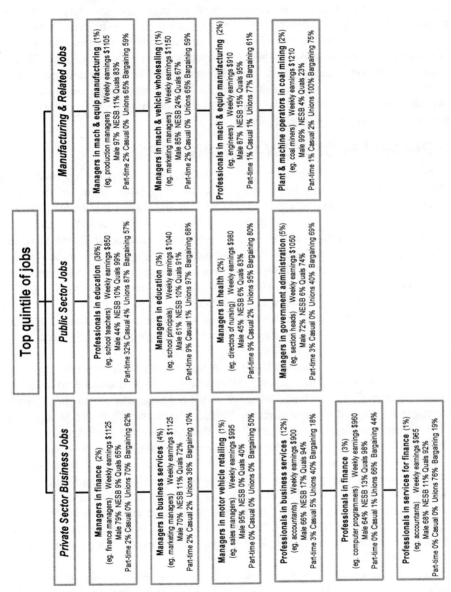

Source: Derived from unpublished AWIRS 1995 employee survey data.

Population: Employees in workplaces with 20 or more employees.

Note: The definition of a job is the intersection between ASCO Major groups and ASIC categories. Percentages in brackets after each job indicates what contribution that job makes to the total number of jobs in the earnings quintile. Earnings are average weekly earnings including overtime. Qualifications refers to post-school credentials. Bargaining refers to proportion of workplaces with enterprise agreements in place. Unions refers to union density in the workplace.

Finally, in the predominantly blue-collar sectors of mining and manufacturing we find an interesting contrast. Here upper quintile earnings range between $910 and $1210 per week. Unlike the other two sectors, high weekly wages are earned by both blue- and white-collar workers. We find professionals, such as engineers, who rely upon their educational qualifications to enhance their earnings, but who also share some of the gains flowing from the general bargaining climate of manufacturing workplaces. But we also find coal miners, a group of workers whose demographic characteristics contribute little to their earnings situation, a group whom overwhelmingly rely on their industry and trade union characteristics for the outcomes they achieve. These workers have the highest level of unionisation (100 per cent) and the highest level of bargaining (75 per cent) of any group of workers in the top quintile of jobs.

THE PROBLEM OF LOW-PAYING JOBS

While the problem of the 'disappearing middle' has now preoccupied economists for a good few years, the problem of the 'working poor' has only more recently surfaced as a serious area of concern. Spurred on by the ACTU's living wage case, economists have begun to look seriously at the issue of low-paying jobs. There is much at stake in this issue. On the one hand, proponents of labour market deregulation look to the United States for inspiration, regularly citing the supposed link between low unemployment and low-paying jobs. In Australia, they argue, high minimum wages have prevented the bottom of the labour market from 'clearing', leaving us stuck with persistently high rates of unemployment. The critics of this view also look to the United States, but they draw a very different picture. Unemployment remains low, partly because large numbers of potential job seekers are locked away in jail (some 1.7 million people), and partly because the economy is so dynamic.

According to economists like Bob Gregory, America's low wages are not responsible for its impressive record of jobs growth. If Australia tried to dismantle its relatively egalitarian labour market institutions, the result would not be greater employment growth, but rather, greater wages dispersion (Gregory 1996, in Harcourt 1997, p. 11). In support of this view, other economists have argued that the responsiveness of employment to moderate changes in low wages amongst American workers 'hovers around zero' (Hancock 1998, p. 22). In other words, changes in the US minimum wage have little real impact on the level of unemployment. We need to look elsewhere for an explanation of America's pattern of jobs growth. It seems fair to conclude that rather than being a social plus, the large numbers of low-paying jobs in the United States are responsible for chronic poverty, homelessness and multiple job holding. When Bill Clinton boasted at a rally about the 11 million new jobs created under his Presidency, one worker in the crowd yelled out, 'Yes, and I've got three of them' (Horin 1997, p. 6s).

This argument about low wages and unemployment has surfaced numerous times in Australia and has recently been summarised lucidly by Keith Hancock. Academics like Peter Dawkins have argued for 'downward flexibility of wages at the lower end of the pay distribution as a means of countering unemployment' (Hancock 1998, p. 22). Business commentators have been blunter: 'if we prefer to keep minimum wages high then we must be clear that it costs jobs' (*Business Review Weekly*, in Hancock 1998, p. 22). Accompanying the BRW article was the graph shown in Figure 4.12 which purported to show that greater employment is associated with greater wage inequality. As Keith Hancock observed, however, 'the relation is feeble' (Hancock 1998, p. 22). Indeed, what the graph invites is not the imposition of a feeble 'line of best fit', but the observation that Japan's employment record is just as good as the USA's, but with nowhere near the same level of wage inequality. Another illuminating observation is that Italy's employment performance is extremely poor, yet it has greater wage inequality than Australia.

Figure 4.12 Employment as a proportion of the population related to wage dispersion

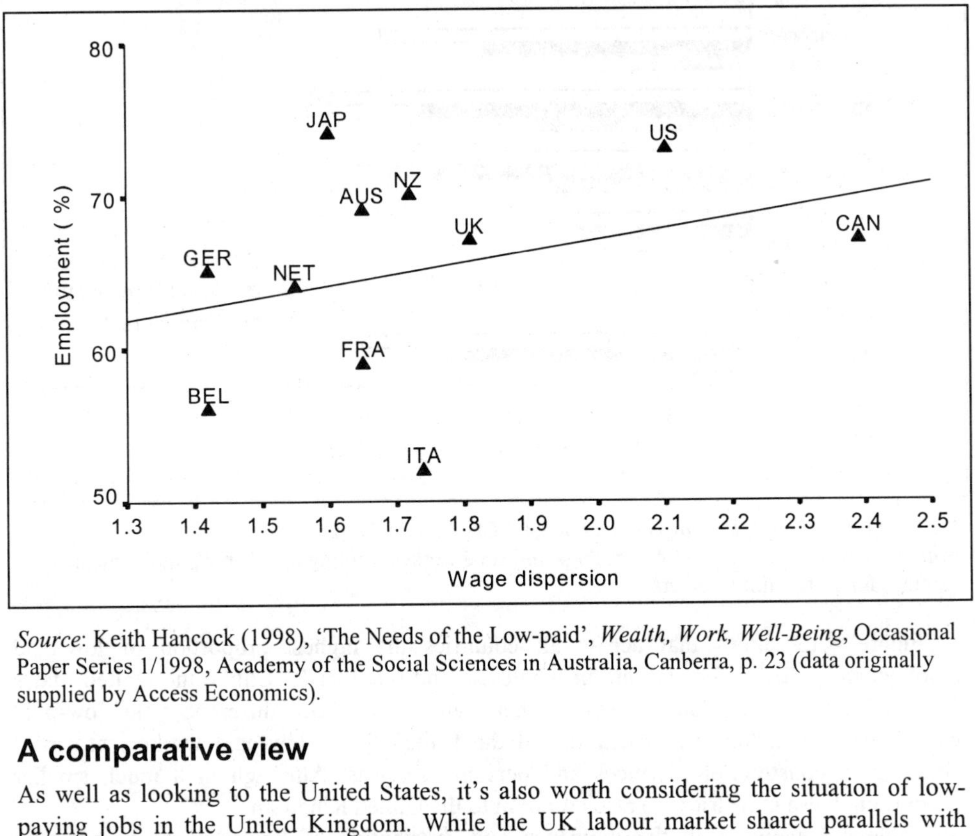

Source: Keith Hancock (1998), 'The Needs of the Low-paid', *Wealth, Work, Well-Being*, Occasional Paper Series 1/1998, Academy of the Social Sciences in Australia, Canberra, p. 23 (data originally supplied by Access Economics).

A comparative view

As well as looking to the United States, it's also worth considering the situation of low-paying jobs in the United Kingdom. While the UK labour market shared parallels with Australia in the 1960s and 1970s, in the 1980s it underwent a radical transformation which left that country without much protection for the lowest-paid workers. In the following data we can see the extent to which industry, occupation, age and sex are factors in the prevalence of low-paid work in Australia, the United States and the United Kingdom.

Figure 4.13 Incidence of low-paid employment by industry by country

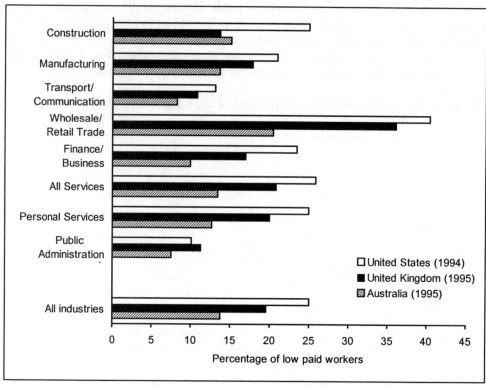

Source: OECD (1996), *Employment Outlook*, OECD, Paris, July, p. 69.
Note: Low-paid employees defined as those full-time workers earning less than 2/3 of the median earnings for all full-time workers.

Figure 4.13 shows that across all countries the highest proportion of low-paid employment is found for workers in wholesale and retail trade. Unlike the United States and the United Kingdom however, there are only small differences in low-paid employment by industry in Australia. In the United States low-paid workers are most common in construction, services and personal services. Although in a much smaller proportion, these industries are also common to the United Kingdom.

Table 4.7 shows both the incidence and distribution of low-paid employment by country. Some of the most interesting differences between the three countries are apparent when low-paid workers are compared by occupational group. The figures for the United States and the United Kingdom are significantly higher across all occupations than for Australia. One of the most significant differences is the proportion of low-paid personal and sales workers in Australia (20 per cent) compared to the United States where more than half the personal service workers are low-paid. The Australian figures for these occupations are also half those of the United Kingdom. Further, there are notable differences between the incidence of low-paid labourers in Australia (19 per cent), the United States (36 per cent) and the United Kingdom (28 per cent). In Australia there is a clustering of low-paid employment in three occupational groups (sales and personal service workers, trade and crafts persons and labourers). In both the United States and the United Kingdom clerical workers also have a high incidence of low-paid employment. Interestingly twice the proportion of professional and technical workers in the United States are considered low-paid compared to Australia where only 4 per cent are low-paid. The data suggests that the arbitration system, as a safety net for low-paid workers in Australia, has prevented the extremes evident in the United States and to a lesser extent the United Kingdom.

Table 4.7 Incidence of low-paid employment by occupation, age and sex

Measure	Country		
	Australia	United Kingdom	United States
Occupation			
Professional/ Technical	4	4	9
Managers	10	6	9
Clerical	13	29	30
Sales	20 *	40	28
Personal services		40	53
Trade/Craft	20	16	18
Labourers	19	28	36
Age			
Less than 25	35	46	63
25- 54	9	15	21
55 and over	13	23	24
Sex			
Male	12	13	20
Female	18	31	33
Total	14	20	25

Source: OECD (1996), *Employment Outlook*, OECD, Paris, July, p. 72–3.
Note: Low-paid workers defined as those full-time workers earning less than 2/3 of the median earnings for all full-time workers. * Figures for sales and personal service workers are reported together in the Australian data

Certainly, the more deregulated the labour market, the worse is the fate of low-paid workers. Looking at a selection of OECD countries (Figure 4.14), we find that the labour markets in the United States and New Zealand treat low-paid workers very harshly. In the last 10 years, amongst men, only high-paid workers have seen their real earnings increase. Both low-paid and median-paid workers have taken considerable earnings reductions. Indeed for the male low-paid workers in both countries, the drop has been in the order of 10 per cent. The situation for women workers was not quite as bad, mainly because median-paid women workers maintained their real earnings.

By way of contrast, European countries like Germany—with a much more regulated labour market—have provided considerable protection to their lowest-paid workers. For both men and women workers, the lowest paid maintained the highest rate of real wage growth over the last 10 years. The situation for low-paid women workers was particularly impressive—a growth in real wages of about 57 per cent.

In the case of Australia, the story outlined earlier in this chapter is apparent. Low-paid male workers fared badly over the decade to 1995, whereas female workers at all levels maintained their real wages. More recent data—reflecting a more deregulated labour market—would show these gender gains beginning to reverse.

Figure 4.14 Real wage growth over the last 10 years for low-, median- and high-paid workers, selected OECD countries

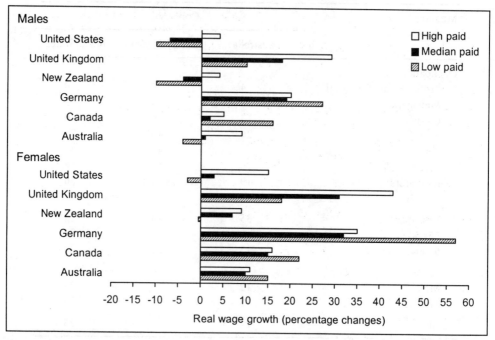

Source: OECD (1996), *Employment Outlook*, OECD, Paris, July, p. 67.

Note: Percentage changes, not annualised. Earnings have been deflated by the consumer price index. Low-paid defined as decile 1; median-paid as decile 5; high-paid as decile 9 (except for men where decile 8 is used). Data has been rescaled to represent a percentage change over 10 years.

Time periods are from 1985 to 1995, except for New Zealand (1984 to 1994), Germany (1983 to 1993), and Canada (1986 to 1994).

The implications of being a low-paid worker

The implications of being a low-paid worker are far-reaching. For many low-paid workers it is a daily struggle to make ends meet. But being a low-paid worker affects more than material consumption levels; it alters the way that these workers value themselves, their opportunities and their general wellbeing. In the 1975 Commission of Inquiry into Poverty, chaired by Professor Henderson, it was argued that:

> an adequate income is fundamental to a person's security, wellbeing and independence. It enables him (sic) to provide housing, education, food, transport and other essentials for himself and his family. An adequate income allows him freedom of choice and freedom to

participate in activities of his choice. It contributes greatly to personal freedom and the extent of opportunities available (cited in Buchanan and Watson 1997, p. 28).

It is very important then to look at the wider implications of low-paid employment, not only for individuals and their families but also for the social costs it imposes on the wider community.

THE ACTU'S LIVING WAGE CLAIM

In an echo of the 1907 Harvester judgment, the ACTU launched 'Living Wage' claims in 1996 and 1998. In the first case, the ACTU were denied their $20 a week claim in favour of an arbitrated safety net adjustment of $10 per week. The reasons given included the potential economic consequences of the higher claim. In the 1996 case (handed down in 1997), the AIRC also rejected the idea that a socially acceptable living standard should be a feature of the Australian wage setting system. Vice President Ross, in his dissenting decision, argued that a higher increase was sustainable and that the Commission should give greater attention to the needs of low-paid workers. He pointed to the social implications of increasing inequality in the community and suggested that:

'given the absence of any institutional restraint on bargaining and executive remuneration there is an inherent unfairness in the proposition that those employees dependent on the award system should bear a disproportionate burden of aggregate wage restraint'.

In the 1998 case, the Commission again rejected the $20 claim made by the ACTU. Instead it delivered wage increases of between $10 and $14 per week, setting the Federal minimum wage to $373.40 per week or $9.83 per hour. In both the 1997 and 1998 judgments the increases were only available to workers who were dependent on the award system for their wages.

Unlike the 1997 judgment, the Commission found that the indirect costs of the 1998 claim would be limited, and suggested that a moderate safety net increase would have little or no effect on the employment opportunities of low-paid workers. They concluded that the claim was unlikely to significantly affect inflation, unemployment or productivity. The Commission also moved towards acknowledging the social implications of wage determination, noting that income inequality was widening in Australia and that many low-paid workers were struggling to make ends meet.

Source: Derived from AIRC, *Safety Net Review—Wages*, April 1997 and April 1998.

An analysis of consumption patterns reveals that low-paid workers make different consumption choices to those on higher incomes. The Household Expenditure Survey allows a comparison of expenditure for varying income levels. Figures 4.15 shows the expenditure for the classic 'Harvester household' consisting of a couple with dependants earning a single income who are presently buying their own home. The first income group (less than $400) approximates consumption for low-paid workers, the second group ($400–$499) is a group which is slightly better off, and the third group is the average for all equivalent household types. While this data is somewhat dated, the relative differences for each item of expenditure remains relevant.

Figure 4.15 Consumption patterns for 'Harvester Households'
(buying their own homes) by level of income, 1988–89

Dollars per week

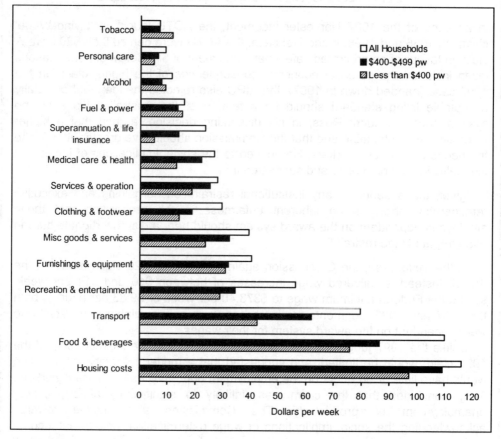

Source: J. Buchanan and I. Watson (1997), 'The Living Wage and the Working Poor' in M. Bittman (ed), *Poverty in Australia: Dimensions and Policies*, SPRC Reports and Proceedings, No. 135, May, p. 35.
Note: The 'Harvester household' refers to the 1907 Harvester decision which set minimum wages for a male worker based on the assumption that he was the head of a single income family consisting of a spouse and dependants.

As Figure 4.15 shows, low incomes have a considerable impact on the expenditure on both the necessities of life and the little luxuries (the discretionary items). Food and beverage expenditure, for example, rises significantly as income rises and to a lesser extent so too does housing expenditure. However, food and beverage expenditure does not continue to rise indefinitely as income rises; rather at higher income levels a substitution of higher quality and luxury food takes place. As Ann Harding found in her study of the consumption patterns of affluent households, 'the affluent were more likely to purchase ham, beef, poultry and seafood, while the average household bought more sausages and processed or canned meat' (Harding and Fischer 1996, p. 5).

LIVING ON A LOW INCOME—EXPERIENCES OF A ROOM ATTENDANT, HOSPITALITY INDUSTRY

I have an approximate household income per week of $380. I spend approximately the following amounts on household expenses each week (this is what has to come out of my income, I don't see any of the money from my husband's income).

- ☐ food/groceries $50
- ☐ mortgage $100
- ☐ bills $50
- ☐ childcare $50
- ☐ transport $20
- ☐ education $20
- ☐ medical expenses $30

When I get a bill I am not expecting I have to hold off paying my regular bills so I can pay it off. I'm presently in debt with my bills, there are over one thousand dollars worth. It's hard with council rates coming up again soon for the house.

If I am short of money I go without things for myself so that the children don't suffer. I feel guilty that I can't afford to let my son go on all the excursions that come up at school. I try to save so he can go every so often. Soon my youngest son will be at school too. That will make things harder. As they get older school costs will escalate. I'll have to do the best I can but it is really going to be hard for us.

I can't afford to have contents insurance on the house which worries me. I don't have any private health insurance for me and my children. I could afford it when I was younger but now I can't. My sons are asthmatic and so I have taken out ambulance insurance - it's the best I can do on the money I've got.

I know that with my job I miss out on a lot socially. All the things that happen on the weekend are out of my reach because I'm working. When I'm not working I'm very tired and I don't have much of a social life. I like to do craft work in my spare time like sewing and decoupage, but I'm usually too exhausted to manage it.

Source: Derived from Australian Liquor Hospitality and Miscellaneous Workers Union, *Affidavit to Living Wage Case*. Reproduced with permission.

CONSUMING AN INCOME—A TALE OF TWO EXTREMES

Fred's story

Fred is in his mid-twenties and works as a factory hand. He lives in a mobile home with his brother who works in the same factory. The brothers are not satisfied with their accommodation because there are broken lights and other problems which the landlord will not fix. Their shared weekly rental is $140.

Fred is employed on an individual contract under the Victorian Employee Relations Act and his take home pay is $232.50 per week. He and his brother (who is on the same rate of pay) do not have enough money to pay the bills when they come in and frequently have to borrow money for food. They rely on donations of clothes from workmates and family and have not been able to afford to go to the cinema for several years. At times Fred has been unable to afford medication for his asthma which consequently has worsened.

Although both brothers were originally employed under a government wage subsidy scheme, they say they have not received any training, and one of Fred's main work tasks is sweeping the floor. Both brothers say their situation is similar to, and perhaps slightly worse, than when they were receiving unemployment benefits.

Source: Brotherhood of Saint Laurence (1996), *Written Submissions to the National Wage Case*, p. 19.

Happy days are here again—for some!

'Happy days are here again—if you are in the richest 5 per cent of the population. After the early 1990s' recession and a slow recovery, the wealthy are cashed-up and spending freely again in a style reminiscent of the 1980s.

The symptoms of the bubble are much the same as during the late 1980s. French champagne sales are up 20 per cent in a year. BMW sales have grown even faster over the past 12 months, while plenty of well-heeled property owners in Sydney and Melbourne have enjoyed price rises of 30 per cent or more in that time.

So far, however, the boom times have been confined to a very narrow segment of the economy.

Those most conspicuously consuming are entrepreneurs, managers and executives—the beneficiaries of globalisation, deregulation, a seven year economic upswing, and the increasingly large premiums being paid by firms for scarce skills.'

Source: Extracted from Stephen Ellis, 'A high five: the rich let the good times roll', *Australian Financial Review*, 2 September 1997, pp. 1 and 11.

Lower-income families spend half as much as the average family on clothing and footwear and transport. Expenditure on medical care is particularly sensitive to income levels with low-income families spending less than half as much as the average family.

Problem areas in particular are those areas not covered by Medicare such as pharmaceuticals (if you don't have a health care card) and dental treatment. Figure 4.15 also shows that low-income families have much lower expenditure on recreation and entertainment than families on an average income, but their consumption on alcohol is considerably higher. This may reflect social or cultural factors or simply that alcohol substitutes for other forms of entertainment at this lower-income level (Buchanan and Watson 1997, p. 31). Lower-income families clearly have a reduced capacity to save and as a result expenditure on superannuation and insurance is also reduced. For families with children consumption is further constrained by the need to make contributions for public education through fundraising and additional fees, the cost of uniforms and childcare costs (Brotherhood of Saint Laurence 1996, pp. 33–43). For some, there is a fear that if they don't pay these 'voluntary contributions' their children will not be able to participate in all of the activities at school. This is difficult for parents who often go without themselves so that their children do not miss out.

Amongst the lowest-paid occupational groups in Australia are childcare workers, nearly one-quarter of whom earned under $11.00 per hour in 1996. They are overwhelmingly women and work in an industry where demand for their services is very sensitive to wage costs. This makes it very hard for childcare workers to bargain for higher wages. A survey conducted for the 1996 Living Wage case highlights the implications of this economic vulnerability for their standard of living. It's often assumed that low-paid women workers are part of a household where other members work, and that their low wages are somehow more acceptable because of this. Not only does this view overlook the basic economic injustice of not rewarding labour adequately, but it also overlooks the reality of female sole breadwinner households. These are situations where women are living alone, or as sole parents, and must manage their households on a single wage. In the case of the childcare workers' survey, over 16 per cent of workers were in this situation. Their economic vulnerability is particularly acute, as Table 4.8 demonstrates.

Table 4.8 Financial difficulties experienced by childcare workers during the last year, Australian Capital Territory 1996

Percentage reporting at least one difficulty in the category

Nature of financial difficulty	Sole breadwinner childcare workers	All childcare workers
	%	%
Inability to meet school-related costs	34	16
Inability to meet housing-related costs	51	36
Inability to meet car-related costs	75	57

Source: ACIRRT and LHMU survey, 1996.

These figures show that between one-third and three-quarters of childcare workers who provided the sole income for their households experienced significant financial difficulties. For one-third of them, their children were affected by way of schooling costs. Half of them experienced problems with housing-related costs and three-quarters reported an inability to meet their car-related costs.

At the core of the issue of low-paid work is a person's standard of living. The case studies in the boxed text in the preceding pages provide a glimpse of what a low income means for individuals and their material wellbeing. In this focus on earning and spending, however, we must not lose sight of the larger picture, of the links between income inequality and society's wellbeing. As the Brotherhood of Saint Laurence succinctly phrased it:

> The emotional and psychological impact of low wages goes to the heart of social democracy. Without freedom of choice, without adequate resources to participate in social activities, low-paid workers are being denied the right to also participate in society as active citizens (Brotherhood of Saint Laurence 1996, pp. 66).

* * *

As the 1980s evolved into the 1990s, the neo-liberal project became more influential in restructuring Australia's system of wage determination. Wages for the weak have fallen, those of the strong have increased. The analysis in this chapter has shown that these outcomes were not simply institutional. Rather, they were rooted in labour market structures, in the way high and low wage jobs are located in distinctive industry and occupational segments of the labour market. Because of this, weakening the institutions of social protection—such as awards, trade unions and the AIRC—could never have produced a 'productivity breakout' as the neo-liberals imagined would happen. Rather, weakening these protections simply exacerbated the market-based inequalities which arise from labour market segmentation. This has had a serious impact on material living standards, especially for low-paid women workers.

It's important to keep in mind, though, that the growth of low-paid jobs in the economy has not just arisen because of the demise of social protection. Important structural changes are also underway. These include changes in the industrial and occupational composition of the labour market, as well as the spread of casual and dependent contractor forms of employment. The challenge for policy involves much more than simply restoring historic principles of wage determination which were based on fairness (such as comparative wage justice). Of course, the spirit behind these principles—decent living standards and comparable pay for similar work—are still relevant. How that spirit might infuse a new approach to determining the level and distribution of work-related earnings is an issue we return to in the last chapter. For the moment it is necessary to examine the closely related issue of working hours. Indeed, effective wages policy must incorporate a sound response to the dramatic changes in working time arrangements which have been unfolding.

CHAPTER 5

Working longer and harder

We saw in Chapter 3 that bargaining over working time arrangements was one of the most common areas where management sought to bring about workplace change. Wage negotiations—discussed at length in the last chapter—were invariably tied to changes in hours of work, usually for the benefit of management. In this chapter we look more closely at the issues of working time arrangements—which has usually meant working longer—and the problem of work intensification—which has meant working harder. We argue that many of the changes which have taken place over the last two decades represent the demise of 'standard' working hours. In the same way that wage outcomes are increasingly fragmenting, so too are the patterns of working time in the economy. By the late 1990s, only about one-third of the workforce fits the mould of the full-time worker doing standard hours, the mould which gave the post-war settlement much of its centre of gravity.

In the nineteenth century, long hours of work were common. A 12 hour day was the lot of most factory workers. Throughout most of the twentieth century, things have been improving. Under the impact of trade union campaigns and state regulation, shorter hours of work were achieved and the idea of paying penalties for working longer, or for work done during 'anti-social' hours, became widespread. Out of these developments grew the notion of 'standard' working time arrangements. These involved an eight hour day worked over a five-day week during 11 months of the year over a 45-year working life. There was a lot at stake in this notion of standard working time because many job entitlements and benefits were built around it. For example, penalty rates and overtime were paid for time worked outside the span of normal hours, while annual recreation leave and sick leave were calculated according to the standard working year.

It's fair to say that during the 1950s and 1960s most full-time workers in Australia fitted into this model of standard working time. This pattern provided people with security and predictability during their working lives. In the 1970s, things began to change in important ways. Unemployment became a major blight on the economic landscape and job security began to disintegrate, a process we chart in much greater detail in the next chapter. For those still in work, the most important change was that people began to work longer and harder. A century of progress seemed to have stalled, and those optimistic musings about the problems of a 'leisure society', so common in the 1960s, seemed like a sick joke by the 1980s. In the mid-1990s we find ourselves in a situation where just over a *third* of the labour force now works standard hours each week. About one-third work overtime and just under one-fifth work part-time. Figure 5.1 summarises the current distribution of working time and shows just how much standard working time has become the preserve of a minority of the labour force.

Amongst the full-time workforce, working longer has become the order of the day. Figure 5.2 shows that since the late 1970s the proportion of full-timers working standard hours of work has dropped significantly and the proportion working very long hours has risen dramatically. In the late 1970s, most full-time workers—about two-thirds—still worked standard hours, that is, from 35 to 40 hours per week. By the late 1990s, this group were in the minority: less than one-half of full-time workers were doing standard hours; the majority were now working extended hours. The proportion of full-timers working very long hours—more than 48 per week—nearly doubled over this time period, jumping from 19 per cent of all full-timers to 32 per cent. Figure 5.2 suggests that the turning point, the period when a new era of long hours got underway, was the end of the 1981 recession. As the economy moved into growth, so too did a new way of working emerge.

We saw in Chapter 3 that enterprise bargaining has focussed on wages and working time arrangements. To gain modest wage increases, workers have had to trade away many long-held conditions, particularly arrangements related to their hours of work. In this chapter, we look more closely at the twin issues of working time arrangements (working longer) and work intensification (working harder) and we demonstrate that enterprise bargaining has been associated with decisive victories by management on both these issues.

Figure 5.1 The current distribution of working time: proportions of the labour force working overtime, standard hours, part-time and who are unemployed, 1995

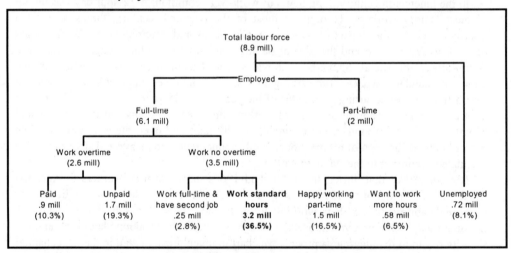

Source: John Buchanan and Sue Bearfield (1997), *Reforming Working Time, Alternatives to Unemployment*, Casualisation and Excessive Hours, Brotherhood of St Laurence, Future of Work Project, Fitzroy, p. 9.

Figure 5.2 Hours worked for full-time workers, 1978–97

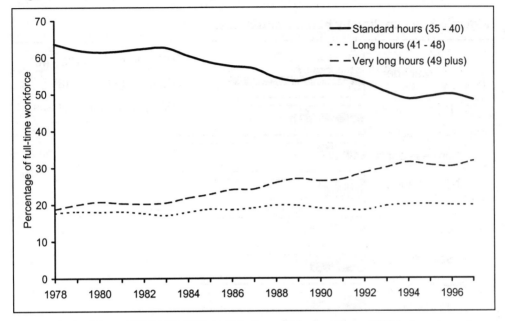

Source: Derived from ABS (1978-1998), *Labour Force Australia*, Cat. no. 6203.0, August surveys.

WORKING LONGER

Who are the people doing these longer hours of work, and where do they work? Overwhelmingly it's managers and professionals who work the longest hours, but there's also a number of blue-collar jobs where long hours are common. Figure 5.3 shows that managers—people whose specific hours of work are the most ill-defined and open-ended— are the occupational group with the largest proportion of people working very long hours. Half of all managers work 49 or more hours per week, and another quarter work between 41 and 48 hours per week. Only a quarter of this occupational category work standard hours. Professionals are also in a similar position. Their work is defined in such a fashion that long hours in the job are very common. It's not a question of knocking off at five, but rather, finishing the task at hand. Consequently, about a quarter of professionals work *very long hours* (49 hours or more), and another quarter work *long hours* (41 to 48 hours).

Most of the other occupational groups are much more likely to be working standard hours, and this reflects the regulated nature of their jobs. They are usually paid for working beyond standard hours—overtime—and this puts a cap on the extent to which their employers are likely to increase their hours of work. There are two occupational groups— salesworkers and plant and machine operators—where this isn't the case. Sales reps often work very long hours because their earnings can be based on how much they sell, and good commissions often come from putting in long hours. Blue-collar workers, like truck drivers and miners, also put in very long hours. The industry picture presented in Figure 5.4

103

certainly bears this out. Apart from agriculture, the industries with the greatest proportions of workers in the very long hours category are mining and transport and storage.

Figure 5.3 Occupation by hours worked, 1993

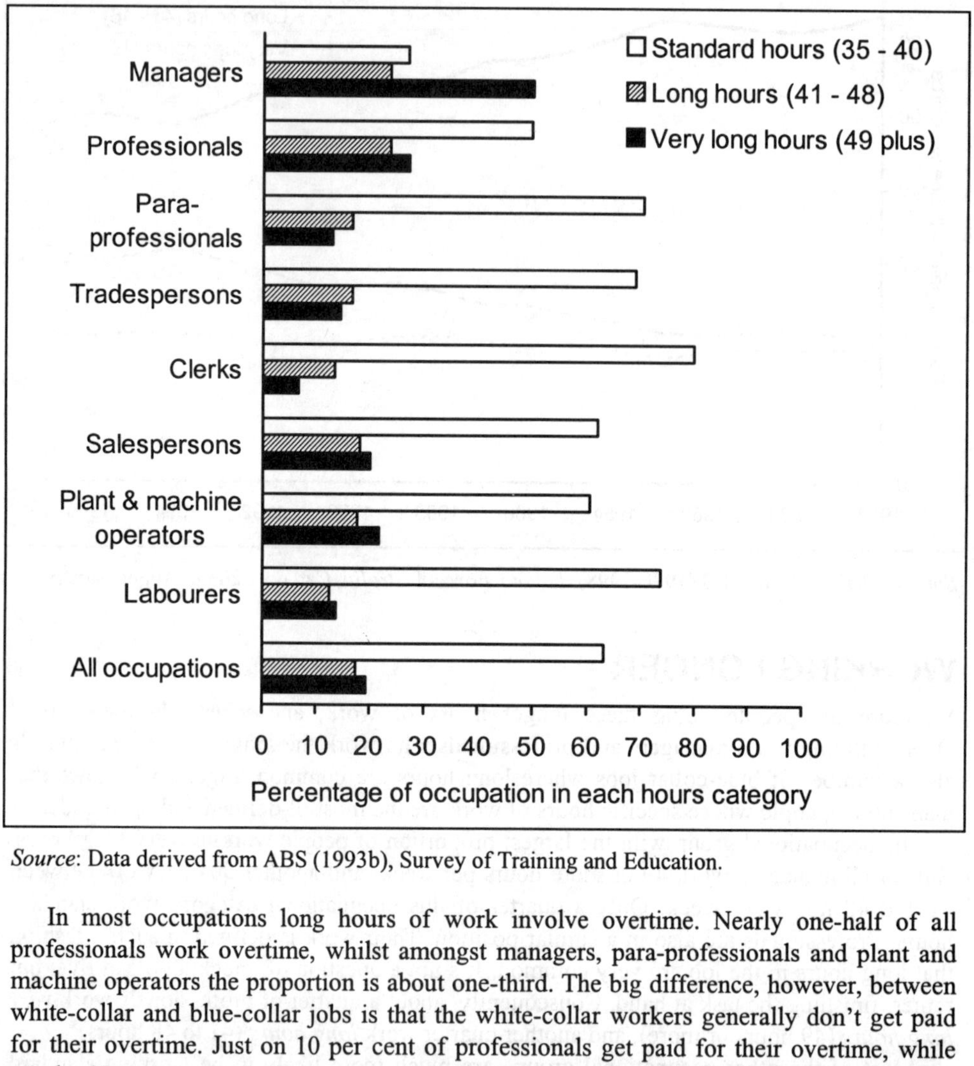

Source: Data derived from ABS (1993b), Survey of Training and Education.

In most occupations long hours of work involve overtime. Nearly one-half of all professionals work overtime, whilst amongst managers, para-professionals and plant and machine operators the proportion is about one-third. The big difference, however, between white-collar and blue-collar jobs is that the white-collar workers generally don't get paid for their overtime. Just on 10 per cent of professionals get paid for their overtime, while nearly 90 per cent of plant and machine operators get paid for theirs. Traditionally, payment for overtime—often at double-time or time-and-a-half rates of pay—is what has kept a lid on increases in working time. It's partly because overtime is not paid that managers and professionals work such long open-ended hours. By contrast, blue-collar and pink-collar jobs are tied more closely to standard working time because their hours are regulated by industrial agreements or awards, and payment of overtime is common.

We shall see below that this traditional regulation of the length of the working day is beginning to break down, as overtime payments are absorbed into annualised payment systems, and as the span of standard hours is redefined away from the traditional eight hour norm. This is one of the reasons why the labour force statistics for the 1990s show people working longer hours, but not a lot of change in the patterns of overtime. Trying to understand people's working patterns by looking at overtime is increasingly outdated. New ways of understanding working time arrangements are needed and one of the goals of this chapter is to advance that understanding.

Figure 5.4 Industry by hours worked, 1993

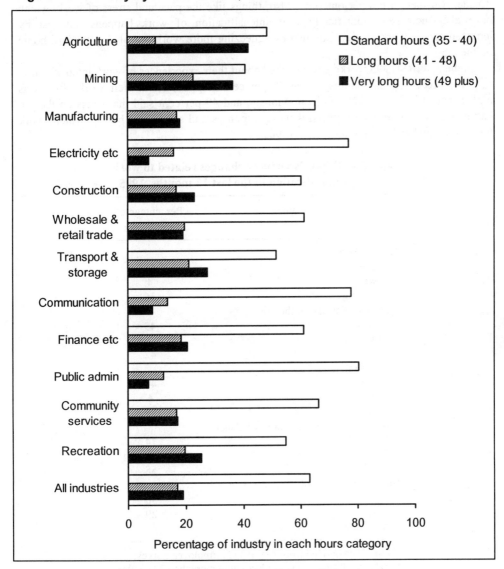

Source: Data derived from ABS (1993b), Survey of Training and Education.

WORKING HARDER

One of the reasons why it's useful to look at this issue of overwork is because it's a good measure of the rapidity of workplace change. In the last decade, the hours of work of both managerial and *non-managerial* occupations has steadily increased. For example, full-time tradespersons increased their average weekly hours of work by nearly three hours between 1986 and 1994, whilst labourers increased theirs by over four and a half hours. Working longer hours then, is certainly a major outcome of workplace change during the last decade. But there are other outcomes also, things like the pace and stress of work, which have also increased dramatically. The intensification of work happens not just by lengthening the working day, but also by squeezing more work out of the standard hours on the job.

In the AWIRS 1995 workers were asked about their experiences of work intensification over the preceding 12 months. Some 58 per cent responded that their work effort was higher than it had been 12 months previously, and 49 per cent said that stress on the job had increased. Table 5.1 summarises these responses and shows just how prevalent work intensification has become in the mid-1990s.

Table 5.1 Worker's views of changes related to work intensification in the last 12 months, 1995

Worker's view of change	Percentage of employees
Work effort	
higher	58
lower	4
no change	36
Amount of stress on the job	
higher	49
lower	7
no change	42
Pace of the job	
higher	46
lower	4
no change	49
Satisfaction with work/family balance	
higher	14
lower	26
no change	58
Satisfaction with job	
higher	30
lower	29
no change	40

Source: Data derived from AWIRS 95, Employee Survey.
Population: Persons in workplaces with more than 20 employees.

One of the common areas of work intensification has been in government utilities—the electricity, water and gas providers—and the education industry. The utilities industry has been subject to massive dislocation: corporatisations and privatisations, organisational restructurings and programs of job shedding and job redesign. And the impact on the workforce has been dramatic. In surveys like the AWIRS 1995, workers are far more likely to respond adversely on issues which measure the impact of change, things like autonomy, promotion and stress. Whereas about one-tenth of all workers reported a decline in their decision-making power, nearly one-fifth of electricity, water and gas workers reported this. Similarly, about 15 per cent of all workers thought that their chances of promotion had declined, but the corresponding figure for the electricity, water and gas industry was 37 per cent. On issues like job stress and decreased job satisfaction, the differences between this industry and all workers was of the order of 10 percentage points.

Education is an industry which has been under immense pressures during the last decade (see boxed text). This industry has been subject to a form of 'creeping privatisation', as resources have shifted from the public sector to private providers. At the same time, 'managerialism' has been unleashed in a series of chaotic restructurings. On top of all of this have been increased social pressures on schools, with expectations that teachers should embrace new technology and cope with social problems related to drugs, unemployment, racism and sexism. It is no surprise then, that AWIRS 1995 shows that workers in education respond in a similar fashion to their colleagues in electricity, gas and water, particularly around issues like increased effort and stress. On the other hand, workers in education are less concerned about issues like promotion, and much more worried about the balance between work and family life, an area where their long hours of work impact so badly.

The problem of work intensification is not just one of perception. Stress also makes people sick. Between 1990 and 1994, stress claims under workers compensation doubled, even though stress is one of those illnesses where workers seldom make claims, preferring to use their sick leave or recreational leave to try to recover (ACTU 1997). In the AWIRS 1995 employee survey, nearly 5 per cent of respondents reported that stress had caused them to be ill—and 15 per cent of this group received workers compensation for their stress and 50 per cent took time off work. The industries which had the worst records for stress-induced illness were: health and community services, personal and other services, and—not surprisingly—education.

Basically, education is an industry where shrinking resources meet dedicated professionals and the outcomes are often disastrous. In Japan they have a word for 'death from overwork'—karoshi—and it was a school teacher's fate that led to an important court ruling in December 1994. The judge ruled that the family of a school teacher, who collapsed at a parent-teacher meeting in 1986 and later died from a brain haemorrhage, should be awarded nearly $160,000 because there was a 'legitimate causal relationship between the teacher's overwork and his death'. The judge criticised school officials for neglecting 'to take proper steps to maintain its employee's health' (*Australian*, 21 December, 1994).

While the Australian legal system has yet to encounter cases like this, evidence for the problem of stress amongst the workforce in Australia surfaces in other quarters. In 1996 the *Sydney Morning Herald* revealed that stress in the office and factory was estimated to be costing $150 million per year in workers compensation payments (3 January, 1996, p. 4).

The president of the Australian Medical Association, Dr David Weedon, observed that 'Economic rationalists have to take some of the blame. Competition, the free market and increased profits have brought a high price'.

EDUCATION IN THE 1990s

Recent surveys in Victorian and New South Wales schools set out to measure levels of teacher stress in independent schools. They found that hours of work were a major factor in contributing to stress. Workloads in both States were much higher than industry standards. Half of all Victorian respondents worked more than 21 hours of direct student contact per week. The figure for NSW was slightly less, at 43 per cent. In Victoria, over half of the respondents reported less than four hours of 'release time', the period of non-contact time used for classroom organisation and lesson preparation. In NSW, the comparable figure was 58 per cent. In both states, many hours at home were spent on school work. Twenty one per cent of Victorian respondents, and 27 per cent of NSW respondents, reported that they worked for more than 11 hours per week at home on school work. Finally, teaching staff were also frequently called back to school in the evenings and on weekends for various kinds of extra-curricular activities.
Source: Spence 1996.

* * *

Research by the New South Wales Teachers' Federation found similar problems in the state school system. A survey carried out in 1995 found that 18 per cent of respondents reported having a medically diagnosed stress disorder. For most teachers, the major problem was excessive workload. In particular, the greater range of tasks expected of teachers, and the lack of time to carry out these additional tasks, were major problems.
Source: NSWTF (1996), *Federation Annual Report*.

* * *

University teachers have also found their workloads increasing dramatically since the Dawkins' 'reforms' of the 1980s. Academics have always prized their 'free', unstructured time: it's when they read, think and write. Yet that is the very time increasingly removed from their control. Not only has their working week increased by up to three hours a week since the late 1970s, but their weekends and their summer break have come under assault by their employers. Summer schools have become pervasive and, through enterprise bargaining negotiations, employers have fought to have their staff work on weekends.
Source: Armitage 1996; Powell 1995.

The public sector has been particularly vulnerable to problems of overwork, because operating budgets have been cut and workforces reduced, but with no commensurate reduction in the workload. In 1993–94, one-quarter of the stress claims approved by Comcare, the Commonwealth Government's workers compensation agency, 'were a direct result of workload and deadline pressures' (*Australian* 8–9 April, 1995, Review section p.

1). While white-collar workers have borne the brunt of public sector cutbacks, blue-collar workers in government instrumentalities have also been savaged, since the constant cycle of restructurings has always led to increased workloads. One supervisor with State Rail found his heart kept pounding for several hours each evening, well after knock-off time. He sought medical advice, but the cause lay in the workplace: his workload had almost doubled when another depot was closed and the work was transferred to his depot: 'I just had this feeling that I would never catch up, no matter what I did. I stayed longer and longer but it just didn't help'. (*Australian* 8–9 April, 1995, Review section p. 1).

THE OVERWORKED AUSTRALIAN

Why are people working longer and harder?

In the early 1990s Juliet Schor released her book, *The Overworked American: The Unexpected Decline of Leisure,* and showed how over the last 20 years American workers increased their working hours by the equivalent of one month per year. Not only managers and professionals, but also low-paid workers, were putting in excessively long hours of work. Indeed one of the reasons why US workers were working longer was that their hourly rates of pay had been falling and they were trying to maintain their accustomed standard of living.

By the late 1980s it's now apparent that an 'overworked Australian' has also emerged on the scene. Unlike their American counterparts, these Australian workers are mostly at the better paid end of the labour market. As we saw in the last chapter, Australia's low-paid workers still earn a living wage and can do this by working standard hours. By contrast, America's working poor could not survive without doing the excessive hours. Despite this important difference, there is little doubt that American workplace trends are beginning to surface in Australia, and that a culture of working long hours has become entrenched in particular occupations and industries.

It's important to recognise that there is this cultural dimension, as well as job-related reasons, for why people in some occupations are inclined to work long hours. Managers, for example, have always worked long hours as part of their career building. In more recent years, however, a workplace culture has grown in which job commitment has been equated with working exceptionally long hours. This is particularly so in industries like banking, law and information technology. Daniel Petre's reflections on working at Microsoft (see boxed text) illustrate this very well. As Petre observes, the running joke at Microsoft was that you only worked half-time. You just had to decide which 12 hours of the day you wanted to work (Petre 1998, pp. 103–4).

Competitive work environments, like those as in the finance sector, often lead to situations where the hours that people work become a major factor in their career advancement:

> The people who work the hours are the ones who advance. Hours are considered in performance appraisal ... Before people just used to work their 40 hours a week. Now it is generally accepted that you are a slacker if you work less than 50. It is competitive, people compete with each other. I have seen a lot of that around here. *Focus group informant.*

WORKING-TIME CULTURE AT MICROSOFT

In his time working at Microsoft in the USA and in Australia, Daniel Petre developed an acute perception of how the corporate culture of working long hours operated. People—not just managers—routinely worked 12 to 14 hours a day and appeared to be happy to work these hours, and to turn up on weekends when needed. It was part of the 'challenge of changing the world through software', not to mention the very generous pay and conditions attached (including stock options which could turn them into millionaires within a few years!).

Managers, however, were also responsible for fostering this culture of overwork. They routinely called early morning (before 8 am) and late-afternoon (after 5 pm) meetings and expected everyone to attend. They also regularly called meetings on weekends. As Petre saw it, Microsoft weren't interested in balance in their worker's lives, they wanted commitment. People who had another focus in their lives—such as their children—were seen as no longer committed, 'as though they had given up on religion'. Petre concluded that 'acting dedicated was as important as performing well'.

The cost to workers of this kind of culture was very plain to see: superficial relations with their spouses and no time with their kids—'lost fathering' as Petre termed it.

Source: Petre (1998), *Father Time: Making Time for Your Children*, Macmillan, Sydney, pp. 44–7; pp. 103–4; p. 106.

With self-employed professionals, a 'culture of long hours' can become so entrenched that it passes as normality, until someone refuses to collude in such practices. Nicole Burns, a young solicitor, left her job with a big Sydney law firm because she decided a 'culture which encouraged working from 7.30 am to midnight was not for her'. Instead she settled for a job in a small solicitor's firm where her working day finished at 6.30 pm. Her former colleagues were shocked at her departure, but for her the decision was clear-cut:

> When I'd come home at night I'd just feel like bursting into tears. All I was doing was working. I lost touch with some friends. I felt depressed and had problems sleeping (Sweet 1996, p. 4).

There can also be a status thing about working long hours, particularly amongst managers. When Penny Sharpels quit her job as a senior human resources manager, she left behind a lifestyle that included regularly working 12–hour days, including weekends. The penny dropped for Ms Sharpels when a colleague 'boasted about having been at work at 7.30 pm on Sunday' and,

> I thought, this is not a status symbol, this shows that you have nothing else to go home to. I started to see that I had swallowed the corporate myth and that it wasn't particularly healthy … There was more to life than just work (Sweet 1996, p. 4).

There is also a problem of course with the 'open-ended' nature of managerial and professional work, the fact that the job never finishes cleanly at 5 pm. As one focus group informant observed: 'Professional hours are focussed on the task rather than the time worked'.

The blurring between a worker's own time and the employer's time can also contribute to overwork. With managers, this has always been a problem. As Daniel Petre explained:

> The company [Microsoft] had perfected a process that is now becoming widespread across both the US and Australia. It has effectively blurred the line between the workplace and the domestic front to the point that work had invaded the home and home had become merely an extension of the work environment (Petre 1998, p. 44).

In more recent years, this blurring has been extended to more and more groups of workers, not just managers and professionals. Even clerical and sales workers, in industries like banking and hospitality, are now expected to train in their own time, to attend meetings in their own time, and to take work home if it's not finished at the end of the working day or shift. As one part-time waitress discovered once she was promoted to supervisor, the world of work soon invades the home:

> On our days off, we do rosters and we have 40 odd staff saying, 'I can't work this and I can't work that ... and I've got to go to Tech on Tuesday, so I can't work and ... blah, blah' ... We never have a night at home without staff ringing us ... Saying, 'I can't work my shift tomorrow. I'm sick, or I've got a cold or ...' *Part-time tourist resort waitress.*

Finally, where work is client-focussed, particularly in the helping professions, increased workloads in an environment of diminishing resources invariably leads to longer hours of work because workers do not want to let their clients down. In schools and hospitals, where operating budgets have been slashed so often that services are close to collapse, this kind of dedication is being sorely tested:

> There is an element of 'working on the goodwill of the staff' and we do not know how long this can last. In a sense, the goodwill of the staff is 'subsidising' the project because we only have enough money to employ people for x hours and yet more and more hours are put into it. In addition, the services for patients are subsidised by worker goodwill and you only hope that the staff provide the services to patients whether this is outside work hours or not. *Manager in the health industry.*

Amongst blue-collar workers, maintaining a reasonable standard of living breeds an 'overtime culture', in which grabbing as much overtime as possible becomes taken for granted. This often suits management, because it means fluctuations in workload can be covered by the existing workforce. There's no need to recruit additional staff if the present workforce is prepared to work longer hours when necessary. Within blue-collar jobs its important to distinguish between those workers caught up in this overtime culture and those whose job is structured in such a way that it enforces long hours. Amongst truck drivers, for example, the driving schedules enforce long hours of work. Here are some examples from one enterprise agreement:

❑ Melbourne to Sydney: 866 kms at 85 kms per hour. To be driven in 10.19 hours and (with allowances) to be paid $223.16;

❑ Sydney to Adelaide: 1418 kms at 85 kms per hour. To be driven in 16.68 hours and (with allowances) to be paid $335.24;

❑ Melbourne to Brisbane: 1681 kms at 85 kms per hour. To be driven in 19.78 hours and (with allowances) to be paid $407.18. (*Source*: Transport Workers Union and Stepnell Transports Enterprise Agreement 1997.)

Coal miners and wharfies, for example, may earn as much as $70,000 to $80,000 a year, but this is heavily dependent on production bonuses and overtime payments. The base rate of earnings may be as low as $35,000. If they don't do the long hours of work, their employment in that industry is 'wasted', and they may as well work somewhere else with lower risks and less physical strain.

There are thus a range of reasons why workers—particularly managers and professionals—are working such long hours. All of these reasons—workplace cultures, diminishing resources, the nature of the labour process, low base rates of pay—have a role to play in explaining the last decade of change. But, in the background, hovering there all the while, is the spectre of the employer, and the new agenda of work intensification and working-time flexibility which firms have been pursuing. Many of the apparently psychological aspects to working long hours—such as competition and status—only emerge so strongly because the pressures on workers to perform have intensified so dramatically during the last decade and fear of losing one's job has become so pronounced. Ultimately it is managers who have used enterprise bargaining, and other industrial relations strategies, to get their workers to work longer and harder. They have been able to do this because many of the traditional protections against overworking have been dismantled during the last decade. As the next section shows, 'hours of work' has been one of the areas of working life most severely deregulated by the success of the neo-liberal project.

The industrial relations context

When it comes to planning their use of labour, employers are interested in *flexibility* and *security*. They want *flexibility* because often the workload fluctuates and they need to cover peaks with adequate amounts of labour. Yet, from a cost point of view, they want to avoid 'carrying' excess labour during business downturns or during quiet times of the day or week. As well as flexibility, employers want the *security* of knowing they will have a labour force able to perform tasks with the appropriate level of skill, at the time required, and in quantities needed to do the job. In the 1950s and 1960s, an era of labour shortages, employers favoured security above all else. They 'hoarded' their labour during business downturns and went in for 'overstaffing' in order to cover their peaks. In the 1990s employers have the luxury of high unemployment, and the curse of high cost pressures. As a result, they have elevated flexibility to the status of a panacea for all their ills. If they can cut costs by cutting back on staff and get away with it, so be it. If they can get that extra drop of labour out of the last five minutes of the day, well and good. If two workers are barely coping with the workload, there's no need to hire a third. In an environment of constant cost-cutting, employer flexibility nearly always means longer hours and greater work intensification.

ENTERPRISE AGREEMENTS AND HOURS OF WORK

Absorbing penalty payments into annualised wages is emerging as an important trend within enterprise agreements. Between 1993 and 1997 the proportion of agreements using this approach increased from 9 per cent to 16 per cent. A landmark example of this approach was the agreement developed by the Sheraton Towers Southgate in Melbourne. The agreement rolled all award penalties into a higher fixed weekly wage. As the company saw it, the new system made administration simpler, helped with equity in rosters, and made the company less sensitive to labour costs at night and on weekends.

Increasing the span of ordinary hours has also been popular with employers, particularly those in the retail industry. Enterprise agreements, in which the span of hours was 12 hours or more, increased between 1993 and 1997 from 25 per cent to 38 per cent. The large retailer, Coles Myer, has moved towards 24-hour trading and has negotiated a workplace agreement which increases the span of ordinary hours from the old standard of 7 am to 6 pm to a new standard of 6 am to 9.30 pm Monday to Friday (with 6 am to 6 pm Saturday and 8 am to 5 pm Sunday). Penalty rates are still paid, but they now apply to overnight working, from 9.30 pm to 6.30 am.

Source: ADAM Database.

ENTERPRISE AGREEMENTS— SOME SAMPLE CLAUSES

'An employee may be required to work for a continuous period of 15 hours, excluding meal breaks, from the time of commencing work each day.'

'Employees may be required to work up to 20 hours overtime per week exclusive of meal breaks, which is deemed to be a reasonable amount of overtime.'

Source: Concrete Mixing Industry Agreement.

'Employees shall work 40 hours per week balanced over a 52 week period. Normal work days shall comprise Monday to Friday of each week excluding public holidays.'

'The commencing and finishing times of each day shall be flexible to enable completion of trading and associated duties.'

Source: Café Operation Agreement.

AWAs AND HOURS OF WORK

☐ An aircraft ground service company, working a seven day operation, has eliminated different overtime rates, weekend and public holiday penalty rates and replaced them with one flat overtime rate for any work done outside the two day shifts. The maximum shift length has been increased from 8 to 10 hours, and maximum time worked before entitled to a break has increased from 5 to 6 hours.

☐ A community organisation working with the disabled has changed the span of ordinary working hours to allow work on Saturdays while payment for overtime has been replaced with time in lieu.

☐ A manufacturing company increased ordinary hours for its laboratory technicians from 35 to 40 hours, and removed penalties and allowances. The workers received a pay increase of 15 per cent and additional annual leave.

Source: Office of Employment Advocate (OEA), *Monthly Updates*, March 1998.

The new industrial relations climate has made this easier for employers for a number of reasons. To begin with, the regulatory framework covering hours of work has always been weak. It has not been part of statutory law, but has been embedded in industrial awards or been part of 'custom and practice'. Consequently, once Australian workplaces began to move towards decentralised bargaining, the industrial instruments which had traditionally regulated hours of work began to be dismantled. For example, in nearly all enterprise agreements, wages and hours of work are the most commonly negotiated items. What's more, most variations in hours of work favour employer flexibility (see boxed text).

Why have workers consented to this weakening in the regulation of hours of work? As we saw in Chapter 3, they have been on the back foot for most of the period of bargaining. Clearly, high levels of unemployment and a weakened labour movement have weakened the bargaining power of the workforce considerably. Secondly, after a decade of falling living standards, most workers have been prepared to 'trade off' various conditions as part of an attempt to catch up on their earnings. Trading off conditions related to hours of work has been one of the most common practices in negotiating enterprise agreements. Finally, workers often get little choice. When it comes to Australian Workplace Agreements (AWAs), there is often little negotiation involved. As the boxed text shows, AWAs have also targeted hours of work.

The extent of the whittling away of conditions is also evident in individual contracts negotiated at the State level. When ACIRRT researchers examined 25 'secret' individual contracts from Western Australia and compared their clauses with the equivalent awards, they found that nominal rates of pay were not cut, but working time arrangements were profoundly changed. These changes included: abolition of penalty rates, no minimum call in times, and overtime paid at a single rate (ACIRRT 1996). Research into 116 secret Victorian contracts revealed similar patterns (Bell 1996).

ASSESSING THE CHANGES

Anecdotal evidence and case study materials are very useful for understanding how patterns of working time are changing but it's also important to keep an eye on the statistical picture and not be misled by unusual cases or assume that the prescriptions outlined in an enterprise agreement always happen on the ground. Fortunately, the AWIRS 1995 employee survey provides some very useful statistical data on working time and work intensification, as well as workers responses to these issues.

Using this AWIRS data, it's possible to measure not only the hours which different categories of people work, but how they feel about it. If we look at the group working very long hours, we find that it divides into two distinct subgroups: the 'consenting-over-worked'—people who are working very long hours and who are happy with their hours—and 'conscripts'—people doing the same hours but who want their hours of work reduced. It's important to realise that the consenting-overworked are not necessarily satisfied about working long hours. They may be 'happy' with the number of hours they work only in so far as those hours are needed to maintain their standard of living. Reducing their hours of work may not be a real choice. Of course, within this group of consenting-overworked are bound to be some 'workaholics', people who have become so wedded to their jobs that they can't bear to stay away for too long. Unfortunately the data does not allow us to distinguish between these different shades within the consenting-overworked. In the case of the conscripts, however, it seems clear that they are working longer hours out of insecurity, often in order to keep their jobs in a competitive labour market, and sometimes in order to meet the needs of their clients in a world of shrinking resources.

Table 5.2 shows how we have arrived at our definitions of these two groups of overworked people. The consenting-overworked are the group found in the columns marked C-O while the group termed conscripts are found in the column marked C. Of course we could draw a similar picture for the group of people working long hours (41 to 48) but the story is more clear-cut by choosing people at the extreme. After all, someone working 42 or 43 hours a week may be so close to the standard working time model that you'd be stretching the point to consider them as overworked. On the other hand, someone regularly working 50 or 60 hours a week is definitely overworked.

In numerical terms, the consenting-overworked make up about 13 per cent of all full-time workers in workplaces with 20 or more employees, while conscripts make up about 8 per cent of workers. The most common jobs found amongst the consenting-overworked are sales and marketing managers, specialist managers, production managers and finance managers. Professionals are particularly prevalent amongst the conscripts and include jobs like business professionals and school teachers. Amongst the consenting-overworked are blue-collar jobs, people working in plant and machine operating occupations like boilermakers and welders, bus and tram drivers, truck drivers and excavating plant operators.

Table 5.2 Occupational background of the overworked

Percentage of occupation in each of the hours categories

Occupation	Normal hours (35-40)			Long hours (41-48)			Very long hours (49 plus)			Total
	Happy with hours	Want less hours	Want more hours	Happy with hours	Want less hours	Want more hours	Happy with hours	Want less hours	Want more hours	
							C-O	C	C-O	
Managers	15	2	0	25	9	0	25	25	0	100
Professionals	28	4	1	27	11	0	15	14	0	100
Para-professionals	45	8	2	22	10	1	8	5	0	100
Tradespersons	36	5	5	27	5	4	12	5	1	100
Clerks	57	9	2	19	6	1	4	2	0	100
Salesworkers	45	4	5	21	5	1	11	8	0	100
Plant & machine ops	30	3	8	27	4	4	16	5	2	100
Labourers	49	4	7	22	2	3	10	2	2	100
All occupations	40	5	3	24	7	2	12	8	1	100

Source: Unpublished data from AWIRS 95, Employee Survey.
Population: Persons in workplaces with more than 20 employees who work full-time.

The people we've defined as overworked are not just people giving up a few extra hours a week to their employer. They are chronically overworked and usually over-stressed, and are struggling to stay on top of the demands of their jobs and survive in a competitive labour market. Both gender and age come into the picture for these two categories of overworked people. The consenting-overworked are far more likely to be men, and to be either in their twenties or past their mid-40s. The conscripts are still overwhelmingly men, but the proportion of women is greater than amongst the consenting-overworked. The conscripts are also more likely to be in their middle years, but this does not seem to be related to raising a family, since workers with dependents are equally likely to be in each camp.

Many of the consenting-overworked are managers, and are therefore spread across a range of industries. This makes it difficult to build a comprehensive industry profile of them. Nevertheless, as Table 5.3 shows, it is possible to isolate concentrations of the consenting-overworked in particular industries. We saw earlier that the consenting-overworked come from both blue-collar and white-collar backgrounds. When we look more closely at where they work, this split becomes self-evident. Mining, construction and transport are where the blue-collar consenting-overworked are found. Property and business services, as well as wholesale trade, are the abodes of the white-collar consenting-overworked. The conscripts are also spread across a range of industries, with two glaring concentrations: mining and education.

Table 5.3 Industry location of the overworked

Industry	Consenting-overworked %	Conscripts %
Mining	**28**	**12**
Manufacturing	**14**	6
Electricity, Gas & Water supply	5	3
Construction	**18**	6
Wholesale Trade	**16**	7
Retail Trade	4	7
Accommodation/Cafes/Restaurants	6	3
Transport & Storage	**20**	7
Communication Services	11	5
Finance & Insurance	10	8
Property & Business Services	**14**	7
Government Administration	5	3
Education	9	**12**
Health & Community Services	5	2
Cultural & Recreational Services	8	4
Personal & Other Service	6	3
All industries	10	6

Source: Unpublished data from AWIRS 95, Employee Survey.
Population: Persons in workplaces with more than 20 employees who work full-time.
Note: Figures in bold are the more dramatic differences between particular industries and all industries.

Responding to workplace change

The consenting-overworked and the conscripts are not just arbitrary categories. The people designated in this way really do have different attitudes to their work and to what is happening in their workplaces. Many of the consenting-overworked seem to thrive on workplace change. Compared to their situation 12 months earlier, they report much more say in decision-making, greater opportunities to use their own ideas and increased chances of promotion. Not surprisingly, they report considerably more job satisfaction than the average response from all workers. Disturbingly, despite working upwards of 50 hours per week, they are no more likely to be dissatisfied with the balance between work and family life than the average level of response.

The conscripts are a very different group. They are very discontented about the balance between work and family life—about two-thirds of all workers in this category register an increase in dissatisfaction with this balance. Across most of the other measures of workplace change they also stand out starkly from the consenting-overworked. Considerably more of the conscripts report that their jobs require more effort, are faster paced and impose more stress than 12 months earlier. There seem to be few bonuses for this group—they are no more likely to feel greater autonomy in their job than the average response. In fact, they are more likely to feel they have less decision-making power than a year before, and that their chances of promotion have fallen during the last year. Not surprisingly then, their job satisfaction has not increased anywhere near the same extent as the consenting-overworked, and as a group they even fall behind the average in this regard. Indeed, they are far more likely to have experienced decreased job satisfaction over the last year than the average response. Figure 5.5 summarises this picture and illustrates dramatically that the consenting-overworked have revelled in the turbulence of the 1990s, whereas the conscripts have been reluctantly dragged along by the rapids of workplace change.

Figure 5.5 How the overworked have responded to workplace change

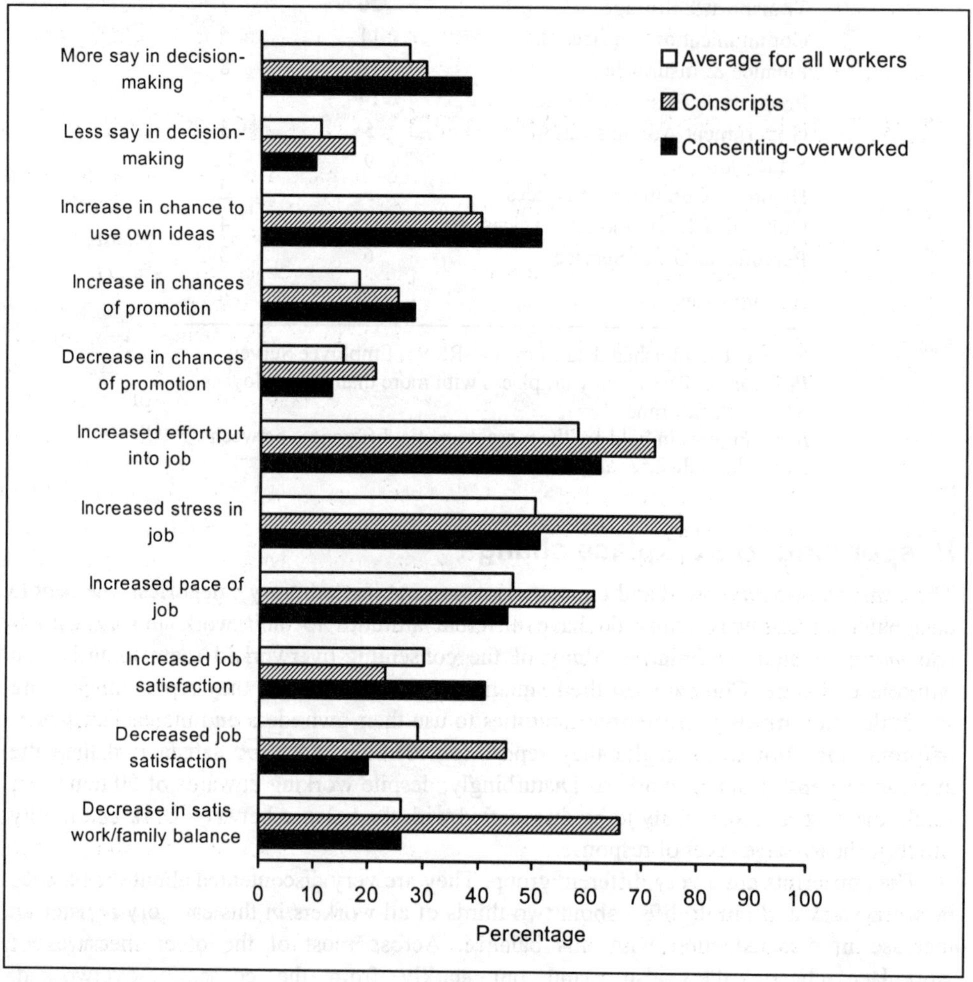

Source: Unpublished data from AWIRS 95, Employee Survey.
Population: Persons in workplaces with more than 20 employees.

There is an interesting gender dimension to this story. We saw earlier that men make up most of the overworked (about three-quarters) and that this is more pronounced amongst the consenting-overworked. On many of the issues just discussed, there are no dramatic differences between men and women—both sexes are responding to workplace change in a similar fashion. However, if we contrast women amongst the consenting-overworked with women conscripts, there are a number of key issues where pronounced gender differences between men and women emerge. Moreover, these are the issues which commentators have traditionally pinpointed as problematic for 'women working in a man's world', that is the higher levels of managerial and professional work. While the women amongst the consenting-overworked respond almost identically to their male colleagues, the female conscripts report more adverse responses in areas like decision-making, their chances to use their own ideas, their job effort, and the job stress they feel. They are also a group for whom the balance between work and family life has taken a battering. Whereas the women amongst the consenting-overworked mirror the men on this measure, the women conscripts stand out more strongly from the men in their discontent.

GOODBYE TO THE STANDARD WORKING WEEK

Working longer, and working harder, can emerge at particular times in a country's economic history. Particularly, during the pickup after an economic downturn, workplaces can find themselves frantically rushing to cope with rising demand. But the picture painted above does not fit into this idea of a short-term response to an economic cycle. The picture above is a long-term one and it signals a secular change in how working time in Australia is organised. Certainly, it started at the end of a recession—in 1983—but it has continued through another economic downturn—in 1990–91—and several upturns. What's most revealing is that these changes to working time have coincided with rapid workplace change across a number of other frontiers, such as increased product competition, enterprise-based bargaining, a weakening of trade union influence on the shopfloor, and increased levels of job insecurity throughout the workforce. *In other words, in workplaces around the country, management has been under pressure to intensify work and has grasped the opportunity provided by a weakened and divided workforce to carry out some fairly dramatic changes. They've been able to do this because the regulatory environment has shifted decisively in their favour. 'Workplace flexibility'—for employers—has become the mantra chanted by most legislators and regulators over the last decade as they have set about weakening the regulatory environment which surrounds working time arrangements.*

Of course, another shift in the balance of power in the workplace could see hours begin to drop, and work intensification ease off. This is unlikely at present, but nevertheless, still possible. What is much harder to change, however, is the new 'regime' of working time arrangements embodied in an increased span of hours and other changes to shift arrangements. The definition of what counts as the working day, and the working week, has been profoundly reshaped during the last decade. In many ways a new culture of working time has emerged, and because it merges with new patterns of shopping and recreation, it will be much harder to overturn. A simple return to the standard working week of the 1970s may not be possible.

Many of the changes to the span of hours may at first glance appear only slight, and they may apply to only some groups of workers. But their significance is much greater than this suggests, because once a new culture of working time begins to permeate society at large, it comes to affect most people in the workforce. For example, once the socially-acceptable limits to the length of the working day have been expanded for some workers, the same limits can potentially apply to all workers. In the early 1990s a significant shift occurred in the hours that workplaces were operating. In 1990 about 42 per cent of workplaces operated for standard hours (that is, up to 40 hours per week). By 1995, this figure had dropped to 31 per cent. Workplaces which operated around the clock had not changed much. Rather, what had taken place was that workplaces with extended hours of operation—from 41 hours to 167 hours per week—increased from 43 per cent of all workplaces to 56 per cent (unpublished AWIRS 1995 data).

Enterprise bargaining has facilitated this expansion in operating hours. About 30 per cent of all agreements on ACIRRT's ADAM database allow for 12-hour spans of work and in some industries—wholesale and retail trade—the figure is 43 per cent. Enterprise agreements have also handed over to management greater discretion about how hours of work are to be worked. About one-quarter of all agreements provide such discretion, while in industries like recreation, and wholesale and retail trade, the figures are well over one-third (ADAM 1997).

To some extent, extended operating hours have generally been a feature of certain kinds of industries, those with workplaces which have a lot of expensive machinery that needs to be worked for long hours to pay its way. In manufacturing, for example, more than half of all workplaces have extended operating hours because of these sorts of reasons. What's interesting about the 1990s, however, is that more and more industries are joining the rush to extend their hours of operation, and most of these are service industries where considerations of expensive capital equipment don't apply. Often these are industries where staying open for longer hours is related to their customers' needs. For example, accommodation and cafes have traditionally operated long hours because of the nature of their service. Even so, in just five years the proportion of such workplaces with extended operating hours jumped from 70 per cent to 85 per cent. Retailing followed a similar pattern: a jump from 78 per cent to 93 per cent. In the last 10 years supermarkets have been at the forefront of the push to redefine what 'a day in the life' means. Late night shopping on Thursdays or Fridays has virtually died because every night is a late night at the supermarket, and because Saturday and Sunday retail trading has obliterated the distinction between weekdays and weekends. This push to extended hours of operation has even encroached on other service industries where customer buying habits don't really matter. In property and business services, for example, the proportion of workplaces with extended operating hours jumped from 38 per cent in 1990 to 60 per cent in 1995. Even in government administration, the figures jumped by over 10 per cent (from 20 per cent to 31 per cent) (all figures from unpublished AWIRS 1995 data).

These changes in hours of operation provide a good example of a new pattern of 'flow-ons'. In the old days of industrial relations, gains won by the metal workers would flow-on to the rest of the workforce. Now, losses suffered in one part of the service sector soon flow-on to other parts of the service sector. For example, once the Shop, Distributive and Allied Workers Union reached agreement with the retail employers on the issue of extended hours of operation, pressure then mounted on the unions which covered the transport and stores workers to accommodate these changes. A similar thing happened in the finance sector. Once management made gains in insurance around the hours issue, pressures from this precedent soon followed in the banking sector.

Once these kinds of changes take place, it's very hard to turn the clock back because a particular 'culture of time' emerges. People's reliance as consumers on extended shopping hours has been fed by the longer hours of work they find themselves doing. In turn, their expectations that workplaces should be open for longer has been fed by these changes in their working and shopping habits.

This 'culture of time' also impinges on people's psychology. We saw earlier that working longer hours has become one of the new terrains of workforce competition, a kind of workplace rivalry around who can work the longest hours. Left unchecked, this kind of competition breeds new expectations about the length of the standard day, about when it's acceptable to knock off work and go home. As one focus group informant observed: everyone 'is watching to see when you leave and you can't possibly leave at 6 or 7 (pm) ... it is outrageous. Then, it's how early can you get in?'

Once known as the 'land of the long weekend', Australia might now well be called the 'land of the lost weekend' (Dusevic 1997). It's not just in weekend shopping that the distinction has been blurred, it's also in the increasing tendency for more workers to take work home on weekends or 'duck in' to work for a few hours on Saturday afternoon. The proportion of workers who now work just Monday to Friday is only 60 per cent, a slight decline from 64 per cent in 1993. In a few years time, about half of all workers will be doing some of their work over the weekend. Many of these will be shift workers or sales assistants, but a sizeable proportion will also be office workers forced to work on weekends to keep up with their workloads:

> [Work] encroaches on your whole family life and then at weekends you have to go in and after a while it becomes expected that you have to go in at least one day of the weekend ...
> *Finance sector focus group participant.*

LAMENTING THE LOST WEEKEND

Elaine Kelly, a 25-year-old weight loss consultant handed in her resignation rather than have to work on Sundays. As she explained:

'If we are not careful not only will weekends and public holidays become quaint, outmoded customs, but this greed, this voraciousness, will spread and eventually take over like a disease. Like our diseased body withers and fails ... so will the structure of our society.'

Ms Kelly sees both family time and leisure time at risk from the new regime of working hours. It's almost a 'mission impossible' getting family and friends together for any celebration.

'We all need Saturday and Sunday', she said, 'to rejuvenate so that we can start the grind again on Monday. If you work weekends ... how can you ever rejuvenate.'

Source: adapted from Anabel Dean (1992), 'The Sunday Shift', *Sydney Morning Herald*, 12 February, p.17).

It's not just family life that suffers when weekends disappear. Structured team sports, for example, require large numbers of people sharing a period of time in common. Other community activities are also at peril when working-time arrangements begin to absorb all of a person's free time. Research into the effects of continuous shifts in coal mining towns in Queensland showed that the community's social life, especially its sporting activities, were seriously eroded by the working-time arrangements which prevailed at the mines (Gibson 1993).

Recent ABS data also shows that voluntary community activities are in serious decline in Australia. Between 1982 and 1995 the volunteer rates for women in Queensland declined from 31 to 24 per cent, while for men the figures were a fall from 26 to 18 per cent. Similar declines occurred in Victoria (ABS 1998b). While the reasons for the female decline are due to increased participation by women in paid employment, the reasons for the male decline are most likely due to the squeeze on free time which the new working-time arrangements have produced.

SELLING THE CHANGES IN WORKING TIME ARRANGEMENTS

The changes to working time arrangements were driven by the desires of employers for flexibility and for cost-cutting. But these changes were sold to the workforce as being beneficial for everyone: they were intended to give flexibility to *both* employers and workers. As one enterprise agreement phrased it:

> [The organisation] will operate a system of flexible hours of duty that will recognise the increasing ability of our employees to take control of their working arrangements. This hours of duty proposal includes the concept of regular hours within a flexitime system. The concepts of core hours and standard day are not features of this system. The system will enable employees to balance personal and customer needs and work their required or normal hours of duty in a flexible manner. The system does not require employees to increase their working hours (Employment Services Sector Agreement).

In practice, however, most of the changes in working time arrangements appear to have provided flexibility to management—particularly in terms of deploying staff to cover periods of peak activity—but have given only limited flexibility to their workers.

There has always been some flexibility in working time arrangements, *but only for some workers*. For most workers, the promise of flexibility has rung hollow. For example, when asked if they could take some time off work to care for a sick family member, a fair proportion of workers could do so by using their own sick leave or holiday leave (42 per cent) and a smaller proportion could take leave without pay to do so (36 per cent). But only 16 per cent —barely one-sixth of all workers—could take time off and then make it up later (unpublished AWIRS 1995 data). In other words, only by drawing on existing leave entitlements or going without pay could workers gain some access to the extra time they needed. There was virtually no flexibility in managing their own time so as to accommodate their family's needs. Those workers who did have some flexibility were primarily managers and professionals. About 29 per cent of the former and 23 per cent of the latter could take off time and make it up later. For salesworkers the comparable figure was just 12 per cent; for plant and machine operators the figure was a very low 8 per cent; and for labourers the figure was 10 per cent. It's important to keep in mind, however, that managers and professionals won their flexibility at considerable cost—the price they paid was working very long hours.

A similar difference between blue-collar and white-collar jobs is apparent in the discretion workers can exercise over their starting and finishing times. About two-thirds of all workers reported that they have some influence over when they start and finish work. For plant and machine operators and labourers, though, the figure is around one-half, whereas for professionals and for clerks the figure is about three-quarters. Clearly, part of the explanation for this lies in the nature of the work, the way it is scheduled around using capital equipment or working in team situations within blue-collar jobs. With white-collar jobs, on the other hand, the task at hand is sitting on the desk, ready to be resumed at the worker's convenience. Those workers with the least bargaining power, such as labourers, can gain very little flexibility, compared with those workers with more skilled labour to sell. This is apparent when we look at para-professionals, workers in jobs where team situations and capital equipment are also considerations. As more skilled workers—and generally well unionised—these people have gained greater control over their starting and finishing times than have labourers (about two-thirds of para-professionals have some discretion compared with only about half of all labourers).

It is difficult to get a feel for how flexibility is changing over time because we have so little data on this. The Australian Bureau of Statistics did measure some aspects of working time flexibility during the 1990s, but the time frame is quite short (4 years) and the changes are only moderate. Nevertheless, this general picture of limited flexibility for workers— particularly blue-collar workers—does appear to be corroborated. For example, the ABS found a 4 per cent increase in the number of workers allowed to work extra hours in order to take time off, but the overall proportion still remains quite low—just 38 per cent. Moreover, at the same time, there was a 5 per cent *decline* in the number of workers entitled to a rostered day off (RDO). Considering that blue-collar occupations make much greater use of RDOs than white-collar jobs, it's clear that flexibility around how one manages the course of the working week (or fortnight) has certainly stalled, if not declined, for less skilled workers (ABS 1997b).

Making workplaces 'family friendly' was certainly part of the rhetoric of working-time 'flexibility'. Have changes in working arrangements brought about by enterprise bargaining made it easier for parents and carers to cope with their family responsibilities? Research by the Australian Institute of Family Studies suggests the answer is No. Christine Kilmartin's study of ABS data suggested that 'working parents, despite their dual responsibilities, have, at best, the same working arrangements and benefits as workers without parenting responsibilities' (Kilmartin 1996, p. 36–37). Women with children under 12 had no more flexibility in their start and finish times than other women, and no more scope to take off time for special events related to their children's needs. A newspaper summary of this research summed up the findings bluntly: 'family friendly workplaces are more myth than reality' (*Australian*, 4 September, 1996).

At first glance, enterprise bargaining does appear to have assisted parents and carers. When managers were asked, in the AWIRS survey, whether their workplaces provided carers' leave or family leave so that their workers could take off time to look after family or household members, a fairly solid 40 per cent replied Yes. Of these, about 30 per cent had introduced this leave as a result of enterprise bargaining. Yet when you look at the picture more closely you find that this is much more a formal entitlement, than an actual reality. When asked what kinds of leave their workers would *actually take*, if they did have to look after someone at home, most managers replied that their workers would take their annual leave, sick leave or unpaid leave. Only 22 per cent of workplaces allowed their workers to use family leave, and only 7 per cent allowed the use of carers' leave. In practice then, little has changed from more traditional approaches to dealing with the family needs of workers.

'Family-friendly' clauses in agreements were one innovation in terms of flexibility which were expected to become popular. However, efforts by governments to encourage the spread of family-friendly measures have fallen flat and the introduction of family-friendly entitlements in enterprise agreements has remained limited. Only 10 per cent of agreements on the ADAM database contained at least one family-friendly measure. In the following discussion we look more closely at this issue.

Enterprise agreements and family-friendly measures

Family-friendly measures at the workplace are those conditions which support or assist workers in managing the dual responsibilities of work and family life. Some of the more obvious provisions include paid maternity and paternity leave (referred to as paid parental leave), paid and unpaid leave for those caring for family members (referred to as personal leave), career break schemes, and employer provided or sponsored childcare services.

It is also reasonable to view flexibility in hours of work arrangements—such as part-time work, job-sharing and work from home schemes—as family-friendly if they are mutually agreed to, and if they are truly directed towards the needs of workers. Other innovative measures that make the work environment more attractive to workers with families—such as the provision of a carer's room at the workplace—can also be found in industrial instruments. Allowing workers to opt in advance for extra leave (available as single day absences), with a proportionate reduction in the overall rate of pay, is another option that has been introduced in some workplaces.

An examination of the frequency of nine types of family-friendly measures in agreements on the ADAM database revealed that only 10 per cent of currently operative agreements contained a provision covering at least one such measure. Nine key variables were examined and, as Table 5.4 shows, unpaid personal leave was the most widespread family-friendly measure (9.4 per cent). Paid personal leave, in addition to that offered under sick leave entitlements, was the next most frequent benefit (3.8 per cent). Job sharing and paid parental leave both appeared with equal frequency (3.2 per cent). The range of paid parental leave offered varies between a minimum of one to a maximum of 18 weeks. The low incidence of other family-friendly provisions shows the unwillingness of employers to agree to implement more innovative strategies.

Table 5.4 Family-friendly provisions in agreements

Provisions	Percentage of agreements
Unpaid personal leave	9.4
Paid personal leave given additional to sick leave component	3.8
Job sharing	3.2
Paid parental leave	3.2
Childcare facilities for the workplace to be examined	1.1
Work from home/telecommuting	0.8
Childcare facilities available at the workplace	0.2
Childcare/elderly care referral service	0.1
Career break schemes	0.1

Source: ADAM Database, March 1998.
Note: Current agreements include all agreements that have not reached their stated expiry date as of 31 December 1997.

Family-friendly provisions are most likely to be found in public administration agreements (19.6 per cent), community service (16.5 per cent) and finance industry agreements (15.3 per cent) and are least likely to be found in manufacturing (5.5 per cent) and recreational and personal service industry agreements (5.8 per cent).

* * *

Throughout the 1980s and especially during the 1990s, the issues of wage rises and changes in the bargaining system dominated the official debate on policies about working life. These were certainly important issues, but they also distracted attention away from a major change which was underway during this period—the restructuring of hours of work. In the area of working time arrangements, the bargaining process had an enormous impact, primarily in rolling back a century of gains. Until the early 1980s, the debate on working time was predominantly about reducing standard hours of work. As productivity increased in society, so the argument ran, hours should be progressively reduced. This was part of the definition of a civilised society. With the dismantling of the post-war settlement, and the ascendancy of the neo-liberal agenda, all that changed. The issue shifted from the length of hours given by the worker to the question of flexibility for the employer, particularly when those hours were to be worked to suit the needs of production or service provision. Concerns with social protection receded—such as the needs of families and communities for shared time in common—and the demands of the market for 'efficiency' came to the fore. This dynamic not only resulted in increased hours of work for the full-time workforce, it also resulted in increasingly fragmented and unpredictable hours of work for a growing number of unemployed and casual workers. It is to this dimension of the restructuring of working life that we now turn.

CHAPTER 6

Job security in a changing labour market

We saw in the last chapter that the standard working week has been in decline. In this chapter we find a parallel decline in the notion of a standard working lifetime.[1] Profound changes in the labour market have rendered almost obsolete the conventional notion of a full-time, permanent job carried out for most of one's working life. Where changes to working time arrangements have provided employers with increased flexibility in *utilising* labour, so too has a dramatic increase in non-standard forms of employment given them similar flexibility in *taking on and dispensing with* labour. The cost for workers, however, is massive job insecurity.

Job insecurity has become one of the most common sources of social anxiety during the late 1990s. The employee survey from AWIRS 1995 found that nearly one-third of workers reported that they felt insecure about their current job, and focus group participants regularly dwell on this issue as one of their main workplace concerns. The causes for this heightened awareness of job insecurity are not hard to find. Some of the reasons lie in the changing nature of the labour market, while others lie in the process of workplace change itself. In this chapter we will explore both these domains. We will show how the persistence of high levels of unemployment has undermined people's confidence in the economy's ability to create employment. At the same time, the growth of precarious and other non-standard forms of employment has heightened people's fears about finding and keeping a 'proper job'. For those in work, the turbulence of workplace change—particularly restructuring, downsizing and privatisation—has weakened people's confidence in their own employment future.

INSECURITY—THE LABOUR MARKET STORY

Unemployment and retrenchments—the backdrop to insecurity

Since the mid-1970s opinion pollsters have regularly asked people whether they think their current job is safe or not. In the late 1970s, about 20 per cent felt their jobs weren't safe. In the late 1990s, about 25 per cent expressed the same sentiment. But a great deal had happened in the meantime. Unemployment had risen from about 5 per cent to settle at over 8 per cent and two major recessions had come and gone. We might have expected the figure for insecurity to have been much higher for the late 1990s. It is quite likely, however, that the definition of security has altered over the last 20 years, a change which reflects people's more sober expectations of the labour market.

Over the last two decades job insecurity has closely tracked unemployment (see Figure 6.1). Interestingly, the peaks in job insecurity precede the peaks in unemployment, presumably because people still in work are aware of increased retrenchments and reduced hirings before they become aware of the extent of unemployment. Figure 6.1 shows that at the beginning of the 1991 recession, job insecurity reached a peak, with over one in three Australians fearing for the future of their job. It is also worth noting that after the 1982 recession, job insecurity settled at a moderate level for about six years (averaging about 18 per cent), whereas after the 1991 recession, job insecurity has remained at a much higher level (averaging about 25 per cent). The reason for this, as we shall see later in this chapter, is that job insecurity has lost its traditional linkage with business cycles and has become an almost permanent feature of the economic landscape.

Since the end of the 1991 recession, unemployment has remained stuck above 8 per cent. To some extent, this reflects the 'do nothing' mentality of governments in Canberra, whose perspective on the labour market has been largely non-interventionist since the mid-1980s. This high level of unemployment is also a feature of advanced economies and the structural changes in employment which they have brought about. Before looking at these structural changes we will briefly describe the current unemployment situation. We do not intend to provide either a comprehensive picture or a more detailed analysis of unemployment in this book. That is beyond our scope. Rather, we are interested in how unemployment has affected workplaces and influenced people's experiences of job insecurity. We are also keen to know what unemployment tells us about where the labour market is heading. Figure 6.2 demonstrates that over the last decade there has been a ratchetting upwards of unemployment in Australia, such that after each recession the unemployment rate has settled at a higher level than the previous recession. At the same time the proportion of the unemployed who are *long-term unemployed* has increased steadily.

Figure 6.1 Job security and unemployment, 1978–97

Unemployment rate as percentage of workforce unemployed.
Insecurity as percentage of respondents who don't think their current job is safe.

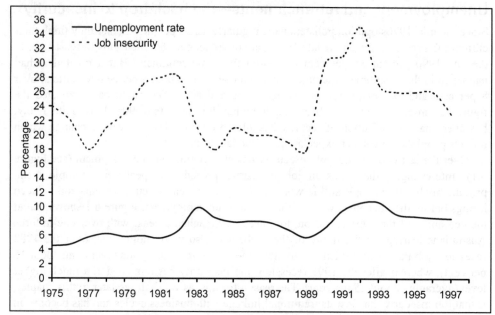

Source: Unemployment rate derived from ABS (1978-1998), *Labour Force Australia*, Cat. no. 6203.0. Job insecurity from Morgan Poll series. (Question asked: 'Do you think your present job is safe, or do you think there's a chance you may become unemployed?')

It's important to keep in mind that the official level of unemployment is only a partial measure of the extent of labour market failure in Australia. In the middle of 1998, the official number of unemployed people was about 800,000. But the real number of unemployed people who would like a job was closer to two million (ABS 1998d). The real unemployment rate is thus closer to 19 per cent than the usually quoted figures of 8 to 9 per cent. Various definitions about when people are able to work, and whether they are currently seeking work, allows the Australian Bureau of Statistics to report the lower figure as the official one.

Workplace surveys show that the people who feel most insecure about their jobs— mainly labourers, plant and machine operators and tradespersons—all work in industries which are highly sensitive to economic downturns and where workplaces routinely use retrenchments when there's a fall in demand for their products. Moreover, the ranks of the unemployed are disproportionately filled with persons who come from a these kinds of blue-collar backgrounds. In a sense, those with the least marketable skills are most at risk of becoming unemployed. Where labour market restructuring comes into the picture is that *getting back into a job* has become so much harder once you've become unemployed. This is especially so for certain groups of people and it has become particularly worse in the late 1990s. We'll look at each of these issues in turn.

Figure 6.2 Unemployment rate and the incidence of long-term unemployment, 1978–97

Unemployment rate as percentage of workforce unemployed.
Incidence of unemployment as percentage of unemployed persons who have been unemployed for 12 months or longer.

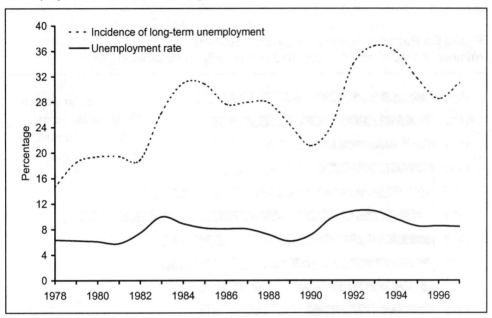

Source: Derived from ABS (1978-1998), *Labour Force Australia*, Cat. no. 6203.0.

Risks of unemployment

Like most advanced economies, Australia's economy has increasingly become service and information-based. For a century, employment opportunities in primary production declined, but in the late 1960s this trend spread to secondary industry as well. In the halcyon days of the mid-1960s, over 30 per cent of the Australian workforce were engaged in manufacturing but by the late 1990s, the figure was just 13 per cent. The casualties of this transition are amongst the most vulnerable members of the workforce. They tend to be male workers aged over 45 who left school early and whose occupational background is blue-collar. If they also happen to be migrants with limited English, they are even more unlikely to regain employment. For example, compared to a male in their prime years (20 to 49 years old), a mature age male is twice as likely to become long-term unemployed. And a migrant with low English language proficiency is three times more likely to become long-term unemployed than a migrant with good English language skills (O'Loughlin and Watson 1997, p. 195).

Job losses from retrenchments and lay-offs have always hit the blue-collar workforce more severely. Figure 6.3 highlights how much blue-collar male workers have borne the brunt of a decade of economic restructuring. What is particularly noteworthy about blue-collar males is that retrenchments peaked during the 1991 recession, but the levels of retrenchments between recession years and growth years have not been really very different. Their labour market fate was consistently bleak throughout the whole decade. By way of contrast, white-collar workers have fared worse in the years since the recession. While retrenchments for this group peaked during the recession, they have also reached high levels in the last two years. In this respect, organisational change, rather than the business cycle, has contributed to these job losses. We return to this theme later in the chapter.

Figure 6.3 Retrenchments and lay-offs, 1986–97
Number of people laid-off/retrenched involuntarily (in thousands)

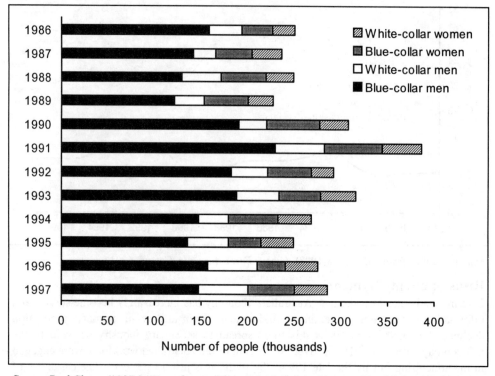

Source: Paul Cleary (1997a), 'How the axe fell on 3.3m', *Sydney Morning Herald*, October 20, 1997, p. 7. Based on ABS data.
Note: Definition of blue-collar is 'semi-skilled' industries; definition of white-collar is 'professional' industries. 1997 figures to August, estimate for full year.

Job losses through retrenchment are closely tied into the business cycle, and they only tell half the story. We also need to look at jobs growth, to see if the losses are compensated elsewhere. In other words, we need to also look at the structure of industry employment. It's clear, for example, that characteristics such as being mature age, blue-collar, or from a migrant background, were not liabilities in finding work during the 1950s and 1960s. This was an era when large infrastructure projects were under construction and when manufacturing was still expanding. But in the 1980s and 1990s, these characteristics have become a liability because the patterns of industry employment have changed dramatically. As Table 6.1 shows, the jobs which have grown most dramatically have been in service industries while the jobs which have declined have predominantly been in blue-collar industries.

Table 6.1 Job losses and gains by industry, 1988–98

Industry	Change in employment - number of persons
Largest number of new jobs	
Property and business services	+ 391,400
Retail trade	+ 201,400
Health and community services	+ 199,400
Accommodation, cafes and restaurants	+ 144,600
Education	+ 120,900
Construction	+ 92,300
Personal and other services	+ 79,300
Cultural and recreational services	+ 61,800
Wholesale trade	+ 58,900
Largest number of lost jobs	
Manufacturing	— 70,000
Textile, clothing, footwear & leather	— 31,500
Machinery & equipment	— 41,400
Metal product	— 19,500
Electricity, gas and water	— 52,200
Rail transport	— 40,100
Insurance	— 20,600
Government administration and defence	— 17,400
Finance	— 16,200

Source: Derived from ABS (1978-1998), *Labour Force Australia*, Cat. no. 6203.0.
Note: New job industries are all at highest level of ANZSIC aggregation. Different levels of aggregation are used in the lost job industries for purposes of clarity.

What is particularly disturbing about Table 6.1 is that manufacturing employment has deteriorated so severely during the last decade. At a time when the labour force as a whole grew by nearly 17 per cent, the manufacturing workforce actually declined by 6 per cent. Even more disturbing is the picture within manufacturing. Declines in tariff protection for the textile, clothing and footwear (TCF) industries has resulted in predictable job losses, with some production moving offshore and other jobs moving into the outworker sector (something we discuss in detail later). This is an area of manufacturing which is very cost-sensitive, one where Australian producers find it hard to compete with cheaper imports. However, the same cannot be said for machinery and equipment and metal products. These are the areas of manufacturing in which innovation should thrive—this is part of the high road to the future discussed in Chapter 2—but the employment profile of these two industry subdivisions is a bleak one indeed. Without more decisive industry policy, the 'high road' to the future looks remote, and the employment consequences disturbing. We return to this theme in the next chapter.

There have, of course, been white-collar job losses, most notably in banking, insurance and government. In the case of the latter, the figures in Table 6.1 disguise the severity of the job reductions over the last few years, particularly at the Commonwealth level. Following the election of the Howard Liberal–National Party Coalition in March 1996, major job shedding got underway. In just two years, between February 1996 and February 1998, some 86,000 Commonwealth Government jobs disappeared (ABS 1998e). The neo-liberal philosophy of 'small government' was being rapidly put into practice.

In the case of banking and finance, the job losses have been closely tied to financial deregulation and technological change. Job shedding has been a major component of industry restructuring, as all the major banks extricated themselves from the morass of bad debts they piled up during the speculative frenzy of the 1980s.

Retrenchments—the experience of losing work

I'd worked for the security firm for over two years. After completing the Wednesday night shift I wasn't told when my next shift would be. The next day I was notified of my retrenchment in the mail. *Jason, retrenchee, workshop, Sydney.*

The response of management and unions to retrenchments in Australia has generally focused on how much is paid out for each worker, rather than what the social costs to workers might be. It is often forgotten that the retrenched worker has to deal not only with the economic hardship from being retrenched, but that they will also have to endure psychological stresses as well.

It is clear that involuntary retrenchment, in the main, is an immensely dislocative experience—not just for all those who lose their jobs, but for their families and local communities. There is nothing from our research and consultation work to suggest that that this dislocation is short lived or superficial or easily smoothed over ... People's jobs are taken away from them and this is a special injustice (Social Justice Consultative Committee 1992, p. 84).

In their study of retrenched workers in Australia, Webber and Campbell (1996, pp. 3–4) emphasise some of the stark consequences that flow from losing one's job. After the initial shock of the job loss, there was the material reality of a loss in income and the need to rationalise expenditure. As time passed, male breadwinners faced psychological problems because of changes in household relations, particularly their loss of self-respect. In effect, the structure of their daily life was overturned and commitments which had been based around working had to be totally reorganised. Social isolation became acute as personal interactions, and involvement in leisure activities, declined.

Some of these problems were the result of long-term unemployment (LTU) itself, and labour market programs which specifically target the LTU for assistance might make a difference to their severity. But other problems were the result of *how retrenchments were handled in the first place*. The Social Justice Consultative Committee reviewed the process of retrenchment and concluded:

A lot of people were highly critical of retrenchment ... they were unhappy about the way they were actually laid off. Reports of orderly factory close-downs or systematic labour shedding ... were rare ... People's comments revealed deep feelings of enormous insensitivity, particularly on the part of middle management, in handling the retrenchment procedure (Social Justice Consultative Committee 1992, p. 31).

A review of overseas findings conducted by Buchanan and Campbell (1992), concluded that firm level initiatives can make a difference to the retrenchment experience for workers, and that employers who adopted innovative approaches to retrenchments also benefited from the process. Benefits of a well managed labour reduction included:

❑ loyalty to the company, including confidence and trust in management;
❑ a reduction in resistance to technical change;
❑ a reduction in staff turnover and improvements in employee relations.

Buchanan and Campbell concluded that it was critically important to avoid damaging morale and productivity, suggesting that a narrow, cost-minimisation approach to reductions in the workforce could in fact prove costly in the long run (1992, p. 73). To appreciate how retrenchments can be carried through in a 'best practice' manner, the boxed text is offered as a case-study.

Regaining employment

Losing one's job is not uncommon in a modern economy, it's one of the side-effects of rapid economic change. In the 1980s and 1990s, globalisation, information technology and organisational restructuring have accentuated this trend, accelerating the rate of change to an extent never seen before. If the jobs which are lost are replaced by new jobs, then the main problems concern labour market mobility, that is, can the former incumbents of the lost jobs slot into the new job opportunities? In general terms, this comes down to an issue of effective labour market programs—of retraining and relocating unemployed workers to enable them to take up the new jobs.

But in the 1990s this adjustment process has failed, and people are finding themselves increasingly stuck in long-term unemployment or revolving through a series of short-term jobs. The reasons for this are twofold. First, many of the new jobs in manufacturing have been reborn overseas, making them inaccessible to former manufacturing workers. Secondly, many of the new jobs are 'precarious', that is, temporary, casual or intermittent. We will examine this issue in greater depth shortly. For the moment we need to appreciate that a growth in this kind of employment leads to quite disastrous effects in the labour market, especially for long-term unemployed people. An important longitudinal study by the ABS has found a large amount of labour market 'churning', the situation where people remain in the labour market but are cycled 'in and out of work without finding a long-term secure job' (ABS 1997d, p. 4). The ABS found that in May 1995, the number of jobseekers totalled 875,000. Between May 1995 and September 1996, about 70 per cent of these people worked for some period of time, but two-thirds of their jobs were casual and 90 per cent were short-term. (1997a, p. 3).

The implications of this are quite profound. Getting into a job remains a considerable hurdle for some of the unemployed—particularly the more vulnerable groups mentioned earlier—*but keeping that job* remains an enormous hurdle for most of the unemployed. Solving the problem of unemployment is no longer an issue of labour market programs—of successfully matching the job losers with the new job opportunities—but is increasingly a problem of the *kinds of jobs on offer* in the labour market. Labour market programs in themselves cannot change the way in which workers are increasingly offered non-standard forms of employment.

THE MOTOR ASSEMBLY COMPANY (MAC)

The Motor Assembly Company (a fictional name) is a case study of a plant closure. Researchers from ACIRRT reviewed the initial closure of the plant, which took place in 1994, and the following case study draws extensively on their report. The conclusions were generally positive, and they deemed the closure an example of 'best practice' by comparison with the normal pattern of plant closures and retrenchments. Indeed, the usual pattern is such that retrenchees are given little notice about their impending lay off, and little assistance in finding subsequent work, factors which limit their opportunities for re-employment. By comparison MAC's procedures in this regard were very good:

❑ workers had six months notice of the closure; and
❑ extensive assistance was given to workers in an effort to enhance their re-employment.

The last point is worth examining in detail, since it marks such a sharp departure from the usual pattern. Together with the union and the government, the company established an Employee Assistance Centre (EAC) which performed a number of important functions:

❑ during the final six months of operations, EAC assisted workers to upgrade various skills and obtain various certificates which could enhance their employability;
❑ EAC staff prepared detailed resumes for all workers and ensured that their records were forwarded to their local Commonwealth Employment Service offices;
❑ EAC staff assisted the workforce to make the most of a government industry re-structuring package (the Passenger Motor Vehicle Labour Adjustment Program) which included extensive retraining provisions;
❑ EAC conducted a targeted mail promotion aimed at potential employers of the current workforce. An invitation was extended to visit the MAC plant and meet the workforce.
❑ EAC brought 100 employers to the MAC plant for a conducted tour of the work site, again attempting to bring current workers and potential employers together

These last two initiatives were particularly innovative, and had been modelled on earlier strategies pursued by other motor vehicle manufacturers. The initial success rate was very high. Of the 420 workers affected by the closure, 260 wanted to continue working, and of these, about 160 had lined up new jobs within a month of the closure. It is important to note, however, that anecdotal evidence gathered later by the ACIRRT researchers in focus groups suggested that subsequent jobs had not lasted long for many of the workers. The literature on retrenchments confirms this possibility, showing that despite initial success in finding new work, many retrenchees eventually find themselves unemployed (and most experience downward occupational mobility in their new jobs.)

NESB immigrant workers composed a significant proportion of the MAC workforce (nearly 40 per cent) and their needs were seen as an important part of the retrenchment process. One of the EAC staff was fluent in three Asian languages, and an important part of the needs assessment process conducted by EAC included English language assessments for 169 employees. Arrangements for Adult Migrant Education Service (AMES) English language training after the closure was set in place by the EAC staff. MAC had itself arranged in-house English language training since the early 1980s, though many employees had successfully worked at MAC speaking minimal English.

The initiatives outlined above show that the employer attempted to minimise the negative employment consequences of the plant shutdown. Nevertheless, it's also true to say that some MAC employment practices had an adverse impact on the long-term prospects for successful re-employment. For example, occupational injuries sustained while working at MAC were a significant barrier to finding work, regardless of skill levels. This was particularly evident amongst the retrenchees who had worked at MAC before the plant was modernised and work practices made safer. However, the greatest difficulty faced by retrenchees, especially mature age workers, was due to the restructuring of the manufacturing industry. The decision to close the plant released a flood of workers into the market with similar characteristics at a time when employer demand for unskilled blue-collar labour was declining.

Source: Derived from an unpublished ACIRRT study on retrenchments.

A changing labour market

The rise of part-time employment

Australia has had two major recessions since the end of the 1970s: in 1982–83 and in 1991. In climbing out of the first recession the Australian economy achieved record jobs growth, some of it due to public sector job creation, some of it due to a private sector boom. By contrast, in climbing out of the second recession, there has been no public sector jobs growth and restrained private sector growth. More significantly, full-time employment grew strongly during the mid-1980s whereas during the 1990s this kind of employment growth has been stagnant. Indeed, Australia did not reach the same level of full employment which existed prior to the 1991 recession until late in 1997. Figure 6.4 demonstrates how flat this recovery has been, and highlights the shortfall in full-time employment growth which has characterised the 1990s.

By way of contrast, part-time employment has been remarkably resistant to cyclical downturns, continuing its long-term upward growth. Between 1966 and 1994, part-time employment growth (5.5 per cent per annum) was well over three and a half times the rate of full-time employment (1.5 per cent per annum) (NBEET 1992, p. 2). Much of this part-time employment growth has been in service sector areas like retail and hospitality and many of the jobs have gone to women re-entering the workforce. In this respect, some of the growth of part-time employment can be viewed as a positive feature of the economy, of a fairer redistribution of work towards people with families and with other commitments. But there is another side to this spectacle of part-time employment growth, a drama in which the players are not offered new choices but are confronted by lost opportunities. One indication of this is the fact that part-time work is increasingly a form of under-employment. The proportion of part-time workers who want to work more hours grew from 17 per cent to 26 per cent between 1986 and 1996. These people are overwhelmingly working in the retail industry, spread largely between food retailing (mainly supermarkets) and personal and household goods retailing. Their occupations are almost entirely made up of cashiers, salesworkers and sales assistants and they are overwhelmingly women.

Figure 6.4 Employment growth, 1978–98

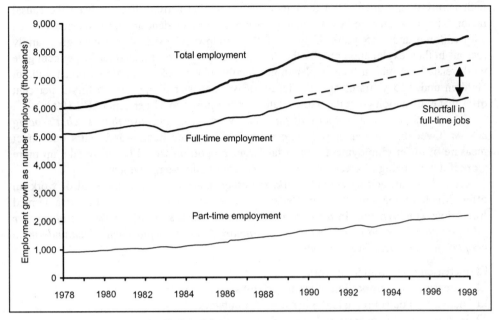

Source: Derived from ABS (1978-1998), *Labour Force Australia*, Cat. no. 6203.0.

Why do people work part-time? For some it's for family reasons or because they're studying. For others, it's a lifestyle thing. For a growing proportion, however, it's because part-time work is the only work available to them. Figures from the Australian Bureau of Statistics allow us to measure quite precisely the extent of these different reasons. Amongst women, about 18 per cent of part-time workers give family reasons as the motivation for working part-time. Amongst men, the comparable figure is fairly insignificant. For men, studying is much more important, and about 22 per cent of part-time workers give that reason. *But, overwhelmingly, for both men and women, the reason most people work part-time is because of work-related reasons, either because there is not enough work available or the job is only offered as a part-time job.* In the case of men, these work-related reasons were given by 61 per cent of part-time workers. For women, the comparable figure was 47 per cent. Looking at the sub-categories more closely, amongst men the 'not enough work available' reason accounted for 31 per cent, and 'job is only part-time' accounted for 26 per cent. The comparable figures for women were 16 per cent and 28 per cent. (All of the above data is from ABS 1997b.)

This lack of symmetry between men and women is important. It shows that men work part-time predominantly because they're studying or because there's a shortage of hours available in the job they're doing. For women, on the other hand, family reasons are more important than studying or a shortage of hours, but still much less important than the fact that only part-time work is on offer. The conventional view says that part-time work, particularly in the service sector, exists because women return to the labour market and seek part-time work due to family commitments. This supply-side explanation has it all wrong. Rather, what happens is that large numbers of jobs are available for women in the service sector, but only if they're willing to work part-time. This arrangement suits women with family commitments, but their own labour market activity has not been the causal factor. The importance of work related reasons is even evident amongst married women with children under 15 years of age. For this group of women, 38 per cent give family reasons in their explanation of why they're working part-time. But another 37 per cent give work-related reasons in their explanation. Finally, if we look at married women without children under 15 years of age, the family-reasons-answer disappears—a tiny 2 per cent offer that explanation—but the work-related answer jumps to 57 per cent (ABS 1997b).

In conclusion, large amounts of part-time work exists because that is what's being offered. Over one-quarter of part-time workers want more hours—and that's one direct measure of under-employment—but a far larger proportion would probably take up more work if it were being offered—an indirect measure of under-employment.

As well as not getting enough work, the other major problem is the kind of work on offer. Much of the growth in non-standard employment has been in the area termed 'precarious employment'. In many respects, *the 1990s is a story about the loss of 'proper jobs', an upward trend in all kinds of non-standard forms of employment which undermine people's job security.* These include:

- ❑ increased casualisation of work;
- ❑ increases in the proportion of temporary jobs;
- ❑ increases in outsourcing and other forms of outwork;
- ❑ increased use of agencies and other labour market intermediaries.

All of these non-standard forms of employment are responsible for creating what some have called an 'irregular workforce' (Harley 1994). Employers have set out to create such a workforce in order to achieve what is called 'numerical flexibility', a capacity to vary their labour inputs to meet patterns of intermittent demand for their product or service. As one commentator put it, this irregular workforce is 'the employer's equivalent of a just-in-time inventory' (Bittman 1991, p. 17).

Figure 6.5 Casual density by industry divisions, 1984 and 1993
Casuals as a percentage of total employees in each industry division

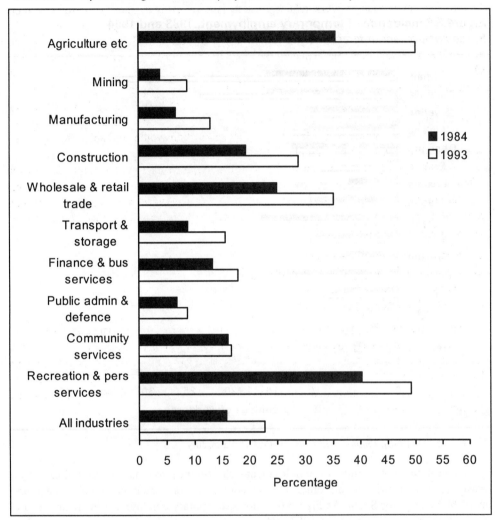

Source: data taken from Campbell (1996a), p. 64. 1984—calculated from ABS, *Employment Benefits Australia*, August 1984; 1984–1992—ABS, *Trade Union Members Australia*, Cat. no. 6325.0; 1993—ABS, *Weekly Earnings of Employees (Distribution) Australia*, unpublished data.

The growth in precarious employment: casuals and temporaries

By 1994 it was estimated that about one-quarter of Australian employees were casuals. The major industries which relied on casual workers were agriculture, construction, retailing and hospitality, but nearly all industries have witnessed significant growth over the last decade in their proportions of casuals (see Figure 6.5). Both men and women have experienced growth in casual employment over the last decade and a half. Amongst men, the proportion of casuals jumped from under 10 per cent to nearly 21 per cent between

1984 and 1997. For women there was also an increase, but of lesser magnitude—from 26 per cent to 32 per cent (Burgess and Campbell 1998, p. 42).[2]

Figure 6.6 Incidence of temporary employment, 1983 and 1994
Percentage of labour force who are temporary workers

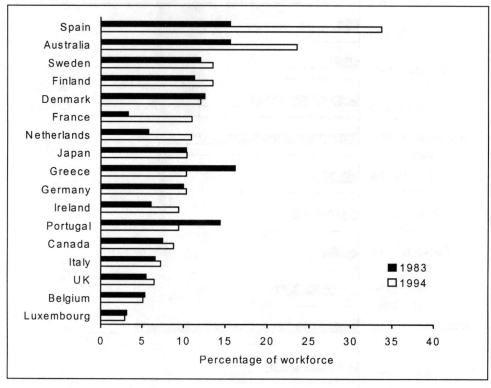

Source: OECD (1996), *Employment Outlook*, OECD, Paris, July, p. 8.

When it comes to temporary employment—short-term jobs—its growth and extent in Australia has outstripped all other OECD countries (for which comparable data are available) except for Spain. As Figure 6.6 shows, temporary employment in Australia rose from 16 to 24 per cent between 1983 and 1994. This occurred at a time when most other OECD countries were keeping their levels of temporary employment stable.

Much of the growth in *part-time* employment since the 1960s has reflected women's increased participation in the workforce. When it comes to permanent part-time work, this development can be viewed as a positive outcome, since it offers greater employment choices to workers. However, the growth in *casual* and *temporary* work is a form of *precarious* employment and has very serious shortcomings for workers.

For a start, job insecurity is far greater for workers in precarious employment. As well as the psychological pressure, such employment can limit a worker's future options because of the financial uncertainty. Bank loans for a home, planning for a family, household budgeting—all take on added stress and uncertainty when you are employed as a casual or a temporary.

Table 6.2 The distinctiveness of casuals in the workplace, Australia 1995

Percentages for each issue

Workplace issues	Casual workers	Non-casuals
Training		
Received job-related training	51	62
Received OH&S training	24	36
Consultation		
Consulted about workplace change	38	59
Given a fair chance to have a say	46	54
Job variety		
Given a lot of influence over type of work done	18	27
Do lots of different tasks	71	85
Satisfaction		
Better off than 12 months earlier as a result of change	34	31
Worse off than 12 months earlier as a result of change	15	25
Think that they get paid fairly for the job	60	44

Source: AWIRS 1995, various questions within the employee survey.
Population: Employees in workplaces with 20 or more employees.

In the job itself, casual employment has definite shortcomings. While the casual monetary loading may partly compensate for the lost leave entitlements, there is little to compensate for the other missing parts of working life. These include training, consultation and job variety. As Table 6.2 shows, across each of these areas of working life, casuals fare considerably worse than non-casual workers. In terms of workplace change, for example, less than 40 per cent were consulted, whereas nearly 60 per cent of non-casual workers were consulted. Interestingly, Table 6.2 also shows that on most of the objective measures of workplace conditions, casuals fare badly, but in terms of subjective assessments, they seem to be more content than the non-casuals. It's possible that casuals have set their job expectations at a lower level than that set by non-casual workers.

Finally, for those workers who are unemployed casual work contributes to the problem of 'labour market churning' we discussed earlier. Analysis of the ABS Survey of Employment and Unemployment Patterns by Burgess and Campbell shows that a 'dualism' in employment destinations had emerged, whereby permanent jobs were more likely to be taken up by people already in permanent jobs, whilst casual jobs were the most likely destination for the unemployed (1998, p. 46). What makes it particularly difficult for the unemployed is that so many of the new jobs emerging in the economy are casual. As Burgess and Campbell noted, of all the new jobs created between 1984 and 1997, over 60 per cent were casual jobs, leading them to conclude: 'Casual employment arrangements have become "typical" of the new jobs being created over the course of the 1990s' (1998, p. 35).

The rise of 'non-employees': outworkers, contractors and agency workers

What we call the 'employment relationship' emerged in the nineteenth century out of the master and servant relationship and coincided with the rise of the free market (Selznick 1969; Fox 1974; Biernacki 1995). It is an important legal relationship because a number of common law duties and obligations flow from it. For example, awards can only be made for employees and certain statutory rights are often based on the existence of an employment relationship. By way of contrast, there is no such relationship between principal and contractor in a contract for service and the same set of obligations and duties do not flow.

Traditionally the divide between the two forms has been quite clear and the employment relationship has dominated work since the advent of industrialisation. However, new forms of work and work relationships have begun to emerge in recent years. In particular, there has been a trend away from the vertical integration of firms which has resulted in increased outsourcing, or contracting out, of significant areas of work. A closer look at the use of contractors is telling: the use of contractors has only increased significantly in certain industries, suggesting that the use of contract labour is being used as a strategic measure. Contract labour has been most heavily utilised in industries like mining and construction, industries with blue-collar workplaces where unions have traditionally been strong and militant. Employers in these industries have not been able to implement numerical flexibility or casualisation, and have therefore chosen to contract in new groups of workers who are not covered by the usual protections.

The panel survey data in AWIRS, which investigated the same firms in 1990 and again in 1995, found that over one-third of firms had contracted out services during the interval between the two surveys. The three areas which were predominantly outsourced were cleaning/laundry services, building/maintenance services, and the production of manufactured components. The industries which were most strongly involved in outsourcing were:

- ❑ electricity, gas and water supply—67 per cent of firms;
- ❑ construction—61 per cent of firms;
- ❑ education—60 per cent of firms; and
- ❑ mining—55 per cent of firms.

While just under one-third of firms in the private sector had engaged in outsourcing, the main proponents of this activity were public sector organisations, particularly government business enterprises (53 per cent), statutory authorities (56 per cent) and state public service departments (53 per cent).

When it comes to defining the contract worker, three broad categories have been suggested: self-employed contractors, employees working for sub-contractors and agency workers (VandenHeuvel and Wooden 1995). A 1994 survey of workplaces conducted by the National Institute of Labour Studies found that firms engaged different categories for different reasons. For example, workplaces made use of sub-contracting firms to access their specialised equipment or skills, and to reduce labour costs. On the other hand, workplaces favoured agency workers to deal with fluctuations in demand for their goods or services. Different kinds of services were also linked to these three forms of contracting out. The self-employed contractors mostly provided computer or other professional/business services, the employees working for sub-contractors usually provided cleaning or maintenance services, and the agency workers mainly offered clerical services.

The reasons why contracting out has grown strongly during the 1990s are not hard to see. For firms, these forms of engaging workers provide the potential to offload the costs of workers compensation, superannuation and payroll tax. For workers, the advantages lie in being able to lower their tax burden and to increase their autonomy (albeit at the cost of their security) (VandenHeuvel and Wooden 1995, p. 1).

Relationships which may once have been considered to be between employer and employee are now not so clear. Would-be employers have tried to construe the contract in such a way so as to avoid an employment relationship arising and have often been very successful. As a result a variety of different 'non-employee' relationships have become more common. The difficulty which arises for individual workers is that it is difficult to enforce their rights because it would mean commencing legal action against a stronger adversary, in an unclear area of the law, where the case would be judged on the individual facts, not some general principle.

The study by VandenHeuvel and Wooden confirms this change. It argues that most of the growth in contractor employment has taken the form of 'dependent' and not 'independent' contractors. The former have a limited client base and are basically dependent on a regular employer for work, much like an employee is dependent on an employer for a wage. Independent contractors, on the other hand, have a greater variety of clients and cannot be regarded as defacto employees.

One outcome of the current approach of the courts has been a steady growth in agency workers who are hired out to employers by labour hire companies. The number of agency workers doubled in Australia between 1990 and 1995 and the number of workplaces using them increased from 14 to 21 per cent (AWIRS 1995). Manpower, one of Australia's largest labour hire companies, has been doubling in size every five years. There are two types of agency worker, one whom could be regarded as an employee and the second where there is no clear employment relationship.

1. *Supplementary labour hire*. Agencies such as Skilled Engineering hire workers and then contract these employees out to companies for short-term employment.

2. *Body hire*. Agencies such as Troubleshooters Available act as a broker by organising sub-contractors to perform work for other companies. An example of this kind of non-employee relationship can be found in the legal judgment known as *BWIU of Australia v Odco Pty Ltd* (1991, 99 ALR 735). Here the court ruled that the hired workers were employed by neither party because an insufficient degree of control had been exercised.

Labour hire arrangements in this second category can be used by companies to avoid entering into an employment relationship and the obligations which usually flow from this. Perhaps the most notorious example of using 'labour hire' arrangements to avoid employer responsibilities to the workforce was the mass sacking of its workforce by Patrick Stevedores during April 1998 (see boxed text).

LABOUR HIRE—GOOD PRACTICE AND BAD

In November 1997, the labour hire company, Manpower Australia, and the peak union body, the ACTU, signed an historic agreement dealing with the future of labour hire. The ACTU won acceptance for full-time, in-house employment by recruiters, but conceded the reality of non-permanent employment. The deal also commits Manpower to training and skills development of employees at all levels, an important issue in the current climate of declining apprenticeship opportunities.

'The agreement committing Manpower to significant training of their employees —which has traditionally not been the case with labour hire companies—will see a system that enables people to access skills no matter where they start', commented the ACTU's spokesperson, Max Ogden.

A spokesperson for Manpower, Chris McKay, suggested, 'The age of the tradesman is returning. Trades nowadays are becoming technology driven. We as a company have a commitment to maintaining and upgrading employees' skills'. Our agreement with the ACTU and also our internal training programs offer good protection to the blue-collar worker'.

Source: Alison Crossweller (1997), 'Blue-collar white-out', *Australian*, 13-14 December.

In April 1998 Patrick Stevedores 'dismissed' its entire workforce in an effort to free its operations from the influence of the Maritime Union of Australia (MUA). These mass sackings were carried out using an elaborate company restructure in which labour hire arrangements were central.

Prior to September 1997, the workforce was employed by four Patrick companies, who owned the assets and conducted the stevedoring business. In September, Patrick restructured its companies so that an 'operational' company took over the business side of stevedoring, and four 'employer' companies took over the provision of labour to the operational company. In effect, after September the workers (without their knowledge) were working for labour hire companies. Moreover, these labour hire companies had virtually no assets—and in the event of the cash flow drying up—no prospects of keeping the workforce employed.

The labour supply agreements between the Patrick employer company and the Patrick operational company specified that these agreements could be terminated without notice if there was any interference or disruption in the supply of labour. Between January and April 1998, a number of industrial disputes erupted between Patrick and the MUA, largely over Patrick's involvement in the Webb Dock scheme (an attempt by the National Farmers Federation (NFF) to create a non-union stevedoring workforce). As a result of this dispute, the Patrick operational company terminated its labour supply agreement with the Patrick employer companies and entered a new labour supply agreement with the NFF-backed company. Because the Patrick employer companies had no assets nor cash flow, their workforce found themselves without jobs.

Source: Based on Blake Dawson Waldron, *Industrial Relations Briefs*, May 1998.

It is clear that management has adopted different employment strategies according to individual labour markets. Some of the service industries with very low levels of 'non-employee' practices have the highest levels of casual employment. Conversely, in some areas of the economy with relatively low levels of casual employment such as manufacturing, construction and mining, these employment types are growing rapidly. Within the manufacturing industry, for instance, labour hire is booming within the metal and engineering industry. Skilled Engineering, one of the largest labour hire companies in Australia, supplies contract labour to over half of Australia's top 100 companies, employs over 5,300 contractors and grew by 27 per cent during 1995–96 (Evatt Foundation 1996). A survey of large Japanese and Australian metal and engineering companies found that 96 per cent of respondent companies had outsourced functions like maintenance work and just 2 per cent of these companies had no plans for further outsourcing in the future (Benson and Ieronimo 1996). Estimates by Drake International for the Victorian labour market suggested that 30 per cent of the blue-collar workforce were being outsourced by recruitment companies (Crossweller 1997, p. 35). One of the hidden costs of this movement towards labour hire is the decline in training opportunities for the workforce. Research by Bob Marshman has found that medium and larger firms only train sufficient workers for their predictable workflow requirements, and rely on labour hire companies to meet their less predictable demands in labour supply (Marshman 1996, p. 13). As a result, employment opportunities for apprentices in the core blue-collar trades has been severely reduced. The ACTU agreement with Manpower Australia to promote training within the labour hire workforce is therefore particularly opportune (see boxed text on previous page).

In the mining and construction industries, the growth of contract employment is linked with anti-union strategies. The use of body hire companies such as Troubleshooters was an effort by building and construction employers to undermine the power of building unions and cut wage standards. In the mining industry contract employment has grown six-fold.[3]

In conclusion, it's clear that there's been a major restructuring of work during the 1990s in which less secure forms of employment have emerged. These include casual and temporary employment and 'non-employee' categories of work such as outwork, contracting and agency work.

Outsourcing—a closer look

The impact of outsourcing on the contractor is uncertain as the outcomes will largely depend on the bargaining power of the contractor. For example, downsizing a bank often involves outsourcing some of its computing functions. The computing contractor hired may be paid well, fully paid for the hours worked and be assured of a regular income for a set period of time. In many cases such contractors will be paid better than employees performing the same work within the bank and will not have to work overtime. The outcomes for this contractor are obviously quite favourable. Take another example. The reduction of tariffs in the textiles clothing and footwear industry (TCF) has resulted in a cost-minimisation approach being taken by a clothing company. In response the company outsources its core function of making clothes to another company, which in turn pays poor wages to its workers. Such an example is examined more closely in the TCF case study (see boxed text). In both cases flexibility, productivity and profitability have increased, but the outcomes for the respective contractors have varied according to their bargaining power.

TEXTILE, CLOTHING AND FOOTWEAR OUTWORKERS

The textile, clothing and footwear (TCF) industries have undergone significant restructuring as a result of tariff reductions. One outcome has been a massive rise in the use of outworkers, as employers seek to lower their costs of production. The TCF industries provide an instructive example of what can happen when cost-cutting is carried to its logical extreme: competition based on the cutting of wages and erosion of conditions. A submission made by the TCF union in 1993 to the Department of Industrial Relations stated in part:

'Massive structural adjustment is occurring in the clothing industry as a result of reductions in protection arising from the Federal Government's TCF Industries Development Plan. Thousands of jobs have been lost in the clothing industry since the start of the Plan. Many of these workers have turned to exploitative outwork as a means of earning an income... As the pace of structural adjustment picks up, so too have we seen a rise in the incidence of outwork.' (TCFUA 1995, p. 6).

The Hidden Cost of Fashion, a report on outworking prepared by the TCF union in 1995, found extremely high levels of outsourcing and exploitation in the industry (TCFUA 1995). Large numbers of clothing manufacturers had ceased to own and operate their own factories and had moved production to outworkers through their distribution centres. The outworkers were most likely to be operating in private homes. It was estimated that the ratio of outworkers to factory workers in the clothing industry was 15 to 1. The union further estimated that there were up to 300,000 outworkers in Australia, operating in an invisible labour market which had been under-reported by agencies such as the Australian Bureau of Statistics and hidden from public view and scrutiny.

The outcome of greatest concern for outworkers was that their isolated position allowed their employers to exploit their labour and breach the award. Outworkers often worked long hours for very little reward: conditions in the industry had deteriorated over the 1990s so that workers would typically work 12 to 18 hours a day, 7 days a week for approximately a third of the award rate of pay. There was no access to the minimum conditions which were available to factory workers. Further, outworkers felt that they had few means to address the problems which they faced. Formal state institutions such as the courts and the industrial tribunals did not provide appropriate avenues of recourse. Workers who replied to the TCF union's nationwide phone-in were typically fearful of their employers and confused as to their rights.

Outworkers—probably the most severely disadvantaged workers in the labour market—are overwhelmingly made up of women from non-English-speaking backgrounds. Of those who contacted the TCF union during the phone-in, 50 per cent were from the Vietnamese community, 20 per cent were from the Chinese community and the remainder was divided between other community groups.

Source: Derived from TCFUA (1995), *The Hidden Cost of Fashion*, Sydney.

INSECURITY—THE WORKPLACE STORY

We have seen that job insecurity has spread because of the parlous state of the labour market in the 1990s. This anxiety has been further compounded by the emergence of new forms of employment relationship which no longer meet traditional expectations about what a 'proper job' looks like. In this section we focus more closely on how insecurity has been experienced at a workplace level, and how workplace change has itself contributed enormously to the problem of employment insecurity.

Historically, job insecurity was tied to business cycles. Workers in manufacturing, for example, always kept a close eye on the 'orders' coming through the door. This was the surest indicator of the health of the economy. Any business downturn quickly rippled through their plant: initially a drop in orders led to a loss of overtime, followed by working shorter hours, followed by stand-downs. When business picked up again, workers could expect to return to their former jobs. In the 1980s and 1990s, this historical pattern was dramatically overhauled and job insecurity became entwined with de-industrialisation and with organisational restructuring.

The exporting of manufacturing jobs to Asia, which we outlined earlier, meant that as the economy pulled out of a business downturn, the former factory jobs were not always waiting for the workers to return to. Many firms had taken the opportunity of a downturn to 'rationalise' their production process. In some cases, this meant new technology; in other cases it meant setting up production overseas. Whatever the case, the outcomes were less jobs for the former workers.

In the case of organisational restructuring, large numbers of jobs were lost purely through management decisions about the future shape of the organisation. The stage of the business cycle had little to do with this process of organisational change, though managers often took advantage of business downturns to implement their strategies for change. As a result the historical link between the health of the economy and job insecurity was broken, and people's fears about their job security became a concomitant to workplace change. Figure 6.7 illustrates this changing relationship between workforce reductions and organisational change. As the impetus towards such change gathered force during the early 1990s, so workplaces began to reduce their employee numbers not because of downturns in demand, but because of restructuring strategies.

Corporate downsizing

The term 'downsizing' entered everyday usage during the late 1980s when American corporations began restructuring. It was used as a euphemism for sacking workers, but in time even the word 'down' became so embarrassing for managers, that new euphemisms like 'right-sizing' were invented. Well before the term became fashionable, the process itself was widespread and well understood. In Australia during the 1970s, blue-collar workers were the most common targets for downsizing, as retrenchment statistics highlighted.

In the 1980s two new developments emerged. First, targeting of blue-collar workers in the *public sector* became more common. Waves of restructuring washed through statutory authorities and utilities, such as the railways and the water and electricity utilities, sweeping blue-collar workers into redundancies and early retirements. Often these workers were mature aged or came from non-English-speaking backgrounds, and their prospects of ever working again were very grim.

Figure 6.7 Main reason for workforce reductions in the year prior to the survey, 1990–95

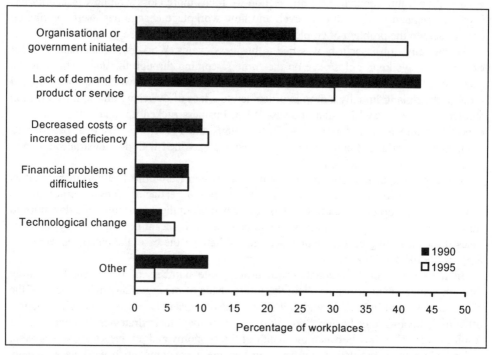

Source: AWIRS 90 and 95 main survey, employee relations management questionnaire.
Population: Workplaces with 20 or more employees where there were workforce reductions in the year prior to the survey. Figures are weighted and based on responses from 635 workplaces in 1990 and 671 workplaces in 1995.

The second new development was that white-collar workers and middle-managers became targets for downsizing (Littler 1997). This often occurred when organisations 'delayered', that is, eliminated intermediate layers of administration and abolished the jobs to be found there. It was during this phase that the term 'downsizing', followed by 'right-sizing', became widespread, and every mention of the term 'restructure' sent shivers down the spines of white-collar workers.

The fears were well-grounded. In just 12 years, between 1986 and 1997, 3.3 million full-time workers were retrenched. Of those, nearly 2 million were blue-collar male jobs (Cleary 1997a, p. 1). By the mid-1990s, more than half of all Australian organisations had been downsized, with the public sector leading the way (Littler 1997). Amongst large corporations, downsizing became almost standard practice. As Table 6.3 shows, between 1990 and 1995 about 55,000 jobs were lost in just 20 large corporations. Most of these firms cut between 20 per cent and 80 per cent of their workforce.

Table 6.3 Corporate downsizing, 1990–95

Company	Jobs lost (Numbers)	As percentage of employees
Ford	7,160	50
Westpac	5,810	17
Nth Broken Hill	4,729	68
Coca-Cola Amatil	3,787	55
Metro Meat	3,017	60
Aust. National Industries	2,855	38
Pasminco	2,687	43
Fosseys	2,408	38
BHP (Slab and Plate Products	2,355	24
TNT	2,334	20
CRA	2,256	15
BHP (Rod and Bar Products)	2,189	38
Amcor Trading	2,175	95
Angliss Group	2,104	82
Shell	1,987	40
BP	1,761	44
BHP (Utah)	1,648	83
BHP (Log Products Division)	1,562	40
Hawker De Havilland	1,443	56
David Syme	1,289	46

Source: University of Southern Queensland, cited in Paul Cleary, 'Manufacturing Hit Hardest', *Sydney Morning Herald*, 22 October, 1997b, p. 6

The AWIRS data provides useful insights into the extent of downsizing during the 1990s. Between 1990 and 1995 managers became much more deliberate in their employment practices and took a much more active role in reducing the size of their workforces. In 1990, 60 per cent of managers reduced the workforce through the passive means of natural attrition. By 1995 this number had fallen to 51 per cent. On the other hand, the use of proactive measures such as redundancies had risen. Compulsory redundancies, favoured by the private sector, rose from 30 per cent to 37 per cent and voluntary redundancies, favoured by the public sector, rose from 19 per cent to 37 per cent over the same period (Morehead et al. 1997, p. 76).

One significant feature of the current trend towards downsizing is that white-collar employees and middle-level managers have been subject to retrenchments in the 1980s and 1990s. Downsizing has been taking place on a number of levels within organisations and has not just been aimed at the production end of the occupational scale (Littler et al. 1997, p. 66). Middle managers, as well as production employees, have felt the impact of downsizing as companies rationalise their internal structures. Organisations have become more focused on their core functions, outsourcing areas which may be done more efficiently through competitive tendering processes. New models of organisational structure have focused attention on the 'unproductive' middle of organisations where neither policy nor product was being created. Administrative areas have been reduced and absorbed into other job classifications. In the process, workplaces have become smaller and more atomistic.

Other surveys of workplaces have also disclosed high levels of restructuring which result in job losses. The internationally comparative surveys conducted by Littler et al. (1997) focused on downsizing trends in Australian and New Zealand firms. The results showed that 44 per cent of organisations had delayered over the past two years. The results were slightly lower in New Zealand which had started downsizing earlier than Australia. It is expected that Australia is currently in the middle of its downsizing phase and that firms and employees will have to live with it 'for the foreseeable future' (1997, p. 69).

The most significant finding of the surveys is that Australian firms were much more likely to have undertaken a number of rounds of downsizing. Rather than cutting employee numbers once, there were often further retrenchments which followed: 44 per cent of firms had downsized three times or more in the two years prior to the survey and 71 per cent had done so twice or more (1997, p. 68). This pattern of downsizing had negative consequences for the morale of workers as well as management.

Restructuring of workplaces

The relationship between restructuring, retrenchments and the ensuing increases in job insecurity can be seen in workplace change and its effects on workforce reduction. It's clear that downsizing has been occurring in conjunction with a number of other changes at a workplace level. Looking at the AWIRS data, for example, it emerges that the most popular forms of change are:

❑ the reorganisation of the workplace structure, which includes changes to the number of management levels; and
❑ changes to the work performed by non-managerial employees, including tasks done.

AWIRS also shows that the largest workplaces, those with over 100 employees, have been the most likely to implement such changes. In particular, of all workplaces with over 100 employees, 83 per cent reported that they had reorganised in the two years prior to the survey, and 64 per cent had changed the tasks of non-managerial employees. This is clear evidence that there is change happening, and that it is most common in large workplaces.

What are the results of these kinds of workplace change? The major effect has been a reduction in the number of workers required to do the same amount of work. New forms of organisational structure, and new forms of work, have directly resulted in the loss of labour. Where the workplace has been reorganised, in 40 per cent of cases there has also been a reduction in the size of the workplace . Where there have been changes in the way work is done, there was a reduction in 27 per cent of cases. *In other words, in the areas where change was most likely to take place, the most jobs were lost.* Retrenchments as a result of downsizing are therefore clearly related to the restructuring of Australian workplaces. In the next section, where we look more closely at workers' perceptions of job insecurity, we will see that these two features—job losses and workplace reorganisation—feature prominently amongst the factors associated with job insecurity.

BANKING IN THE 1990S

The banking sector illustrates dramatically how downsizing has been driven by both technological change and organisational restructuring. Between 1991 and 1997 about 30,000 full-time jobs were lost in the banking sector and a similar number are predicted to be lost over the next seven years (Cleary 1997a, p. 1). Increased use of automatic teller machines (ATMs) and of banking services located in retail outlets (EFTPOS) has provided banks with the opportunity to reduce the counter staff in their branches. At the same time, branch closures have become widespread, as banks concentrate their services on the more lucrative areas of business, such as lending and investment services. These changes have lead to healthy bank profits—most have increased between fourfold and ninefold—and increased job insecurity and work intensification for the banking workforce.

New technology and banking 1995 to 1997

	1995	1996	1997
ATM machines	6,175	7,118	7,816
EFTPOS terminals	68,034	116,704	169,739

Source: Peter Witts (1998), 'Banks Rule, Okay?', *Weekend Australian*, 23.24 May, p. 5.

Bank profits 1986/87 and 1996/97

Bank	Net profit	
	1986/87	1996/1997
Westpac	$244 million	$1.3 billion
ANZ	$226 million	$1.0 billion
National Australia Bank	$253 million	$2.2 billion
Commonwealth Bank of Australia	$226 million	$1.1 billion

Source: Peter Witts (1998), 'Banks Rule, Okay?', *Weekend Australian*, 23.24 May, p. 5.

These themes emerged strongly in a case study carried out by ACIRRT at one of the major banks. The following material is taken from focus groups which were conducted with various areas of the organisation. One of the most common reasons cited for discontent with working at the bank was understaffing. Most interviewees reported staff shortages. In one group, staff shortages were so chronic that the quality of service was suffering:

'There are not enough staff to do existing duties let alone help out new starters—sometimes nobody in the whole branch knows how to answer a query—a manager may be out to lunch—this impacts on the level of customer service.'

'There are not enough warm bodies. Because they get it done anyway with unpaid overtime the bank thinks it is possible to do it with less staff. One example is having 4 staff (at the branch), one is being a teller, one is with a customer, one at lunch and if you're the fourth, you're stuffed! There used to be relief tellers over lunch time but even this has now gone.'

In the Business Banking section understaffing has caused a situation where there is a lack of experienced staff to cover workloads. In some cases members are doing twice the workload, at higher levels, with no higher duties payments or recognition. In the Financial Services section the response was very similar— staffing numbers were stagnant but the amount of work was always growing. To overcome this staff put in extra time and effort but they were not getting any monetary gain or recognition for it. For instance, many people got into a routine of working half an hour of unpaid overtime each day. One member felt that as a result: 'the bank gets a lot of advantage out of that because people don't put their foot down'.

In the Customer Service Centre the problems associated with understaffing were made worse by outdated technology. Understaffing in other areas of the bank tended to compound their own problems. For example most branches referred enquires to the service centres to compensate for their own inadequate branch staffing and inadequate training. This was particularly problematic as there was a general perception overall that there were too few service centres.

As a consequence of understaffing and workplace changes at the bank most groups reported that they were experiencing increasing work intensification. In some units, such as Financial Services, it was considered the issue of greatest importance and was constantly mentioned by the focus group. The group stated that part of the problem was that the 'other duties' part of their job description was constantly being expanded, so that every month they were picking up another task which then became part of their job. They claimed that even if they worked overtime, they couldn't get through their work.

In the Customer Service Centre the joint problems of insufficient staffing and increasing workload could be traced to an inefficient rostering system. Under the present arrangements a majority of the most experienced full-time staff left at 5 o'clock, despite the concentration of calls after 6 o'clock when customers returned home from work and opened their mail. This meant that one of their busiest periods was serviced by the least qualified staff.

The shift to a sales culture also increased the workload for many employees. In Personal Banking in the City one member remarked:

'As the teller your job is to get rid of customers as quickly as possible, but now you have to try to sell them something. Management opportunities have dropped off and now it just seems like everything is sell sell sell. The push to make targets every week, some staff are supposed to be helping out in the branch but they never have any time. Either that or they spend their whole time doing branch stuff and have no time for doing lending.'

The links between job insecurity and workplace change— workers' perceptions

AWIRS 1995 not only asked managers about what was happening in their workplaces but it also asked a large number of employees how they felt about what was happening to them at work. One of the key questions asked whether they agreed or disagreed with the statement: 'I feel insecure about my future here'. Using responses to this question we have analysed a range of workplace and demographic features to isolate the main contributing factors associated with job insecurity. These are summarised in Table 6.4.

Heading the list are occupational and industry features, specifically blue-collar workers employed in the pubic infrastructure utilities. These results show that workers in public infrastructure utilities are twice as likely as workers in manufacturing to feel insecure about their futures. Labourers and plant and machine operators are nearly one-and-three-quarters more likely to feel insecure, compared with managers. These figures should come as no surprise. We saw earlier that nearly 60,000 jobs were lost in the public infrastructure utilities in the 10 years leading up to 1994 and that these industries have been subject to immense turbulence. Moreover, we saw in the last chapter that workers in this industry sector were subject to some of the highest levels of work intensification and were amongst the most dissatisfied members of the workforce.

Table 6.4 Main factors associated with job insecurity

Factor	Relative odds
Increased insecurity	
Industry location - electricity, gas & water utilities	1.9
Occupation - labourer	1.7
Occupation - plant & machine operators	1.7
Occupation - tradesperson	1.6
Workplace with job losses in last 12 mths	1.5
Workplaces with change in last 12 mths	1.3
Casual worker	1.3
Union member	1.3
Decreased insecurity	
Industry location - hospitality	0.8
Private sector workplace	0.7
Given fair say about changes in last 12 mths	0.4

Source: Logistic regression estimates calculated from AWIRS 95
Note: Insecurity is measured as agreement with question:
'I feel insecure about my future here' in AWIRS 95 employee survey.

It is also noteworthy that, irrespective of industry and occupation, workplaces which had experienced job losses in the last 12 months were one-and-a-half-times more likely to have employees feeling insecure, compared with workplaces which hadn't experienced job losses. Finally, workplaces which had undergone change during the last 12 months were also much more likely to engender job insecurity than those workplaces which hadn't undergone change.

By way of contrast, workplaces in the hospitality industry, and private sector workplaces in general, were places where employees were less likely to feel insecure about their jobs. The reasons for this are the strong jobs growth that has been occurring in hospitality over the last decade, and the fact that the public sector has borne the brunt of major restructuring during the 1990s. Finally, those workers who felt they had been given a fair chance to have a say about the changes that had occurred in their workplaces were far less likely to feel insecure about their jobs. Clearly, proper consultation and workplace change need to go hand-in-hand if problems of job insecurity are to be prevented at a workplace level.

* * *

Economic journalists, Larry Elliott and Dan Atkinson, have called our current era, 'The Age of Insecurity'. Their definition of this phenomenon serves as a succinct conclusion to many of the themes explored in this chapter:

> At the centre of the new economic system in the Age of Insecurity is the rotating worker, forever in danger of being revolved out into the market to be replaced by cheaper labour from outside. The internal market, the process whereby employees live in a state of constant competition against each other and against external contractors, is the final development in the transformation of work from a sort of quasi-tenancy from which the employee could be evicted only on payment of redundancy money into a fleeting, transitory experience, infused with terror at the prospect of its ending, akin to a teenage love-affair (1998, p. 76).

In Australia, the demise of job security highlights just how stark are the consequences of dismantling the post-war settlement. If nothing else, that settlement provided both full employment and stable employment for the population. As we've seen in this chapter, insecurity in the labour market is experienced differently by different people. For some workers it is a problem of moving between unemployment and casual work. For others it is a problem of jobs being outsourced or workers being enticed (or coerced) into becoming 'dependant contractors'.

No section of the workforce has been immune from these developments—even managers have suffered through downsizing and restructuring in their organisations. The restructuring of workplaces has been systematic and widespread in Australia. As a result, managers—as individuals—have felt the blowtorch of change. Like their workforce, they too have been subject to the vagaries and uncertainties of workplace change in the 1990s. This vulnerability of the individual manager stands in stark contrast to the growing power of the management function. As all the chapters have shown, the dismantling of the post-war settlement and the ascendancy of the neo-liberal project has seen management garner greater power unto itself. Workers, both individually and collectively, have been the losers in most cases. It's important to realise, then, that workplace problems do not arise simply because of the 'bad behaviour' of individual managers. Similarly, they cannot be solved by changing individual managers. Rather, the problems arise from systemic features of the workplace, features which include the lack of consultation and collaboration between all parties in the workplace. The final chapter explains how a new approach to working life might deal with these issues.

Notes

1   As two of the foremost researchers in this field, Burgess and Campbell have noted: 'there is a direct link between the shift towards non-standard employment and the deregulation of working time, with "standard" working hours dissolving in unison with standard employment arrangements' (1998, p. 32).

2   Casuals are defined by an employer's obligation to provide continuing employment. At law casuals have no more legal security of tenure longer than a day. The statistical measure of this type of employment is whether a worker is entitled to sickness, holiday and long service leave. Casuals typically do not get these types of leave but instead receive some kind of allowance added to their hourly rate to compensate. Temporaries can be defined as persons engaged for a fixed term of employment, often to cover the absence of a permanent employee who is on leave. They have more certainty about their length of tenure, but with no prospect of permanency.

3   The mining giant CRA has relied on individual contracts of service, not contracts for service, in its campaign against the unions. Western Mining has led the charge with contracts for service.

CHAPTER 7

Managing work in the future: new directions for policy

We've now examined in great detail the changing nature of work in Australia. Now it's time to consider our options for the future. We're not going to summarise all of the various policy options currently on offer. That's already been done comprehensively by others (e.g. Schmid et al. 1997). Rather, we will highlight new approaches to the problems identified in this book. Indeed, many of our suggestions arise from insights we've gathered during our field work workplace and labour market initiatives which have not often received the attention they deserve. Hence, like the rest of this book, our findings on policy primarily arise from our empirical work. Before looking at some of these policy options, we'll briefly reflect on the key findings of the previous chapters.

THE ARGUMENT IN BRIEF

Working life in Australia, as in most other countries, is being transformed. This was clearly evident in the first chapter on the human face of workplace change. We showed that there have been a few winners, but for most people, change has been for the worse. Our key analytical finding is that this outcome has not been inevitable. As Chapter 2 demonstrated, change is inevitable, but the *precise form it takes* is not. Economics and public policy are always entwined. If Labor had not embraced the neo-liberal project, Australia's economic direction would have been quite different. When musing on the 'what ifs' of life, the benchmark should never be a static past, but rather, the alternative futures which might have been chosen. Chapter 2 showed that the changing structure of the world economy and Australia's place within it created pressure for change. As in other advanced economies the responses to this pressure did not happen in a vacuum, but had to take account of the historical circumstances prevailing in a particular national setting. We discussed this in terms of the dismantling of the Australian post-war settlement and the emergence of a new balance between the forces of the market and social protection. To date the forces of the market have won hands down at the expense of social protection.

These developments resulted in a move away from the traditional approach to regulating work based on awards to one based on enterprise bargaining. At the time this development was supported by most major industrial and political organisations. They believed more decentralised and less regulated bargaining would enable changes at work to contribute to meeting the new economic challenges. However, as Chapter 3 revealed, this has not been the case. Instead of new and dynamic approaches to managing workplace change—such as greater workplace negotiation and consultation—we have seen a reduction in levels of social protection and an increase in the space available for market and management forces to determine the nature of working life. As such enterprise bargaining has been part of the problem, not part of the solution.

The outcomes we've seen emerge from these developments have been dramatic. As Chapter 4 revealed, both wage outcomes and the wage-fixing system have become fragmented. As a result, wage-based inequality is on the rise, and this is occurring *within* as well as *between* industries and occupations. As noted in that chapter, these outcomes are not simply a legacy of the reduced role of awards. Rather they arise from the interplay of a changing wage-fixing system and the dynamics of labour market segmentation, the way in which the labour market is itself splintered into many niches.

Changes in hours of work have been just as dramatic. As Chapter 5 revealed, growing numbers of people are working extended hours. For many, especially professional and managerial workers, these hours are much longer than they would prefer. In addition, work intensification is on the rise. In short, for many full-time workers the quality of working hours is deteriorating.

Chapter 6 broadened this perspective to include those without any work, as well as those working part-time, or casual or on various forms of contract. It examined rising levels of insecurity at work and showed that at the heart of this development has been the steady rise in the underlying rate of unemployment. But the problem is more complex than this. The rise in casual and contract forms of employment now appear to be just as dramatic in their impact. And the growing fashion for retrenchments, outsourcing and reliance of agency/labour hire arrangements is radically changing the landscape of previously 'permanent' jobs.

HOW CAN WE RESPOND TO THESE DEVELOPMENTS?

The globalisation dilemma

The current policy debate is couched as if there are only two possible responses: move further down the road of neo-liberal 'reform' or 'turn back the clock'. Both approaches are flawed.

The most vocal advocates for 'reform' argue 'There Is No Alternative' (TINA) to the neo-liberal prescriptions of deregulation and decentralisation, and that we just have to accept their outcomes, namely growing inequality and precarious forms of employment. For them globalisation is an irresistible force that dictates policy priorities. Governments must surrender to this irresistible force if their economies are to prosper. Otherwise they will face the punishing judgment of foreign exchange markets and those making decisions on foreign direct investment. Unless government's surrender their policy autonomy they can expect their nation to be left out of future world economic growth. In short, the forces of globalisation are inevitable, the only choice is to 'surrender to them or die'.

As time has passed, the neo-liberal promises about the benefits of globalisation have lost credibility. Far from delivering universal benefits the globalisation process, as managed on the basis of neo-liberal prescriptions, has been associated with profound economic and social dislocation. In the advanced industrial nations traditional industries such as manufacturing have experienced major shakeouts, with large scale job shedding. In some cases, entire branches of production have disappeared, such as steel making. In addition the public sector has been drastically restructured. The increased preoccupation with 'share holder value' has driven a huge amount of change within organisations and workplaces so that the disciplines of international markets—be they for products, shares or foreign exchange—are felt by an increasing proportion of the workforce. Competition policy, in particular, was intended (allegedly) to increase the nation's international competitiveness, but instead has brought all the uncertainties associated with unstable market relations.

The dislocation created by these developments has spawned a growing interest in 'winding the clock back' and protecting nations and communities from the ravages of unbridled competition. This has been evident in Europe and the United States as well as Australia.[1] The clearest local manifestation of this phenomenon has been the emergence of Pauline Hanson and the 'One Nation Party'. To date this party's controversial policies on race relations have received most attention. Research reveals that support for this party is not solely based on this part of the platform. Rather the policy mix of protection of Australia from all foreign threats—people, capital or cheap imported goods—is regarded as the true foundation for its standing. Indeed, the party's policy prescriptions are best understood as a call for the full restoration of the kind of 'new protectionism' which accompanied the turn-of-the-century Federation social settlement (see Chapter 2). Seen in this light One Nation's platform has deep historical roots: protection for industry (like the old policy on tariffs), protection from foreign labour (like the old white Australia policy) as well as recognition of the need for employees to be protected from the vagaries of the market by unions and state imposed standards concerning wages and conditions (like the old vision behind industrial arbitration).[2]

What are the implications of these rival accounts of the globalisation process? The neo-liberal position is flawed on both efficiency and fairness grounds. The poor economic outcomes associated with this doctrine are now being comprehensively documented. The most obvious legacies of this policy project are low rates of productivity growth, growth in low-wage jobs and high levels of economic instability associated with a myopic obsession with 'shareholder value' (see for example: Henwood 1997; Martin and Schumann 1997; Mishel, Bernstein and Schmitt 1997; Moody 1997; Elliott and Atkinson 1998). Given the dislocation and resentment this project is now generating it is clear that this is socially undesirable and, potentially, politically unsustainable in the longer term. Significant social upheavals have already occurred in Europe and the United States. These are unlikely to abate, and indeed they appear likely to intensify as the neo-liberal approach to globalisation gathers pace.

The protectionist reaction is just as undesirable and just as unsustainable. The policies on race and immigration are highly divisive. The economic policies are likely to result in retaliatory trade measures from other countries. Given that around 20 per cent of Australia's GDP is exported (ABS 1998a) retaliation is potentially very damaging to national income. In addition questions remain as to how Australia would maintain overall living standards if consumers were forced to buy domestically produced goods which are currently imported.

Given the above reasoning, the major challenge for policy is not to choose between 'accepting' or 'rejecting' globalisation. Rather the challenge is to identify how and under what conditions Australia should globalise. Clearly a complete answer to this question is beyond the scope of this book. It is worth noting, however, that there is a growing literature which shows that a small country like Australia can successfully engage with the new global realities and still achieve desirable social and economic outcomes at the same time.

The key idea informing this growing literature is the notion that the market is a *good servant* but a *bad master* of social and economic development.[3] As such, the challenge which arises is how to work with market forces, not how to 'liberate' them or 'reject' them. Hirst and Thompson (1996), for example, argue that when responding to the challenge of globalisation it is important to distinguish between different economic settings or levels. What works at one level will not necessarily be appropriate at another. The top level they identify is the relations between the dominant world economies (defined as those that convene regularly at G8 meetings). Below this level are the institutions of multilateral trade such as the World Trade Organisation. Superimposed between this level and national economies are trade blocs such as NAFTA and the European Union. Finally, below the national level are geographic regions (Hirst and Thomson 1996, chs. 6 and 8). When thinking about policies concerning global economic forces account needs to be taken of developments at all these levels. As such, universal prescriptions such as 'free trade' or 'protection' are of limited use in guiding policy. Rather what is needed are specific proposals for each level. For example, some commitment to co-ordinated economic expansion is needed at the G8 level; a notion of fair trade (not just free trade) is needed at the World Trade Organisation (WTO); and agreements concerning market access between trading blocs is needed at this level.

An emerging refrain throughout the 'market as good servant but poor master' literature is that the nation state still continues to have an important role in today's world. Karel Williams and his colleagues reflect this line of thinking and draw extensively on original research into the nature of one of the most globalised parts of manufacturing—the car industry. The management literature is replete with exhortations for managers and policy makers to emulate the 'leaders' if they (and their nations) are to succeed in world markets. Yet Williams and his colleagues show that it is simply not possible for one country to emulate another in order to survive in the world trading system. As they put it:

> ... the effects of management action are bounded by the extent to which ... many costs are fixed or at least determined by the structural variables within particular social settlements ... The lesson of Japanese competition up to the mid 1980s, and of Korean competition in the 1990s, is simple: *the advanced countries which pay high wages and work short hours are threatened by low-wage competition which cannot be met by any conceivable form of productive intervention to improve efficiency* (Williams et al. 1994, p. 243).

For Williams and his colleagues the policy implications of this are clear. We need to shift from a preoccupation with 'emulating successful competitors' and instead focus on the challenge of responding to low-wage competition. This is not a matter of being indifferent to the requirements for poorer nations to develop through trade. As they put it 'the issue is not whether we block Third World Development but whether we countenance the recreation of the Third World in the First' (Williams et al. 1995 p. 92). How this might be achieved in Australia has been considered in recent work done for the Anglican Church's social policy agency, the Brotherhood of St Laurence. As Sue Jackson (1996) has noted in a paper prepared for the Brotherhood, Australia needs to take an active approach to minimising the constraints arising from globalisation. The threat of competition from developing countries is often cited as a reason for reducing Australian wages and living standards. Our emphasis should rather be on improving conditions and living standards in those countries. Australia could take a lead in this regard by seeking to have an appropriate social charter incorporated into international agreements such as GATT and APEC. This would be consistent with and could draw on efforts in Europe to develop a social charter for the European Community (Jackson 1996 p. 25).

Similar sentiments have been developed by leading writers on globalisation such as Martin and Schumann (1997, pp. 235–43).

Putting workplace 'reform' in context

One of the major problems with current policy concerning working life is that too much has been expected of it. As product and capital markets have been 'deregulated' high expectations have been raised about the role of workplace change as the basis for increased competitiveness. In the last phase of the Accord unions and government talked of a 'workplace-change-led' recovery. The assumption of the best practice program was that all other policy settings were essentially in place—the only remaining challenge was to identify and diffuse best practice to enterprises. In the 1993 and 1996 elections the Federal Coalition saw 'labour market reform' as central to unleashing a 'productivity breakout' (see for example Fightback (1992), Jobsback (1992) and the 1996 policy on 'fair work, fair pay'). This was based in part on work done by the Business Council of Australia which estimated that productivity would improve in the order of 25 per cent if a truly enterprise-based system were established (BCA 1989, pp. 25, 60).

The preoccupation with workplace 'reform' and changes to working life as the pivotal policy areas for competitive success is misleading and unhelpful. Labour is only one factor of production. To put the matter starkly—the best trained, most flexible and cheapest workforce in the world cannot make up for inadequacies in the operation of capital markets and policies and institutions concerning industry development. At best industrial relations policy and labour market policy can complement a wider policy mix. They can never work effectively in the context of a deficient policy framework.

It's crucial that we come up with a more effective policy mix where the common elements involve blending market and non-market mechanisms. The goal is to ensure Australia manages its growing insertion in the world economy in an intelligent way that enhances both economic growth and fairness. Unless a policy mix of this type prevails Australia will be condemned to experiencing still more of the harmful labour market outcomes documented in this book. On the other hand, if a more innovative approach is adopted, we have the real potential of creating a more promising future. This entails two considerations. First, we need to get macro-economic policy right and then we need to look more closely at developing a new approach to working life issues.

Getting the macro-policy right

As we saw in Chapter 2, the decline of Keynesianism was associated with policy makers giving up on managing the macro-economy. Initially this took the form of monetarism, and later, micro-economic reform. In effect, economic management at a national level was reduced to simply setting up an environment conducive to capital flows. The market, it was assumed, could be left to manage the economy. But this opting out by governments, as the foregoing chapters have dramatically shown, has left Australia with a legacy of high unemployment, a declining manufacturing sector, large amounts of unproductive investment, and deteriorating living and working standards. While most of this policy chapter is concerned with developing a new approach to working life, we also believe it is essential that macro-economic policy-making be resurrected. In particular, a genuine response to unemployment is needed, as well as more effective policies for industry development and for investment.

Dealing with unemployment

Previous work carried out by ACIRRT on long-term unemployment amongst NESB immigrants has suggested that the solution to unemployment requires a commitment from the state to public sector expansion and the revitalisation of manufacturing industry. While the interested reader may consult O'Loughlin and Watson (1997), a brief overview of these arguments is offered here. An important part of the ACIRRT case rests on work carried out by economists John Quiggin and John Langmore (1994). The Quiggin and Langmore proposals are located within a broadly Keynesian demand management strategy which emphasises the employment generating aspects of public expenditure in community services.

For Langmore and Quiggin, one of the main reasons for the growth in unemployment during the last two decades has been cutbacks in government expenditure, particularly Commonwealth funding for the states which has fallen from 9.5 per cent of GDP in the mid-1970s to 4.9 per cent in the early 1990s (1994, p. 3). They see increased spending on health, education and infrastructure as not only directly generating employment, but also as contributing to the 'vitality of the economy' and thereby guaranteeing its long term expansion. Langmore and Quiggin also argue that increased spending must be accompanied by industry and regional policies which are formulated not on the presumption of competitive markets, but rather on the need for private and public sectors to co-operate effectively (1994, pp. 4–5).

This expansion in public sector employment is presented within the context of a number of other proposals (1994, pp. 117–118). These include:

1. expanding labour market programs, with a job guarantee for the long-term unemployed;
2. an incomes policy based on the Accord; and
3. progressive taxation reform.

These measures are designed to ensure that the long-term unemployed benefit from the expansion in employment (point 1) and to counter the inflationary effects of expanded public expenditure on job creation (points 2 and 3).

For Langmore and Quiggin jobs lost through technology and structural change in traditional employment areas should be offset by an expansion of jobs in health, education, welfare, research, the arts and environmental services (1994, p. 80). These are all areas which are largely publicly funded and the winding back of public expenditures over the last decade has prevented such an expansion.

One critic of this strategy has argued that 'it is difficult to believe that the currently unemployed can slot into public sector jobs in community services such as education and health very easily' (Kenyon 1993, p. 21). However, this objection is misguided. The Langmore and Quiggin position also envisages an expansion in the construction of public infrastructure, an employment area ideally suited to male, low-skilled long-term unemployed. Moreover, an expansion of employment in health and education would not just entail increased recruitment of professionals and para-professionals, but would also create jobs for ancillary positions like cleaning, administration, support and food preparation. The workers needed to fill these positions could also be drawn from the ranks of the long-term unemployed, both men and women. Finally, increased employment in these areas would also draw qualified workers from other sectors of the economy where they may be currently under-employed, and their departure would open up possibilities for unemployed workers in the jobs they vacate. In 1993, about 15 per cent of persons with teaching qualifications were employed in lower level positions, mostly sales and clerical jobs, and over one-quarter of persons with health qualifications were similarly under-employed (ABS 1993a).

The real dilemma concerning the Langmore and Quiggin proposals lie not in the viability of their employment generating aspects, but at the level of macro-economic constraints. The legacy of the Hawke and Keating governments, particularly the serious current account deficit and the weakening of opportunities to increase taxation revenue, have limited the scope for Keynesian-style expansionary policies. Langmore and Quiggin are aware of this dilemma and suggest that increased taxation be used to fund their proposals, and that one of the consequences of this strategy would be a reduction in the current account deficit because 'a significant proportion of discretionary spending goes on imports' (1994, p. 121).

Ultimately, the question of unemployment is a question of political will, not technical difficulties. If the community is prepared to pay, through higher taxation, for full employment, then full employment is possible. Unfortunately, a decade of tax cuts, or promises of tax cuts, have created a climate in which reform of taxation to increase revenues in an equitable fashion is seen as too difficult. Yet Australia remains one of the lowest taxing OECD countries, and the scope is certainly there for significantly increasing revenue (by about 12 billion dollars, according to Langmore and Quiggin, 1994, p. 156). Findings by the Australian Taxation Office, which show that multinational corporations pay effectively no income tax in Australia, also highlight the haemorrhaging of government revenue which current taxation policies have allowed. Finally, increased taxation revenue need not be the only source of funding for public sector employment creation. B. A. Santamaria, for example, argued over many years for an increase in Commonwealth funding of national infrastructure projects to be paid for by an issue of low interest Commonwealth bonds.

As both Chapters 2 and 6 demonstrated, the deindustrialisation of the Australian economy has been responsible for a significant proportion of unemployment and particular groups of workers—predominantly mature age blue-collar workers—have been most severely affected. Is it feasible to expect this process to be slowed, or even halted? Can

Australian manufacturing be revived? Exploring these questions entails revisiting some of the globalisation themes discussed earlier.

Industry policy

Some of the most interesting work on how Australian manufacturing industry should respond to globalisation has been undertaken by employer organisations such as the Australian Industry Group, an organisation formed out of the old Metal Trades Industry Association (MTIA) and the Australian Chamber of Manufactures. In 1997 the MTIA conducted a major study, based primarily on interviews with 170 top executives involved in making investment decisions, about where to locate manufacturing investment. One of its major findings was that Australian governments have failed to adapt 'policy to the challenges of globalisation' (MTIA 1997, p. 13). In saying this the executives were not calling for more deregulation or freer markets. On the contrary, most accepted that tariffs had been cut almost as far as they could go. As the report noted 'most companies are now looking for a new phase in industry policy' (MTIA 1997, p. 26) The elements of what made a good industry policy were described as a set of government initiatives which:

❑ address global trends and markets rather than domestic markets and issues;
❑ support companies in areas that are crucial to their competitive advantage: low cost production, R&D, and market access;
❑ be delivered within a comprehensive and long-term framework;
❑ include a focus on fostering industry clusters with strong growth potential, common requirements, and gains from interaction between firms in the cluster;
❑ make effective use of tax breaks, grants, and other industry supports to foster priority industry development;
❑ be based on good delivery: this means strong central coordination, fast response to corporate needs, and targeted marketing; and
❑ achieve a balance between social and industry objectives that ensures good progress in both areas (1997, p. 25).

Specific recommendations for the future included sound macro-economic management, further tax and industrial relations 'reform', investment incentives (especially for research and development) and integration with the emerging Asian Free Trade Area. Most importantly the report noted the need for government to break with the ad hoc approach to industry development that has prevailed in the past. Drawing on the lessons of recent successful industry policy experiences (such as in Ireland), the report also called for the establishment of a powerful Australian investment agency. Such a body would have the capacity to attract new investment and provide strong, central coordination of industry policy agencies at State and Federal level. The underlying message of the report was that globalisation had changed the nature of world trade. Only those countries which worked creatively with the market would realise potential gains. Those that waited for free markets to deliver prosperity would be left behind. Similar ideas have been developed by the Australian Business Foundation (1997) and the Australian Manufacturing Workers Union (1997).

Rethinking the role of fairness

Fundamental thinking concerning the role of *fairness* in economic development has also been taking place. Froud and her colleagues have recently argued that:

> Redistribution is not just a fading ethical imperative for the better off who can't pay, won't pay for the less fortunate. It is a structural necessity because growing inequality influences the composition of demand, upsets the relative prices of goods and services, and thereby creates those who are less fortunate. Without redistribution, late capitalist advanced societies represent an experimental combination of cheap services and low wage imports which create heaven for the rich and hell for the poor who must coexist in one political system whose democratic future seems increasingly less certain (1997, p. 32).

Sentiments such as this have also been echoed by a number of major business leaders. Percy Barnevick, head of ABB, one of the largest engineering companies in the world, has observed:

> If companies do not rise to the challenge of poverty and unemployment, the tensions between the haves and the have nots will lead to a marked rise in violence and terrorism. (*Die Woche* April 30, 1996, cited in Martin and Schumann 1997, p. 231).

Klaus Schwab, a founder and president of the World Economic Forum in Davos, Switzerland has come to similar conclusions. According to him current developments are 'multiplying the human and social costs of the globalization to a level that tests the social fabric of democracies in an unprecedented way'. He notes that economic and political leaders now need to confront the 'challenge of demonstrating how the new global capitalism can function to the benefit of the majority [of the population] and not only for corporate managers and investors.' (*International Herald Tribune*, February 1, 1996, cited in Martin and Schumann 1997, p. 231). Amongst policy researchers suggestions on how this can be achieved have focussed primarily on the redistribution of income and on labour market restructuring. As Froud and colleagues put it, the imperative is to change not just the level, but also the composition of demand by:

> limiting the claims of the capital market against the product market and pegging payments to shareholders. In a different context, it may be time to revive Keynes' (1936) proposals for the euthanasia of the rentier (Froud et al. 1997, p. 32; see also Henwood 1997, ch 7 and Elliott and Atkinson 1998, ch. 8).

In Australia specific suggestions on how the tax system can work more efficiently and fairly have been identified on the basis of comprehensive research by Australian Councial of Social Services (ACOSS). These specific proposals include closing tax loop holes and rationalising indirect taxes. They have identified three initiatives which alone would raise $2.5 billion: restricting deductions for negatively geared investment in non-productive assets (i.e. property and shares); taxing trusts in a similar way to companies; and overhauling superannuation tax breaks which only benefit high income earners (ACOSS 1998). The work done for the Brotherhood of St Laurence cited above also flagged the need to use tax policy to curtail speculative international financial flows which provide few economic benefits but which destabilise the real economy. As it notes, 'this could be achieved by the imposition of some form of levy on foreign exchange transaction' (Jackson 1996, p. 4; support for the so-called Tobin tax is also outlined in Henwood 1997 and Martin and Schuman 1997).

To date many of these researchers and policy developers have worked in isolation. However, as time passes, a coherent set of practical policy proposals is emerging based on a new vision of the importance of co-ordination within a national economy to meet the growing challenges of global competition. State intervention is being increasingly recognised as important, not simply as the direct provider of services but as the broker or facilitator of innovation. By helping establish new forms of co-ordination between different parts of society, especially within the private sector, state policy can ensure overall outcomes reflect more than the sum of the parts. These policy proposals offer the prospect of a better balance between the forces of the market and social protection. As such they offer a viable way forward, one which goes beyond the neo-liberal cant that 'there is no alternative' to growing inequality and instability, and one which also avoids defensive calls for 'turning back the clock'.

A NEW AGENDA FOR POLICY AT WORK

When devising a new approach to working life, our priority must be to address concrete problems in an innovative way. Such an approach requires that the core assumptions underpinning policy are carefully assessed. In particular we must consider: do they provide an adequate understanding of the major work-related problems of our times? The empirical findings concerning wages, hours and job security identified in Chapters 4, 5 and 6 raise questions about the adequacy of the current assumptions informing policy. These assumptions concern the most basic features of working life:

- ❑ who is providing labour?
- ❑ who provides jobs and associated benefits?
- ❑ what is the framework regulating these activities?

For most of this century, policy concerning issues at work has been informed by the assumptions of the 'classical wage earner model'. This has meant that most attention has been devoted to specifying rights and obligations for '*employees*' and '*employers*' operating primarily in the context of an '*award*' system. Social security was provided as a buffer (Chifley's 'bridge'), primarily as a form of support when an employee's status shifted from 'fully employed' to 'unemployed'.

It has been evident throughout this book that these categories no longer have the purchase they once had on labour market practice. Chapter 6 revealed that growing numbers of workers are either contractors or second-class employees (e.g. casuals). Growing numbers of businesses are actively seeking to avoid the responsibility of providing direct employment and work-related entitlements. Finally, the assumptions concerning the mix of industrial and social security rights no longer works as intended. This latter development has arisen not simply because of the rise in the underlying rate of unemployment. It has also arisen from a growing number of people wish to strike a different balance between work and other activities in life by working part-time. If policy about work-related issues is to engage more effectively with these new realities the basic categories underpinning it need to change.

Table 7.1 Redefining policy about work: a comparison between the 'classical wage earner' model and the 'working life' model

Role performed in working life	Current assumptions of the 'wage earner model'	Current challenges for policy	New assumptions of the 'working life model'	Examples of new initiatives needed
Provider of labour	Permanent employee	• Growth in non-employees workers • Growth in casuals	Worker	• Standardise rights to entitlements regardless of legal status (e.g. S106 of the NSW Industrial Relations Act)
Provider of jobs and employment benefits	A single employer conceived as the owner of the enterprise in which labour is expended	• Fragmentation of enterprises • Growth in atypical jobs • Growth in labour hire/agency employment	Multiple employers providing benefits that are supported by portability and pooling arrangements	• Increase portability of entitlements like parental, long service leave and sick leave (e.g. construction industry model of long service leave and the management of superannuation entitlements more generally). • Promote socially responsible labour hire/pooling arrangments (e.g. group training model)
Framework for regulating working life	Awards specifying rights at work and an array of ad hoc entitlements for when the person is not employed	• Growing interest in better matching work with other life interests (eg education, parenting, retirement, training, unemployment) • Career development often requires movement between employers as well as out of work (eg. education)	Integration of industrial and social policy rights on basis of notion of life cycle rights	• Better dovetailing of IR, Social Security, Superannuation and Vocational Education policy, especially concerning income support for time away from work • Consider extending availability and length of long service leave for career development purposes • Part time work as well as income support needs to be reconceptualised in this framework around the notion of transitional labour markets

In place of the classical wage earner model we propose a more encompassing 'working life model.' At the core of this model is a different conception of the essential elements of our system of employment. What we should focus on are *workers* defined more broadly as *people who work* for *multiple employers* over the course of key phases of their life cycle, within the context of *integrated industrial and social security rights* provided by the state. Table 7.1 summaries the differences between the old framework and our proposed new model of working life. The key features of this table, especially concerning their implications for policy are considered in the following commentary.

The providers of labour: from employees to workers

One of the most fundamental dimensions of work concerns the legal status of the worker. For most of this century, rights for most workers have been defined on the basis of their status as an employee, that is, as a person employed on the basis of a contract of service by an employer. The development of comprehensive legal rights, obligations and protections arose from this status.

The once near-total domination of 'employees' as the people providing labour is now in decline. While many workers are still employees, much of the growth in employment, especially in the early 1990s took the form of contractors. At the same time, we should note that the employee classification itself has become increasingly differentiated. As late as the 1970s most employees were full-time and 'permanent'. Developments in the 1980s and 1990s reveal, however, that employees of this nature are in secular decline, with casuals and part-timers on the rise. Clearly the category of 'employees' needs rethinking if policy is to have a more effective purchase in the future.

How should the inadequacy of the traditional notions of employee status be managed? Ideally, a worker's rights and entitlements should be defined on the basis of *the effort expended in the production of a good or service for which payment of some kind is received*. In place of the 'employee' we believe it makes far more sense to deal with the concept 'worker' (also see Ewing 1996). Such arrangements should cut through the fictions of contracts *of* service and contracts *for* service, 'award free' employees and 'casual' workers. A precedent for such an approach is provided by over 40 years of experience in the NSW jurisdiction in dealing with independent contractors, especially in road transport. The latest version of this approach to a sensible definition of 'worker' can be found in S106 of the NSW *Industrial Relations Act 1996*. This provision confers jurisdiction on the NSW Industrial Relations Commission to deal with what are termed 'unfair contracts'. All that is required for this provision to operate is that a contract exist and that it is one that concerns 'a person perform[ing] work in an industry'.[4] This has provided independent contractors as well as many professional and managerial workers with some protections which they normally do not enjoy because they lack 'employee status' required for many awards and statutory entitlements (Nomchong 1998, pp. 2-3).[5]

Changes to industrial law alone are unlikely to be adequate. Much of the growth in contractor employment has been underpinned by taxation law and practice (Buchanan and Cameron 1998). This has especially been the case in industries such as construction. In this sector special tax arrangements devised initially to capture taxation revenue from the black economy have unintentionally facilitated the easy shift of workers from 'Pay As You Earn' (PAYE) employees to contractors. This development has not just undermined the efficacy of awards. Losses to tax revenue from this industry alone arising from the shift in workers status have been estimated to be between $500 and one billion dollars per annum (Buchanan and Cameron 1998). Relatively modest changes to taxation administration such as stricter reporting and auditing requirements could address this situation. Such initiatives would simultaneously work to restore the integrity and fairness in the industrial relations and taxation systems. As such they would provide a good complement to the more comprehensive reforms concerning the characterisation of workers proposed in the preceding paragraph.

Providers of jobs and employment benefits: augmenting the enterprise with portability and pooling arrangements

The second fundamental assumption underpinning work-related policy concerns who provides jobs and employment benefits, that is, the enterprise. In recent years industrial relations policy has become 'more enterprise focussed' than ever. The irony of this development is that, at the same time, enterprises have become less employment focussed. One of the major outcomes of organisational restructuring in Australian workplaces and enterprises is a declining commitment to the workforce over the longer term, particularly with regard to training, skills development and job security. How are we to respond?

Clearly the enterprise as traditionally conceived no longer provides, on its own, a sound basis for managing employer obligations for a growing number of workers. Complementary mechanisms need to be developed. These are proposed not to provide employers with more options to wriggle out of their obligations to workers. Rather they have been devised to address the growing problems concerning portability of entitlements between employers and sharing the risk associated with less secure forms of employment.

The issue of portability and security of entitlements is particularly important for workers' rights to maternity/paternity leave, sick leave, long service leave and redundancy payments. Workers who move regularly between organisations or enterprises rarely manage to accrue these kinds of rights. They are also entitlements which are highly vulnerable when firms close down. Defining such entitlements purely with reference to 'the enterprise' is often meaningless. It is important that such entitlements earned by workers are enforceable against more secure entities. A good example of such an arrangement is provided by the long service leave arrangements that apply in the construction industry. These ensure that all workers, employees and contractors, accrue long service leave entitlements on the basis of hours worked. Given the unstable and transient nature of many employers in the industry, as well as the high turnover of staff, this system offers the best way of protecting building workers' rights. Because more industries are now taking on the characteristics of the unstable forms of employment characteristic of construction, this system provides a potentially valuable model for other sectors. The development of portable superannuation arrangements in the 1980s and early 1990s provides another example of how work-based entitlements can be freed from the rigidity of relying on one employer to manage the entitlement.

As well as the question of portability of entitlements is the issue of pooling risk. Currently most corporate restructuring involves companies pushing more of the risks and uncertainty surrounding work onto workers. This is the outcome of new forms of competition. While it's important to get organisations to become individually more 'responsible', it's also useful to find more effective ways of *managing the risks* associated with employment on a fairer, shared basis. A number of researchers in Europe have argued that formally organised 'employment pools' offer a way of addressing this problem (see Casten von Otter, 1995). An example of how such pools work locally is provided by group training schemes. Under these arrangements, apprentices and trainees are indentured to a group scheme, but their training and employment is provided by a host employer who hires them out for certain blocks of work. The schemes work well to ensure that organisations have access to the labour they need, when they need it. They also ensure that a larger number of employers are involved in training new labour than would otherwise be the case. Group training arrangements currently only apply to new entrants to the workforce taking up apprenticeships or traineeships, but they could work equally well for all categories of worker wherever conditions of irregular labour demand make it feasible. Of course, a version of this exists already, in the form of labour hire agencies and temporary work agencies. They provide a similar pooling service but often at less attractive conditions of employment for the workers involved. The group training schemes offers a superior model of how such labour pooling arrangements could work in the future (further details on Group Training can be found in Australia Parliament 1995; ACIRRT 1997).

Augmenting the enterprise with portability and pooling arrangements has the potential to improve options available for both workers and management. The benefits for workers are clear. For management they offer the potential for increasing available supplies of skilled labour that can be drawn on to meet unexpected fluctuations in demand in a way that improves efficiency and fairness simultaneously. They provide a clear example of how choice and flexibility within the enterprise can be increased through the better co-ordination of activities and organisations beyond it. In short, they provide management with flexibility without ongoing costs and uncertainties of current arrangements.

The framework: from awards and ad hoc income support to integration of industrial and social security rights over the life cycle

Finally, it is important to consider the nature of the framework regulating work. The assumptions underpinning the classical wage earner model no longer hold true. The rise in the underlying rate of unemployment means that state structures geared to maintaining labour standards for people at work, and income support for brief spells when out of work, is now stretched to the limit. Fewer 'permanent jobs for life' are now available, evident in the rise in casual employment. In addition, internal labour markets are being dismantled, especially in industries such as banking and the public service. As a result 'career development' often requires movement between employers, as well as time out of the workforce and in full-time education and training. Moreover, there is declining interest amongst workers in having a single, full-time permanent job for life. Instead, there is a growing demand in matching work with different life priorities such as education, parenting, care for aged relatives and retirement. These developments in the nature of the jobs available, and in the changing aspirations of workers, raise questions about access to entitlements. How are things like quality part-time work, flexible career paths and rights to leave for key life transitions to be managed? In particular, the challenge is to identify how best to realign wages, industrial relations policy and social policy.

Researcher Gunter Schmid from West Germany has proposed that policy concerning work and the labour market needs to be broadened to ensure it addresses the issues identified above. In particular, Schmid proposes the idea of 'transitional labour markets', that is, institutional arrangements which provide decent job opportunities for those wishing to deviate from 'standard time employment' at various stages of their lives (Schmid 1995, 1996, European Academy of the Urban Environment 1998). Schmid devotes most attention to 5 different types of transitional labour markets. These concern the transitions between:

1. education, training and employment;
2. domestic work or private activities and gainful employment;
3. short-time work and full-time work;
4. unemployment and employment; and
5. full-time work and retirement.

Many workers involved in such transitions have only a marginal or precarious attachment to the mainstream labour market. Schmid argues that, given the growing proportion of the labour force working in such situations, it is essential that policies and practices be developed to improve the operation of such 'transitional labour markets'. He sees the formalisation of transitional labour markets as an alternative to the growth of the 'secondary' labour market. In the United States the secondary labour market takes the form of unsubsidised, low-wage jobs. In Europe (and Australia) it takes the form of an ever growing group dependent on social security payments. For Schmid, transitional labour markets are a mechanism which could grow in recessions and contract during booms, thereby dampening the more extreme effects of swings in the economic cycle.

However, the real attraction of Schmid's proposals is that he offers an alternative approach to employment reform which involves more than simply advocating the creation of full-time, permanent jobs. While such jobs should be available to all (as we argued above), policy also needs to address all the other facets of labour market change, not just the shamefully high level of unemployment.

Schmid's ideas are potentially relevant for contemporary Australia. If workers are to have a real choice in balancing work and other commitments/interests, it is essential that supportive structures are established to minimise the losses associated with exercising such choices. For example, workers going part-time to help with parenting face immediate financial loss (fewer hours worked, fewer wages); reductions in employment-based entitlements (such as superannuation and long service leave); and serious disruptions to career advancement (because many 'career' jobs are not available on a part-time basis). Because of this there is a strong case for extending rights to income support to supplement key transitions in life. It's also necessary to improve the quality of part-time jobs to make them more attractive for people wishing to strike a different balance between work and other aspects of life. Key transitions deserving consideration for better 'management' are listed below.

❑ *School and tertiary education to work.* As well as increasing the levels of allowances paid to people in this situation, policy should also look at improving the quality of part-time work available. Better rostering, pooling and portability arrangements could facilitate such an outcome

❑ *Employment to unemployment.* Consideration needs to be given to developing income support associated with short-time working. Faced with a downturn in demand, companies could move to a system of short-time work to share the available work around. More often than not workers are retrenched because short-time work results in non-viable levels of take-home-pay for many low-paid workers. An alternative would be for workers working short-time to be entitled to unemployment benefit for the time they are off work. Such schemes work well in Germany and have been trialed in the United States and Canada. There is a case for extending our social security entitlements to 'part-time' unemployment of this nature.

❑ *The transition to parenthood.* The birth of a child can have a major impact on people's lives. The right to work part-time, as well as some kind of 'new parenting' benefit, could improve the quality of child rearing significantly and also ease the pressure on young parents.

❑ *The transition to retirement.* Too often it seems workers near the end of their careers are either retrenched and end up unemployed or retire early. Many indicate that they do not wish to finish their work life early or to work full-time until they retire. Phased retirement, involving a blend of part-time work and access to pensions would be a desirable alternative. Such choices will only really be available if (a) employers agree to change their approaches to employing older workers on a part-time basis and (b) if income support is available to ease the financial burden of such a transition.

Revamping the assumptions about the key elements of our system of employment will ensure that the concepts informing policy correspond more closely to reality. But more than this, getting the basic categories right for understanding today's labour market realities gives us the conceptual tools needed for thinking through new and better ways of addressing the key problems identified in this book. As Chapters 4, 5 and 6 revealed there are now major challenges concerning wages, hours of work and employment security that need to be addressed. Our responses to these issues are summarised in Table 7.2. This Table outlines the key features of what a new approach to working life might look like. Again the key features of this table, especially concerning their implications for policy, are considered in the accompanying commentary.

Table 7.2: Rethinking priorities concerning wages, hours and employment security: current and 'working life' policy approaches compared

Key dimensions of working life	Current bases for determining rights and obligations	Current challenges for policy	Proposed new bases for defining rights and obligations	Examples of new initiatives needed
Wages	Safety Net Adustments and enterprise bargaining	• Growing inequality amongst employees (e.g. working poor and the unskilled) as well as between employees and other categories of workers	Universal standards for remuneration for work, effort or task	• Standards set at 'civilised' not minimalist levels • Fair relativities encompassing high as well as low income earners
Working time entitlements	The full-time, standard worker model	• Demise of full-time work increasing irregular hours of work for all with jobs	Work scheduling arrangements	• Develop substantive and procedural rights concerning shift lengths, frequency, rest breaks, maximum hours per week, month and year and allocation
Employment security	Full employment Employment protection laws	• Demise of job for life • Risks and uncertainties surrounding employment increasingly pushed onto employees • Rising underlying rate of unemployment	Portability and pooling arrangements to complement wider range of measures	• Increase portability and pooling arrangements • Can only be achieved with all the above and successful adoption of wider policy mix delivering inclusive full employment

Wages: revamping the foundations for a new era

In recent times it has been fashionable to argue that award standards should only provide a minimal 'safety net' for those labour market 'losers' who cannot settle an enterprise agreement. The undesirable outcomes of this policy stance were clearly illustrated in Chapter 4. At ACIRRT we believe that basic labour market standards should provide a central reference point for work-related issues and beyond (such as social policy) (Buchanan and Watson 1997, p. 32–34). Indeed, we would argue that *the treatment of people at work is one of the leading indicators of a civilised society*. As such standards should not be regarded a residual for labour market 'losers', but rather provide a basis for cohesion and integration in the labour market. This will, however, require a dramatic rethinking of how such standards are developed and applied in practice.

In particular, basic wage levels need to be totally rethought. In the early days of arbitration the 'Basic Wage' was established as essentially a family wage for the male bread winner and lower rates were deliberately set for women as a result (Macintyre 1986). In the course of the 1960s and 1970s, major gains were made in rectifying gender-based wage inequalities, but problems still remain. Women still suffer discrimination in the wages system, an issue currently under review in the NSW jurisdiction (NSW DIR 1997; Heiler 1998). More importantly the foundations for wages policy for contemporary conditions have not been properly developed. In the 1997 Living Wage Case, the AIRC rejected the idea that changing labour conditions should play a part in the setting of basic wage levels. They preferred instead to treat the case as just another Safety Net Adjustment. In the 1998 Living Wage Case, the ground began to shift, and the issue of growing income inequality entered the equation. At present, then, the consequences of polarising incomes and fragmenting wage-fixing mechanisms have not been adequately addressed. If wages policy is to have a coherent foundation as one of the key elements of working life policy, this issue will need to be re-examined. In particular:

❑ what is the unit for calculating a living wage: individual or household?
❑ how does the wages system link with the social security system?
❑ how are living standards for a civilised society to measured?

Considerable materials are now available for addressing issues such as these. The Social Policy Research Centre, for example, has completed a comprehensive study of the 'budget standards' required for basic and adequate living standards (SPRC 1998). This provides a powerful resource for putting wages policy on a more coherent footing. In addition more attention needs to be given to the management of wage relativities. Within the award system the 'minimum rates adjustment process' provides a coherent framework for setting relativities for minimum rates of pay for the waged workforce. These principles need to be extended to others in the workforce. The large salaries of top income earners have attracted considerable attention in recent times. Instead of being a source of public comment and complaint these need to be seriously addressed and encompassed within the framework of wages policy applying more generally. Many years ago the Noble Laureate, James Tobin, explored the possibility of using the tax system to regulate excess wage movements (see for example Withers 1982, Neale 1986 and Alexander 1989). This debate needs to be revived. In this context we note with interest recent reports that the non-executive directors of Australia's largest companies do not think remuneration should be linked to performance (Carr 1998, p. 19). Clearly the time is ripe for a rational debate about the management of remuneration relativities for the top end of the labour market, not just the bottom. Such a debate will require a dramatic rethinking of how remunerations standards are developed and applied in practice. For example, instead of having awards set standards for employees we could consider having more generally applicable 'work orders' which have the potential to encompass tax penalties for upper income workers who grant themselves increases in income that exceed community standards.

We believe it is essential that remuneration levels are based on principles of civilised living standards and fair relativities, rather than the capacity of particular employers to pay. In recent times it has been suggested that wages should fall to 'market clearing' levels and that people should be prevented from starving by government payment of a guaranteed minimum income (GMI) or tax credit (e.g. Dawkins et al. 1997). This is an invitation to promote a plethora of low-wage jobs and attract scarce capital into a low productivity sector. We regard such a policy as undesirable on a number of grounds. First, it represents a massive subsidy from the public sector to employers, they do not have to pay the full cost of maintaining the livelihoods of their workforce. Secondly, it does not address the problem of low pay and inequality at its source. *Many problems associated with living standards originate in the labour market and need to be addressed there.* A GMI or tax credit would simply promote the generation of further low-paid jobs. Far from being a solution it would simply exacerbate problems of low wage, low productivity employment (see Polanyi 1957 and Apps 1997).

Hours: augmenting the full-time worker model with work scheduling rights

As we have seen, changes in working time have been profound. Many of the assumptions concerning working time rights have not kept pace with these changes. The notion of 'standard' working time arrangements is well understood. It involves an eight-hour day worked over a five-day work week during 11 months of the year over a 45-year working life. Many labour market regulations, work-related entitlements and social benefits are built around this model of working time. For example:

- ❑ the eight-hour day is usually defined as falling within a span of 'normal' hours—work performed outside this span attracts a penalty or loading for working during what is commonly referred to as 'anti-social' hours;
- ❑ the five-day work week provides the basis for calculating overtime entitlements—hours worked in excess of the 'the standard working week' attract overtime penalties;
- ❑ rights to annual recreation leave, sick leave and other forms of leave are calculated on the basis of the standard working year; and
- ❑ superannuation and long service leave entitlements are calculated on the basis of assumptions about job tenure and length of service with particular employers.

How should policy respond to changes of the type outlined in Chapter 5? Our argument is that the demise of the standard working time model and people's changing preference does not mean there is a need to abolish working time standards. Universal working time rights and agreements may need to be implemented at workplace and industry level. In this context we believe the traditional approach to regulating working time needs to be augmented with substantive and procedural rights concerning work scheduling. Key issues surrounding work scheduling which could be subjects of basic standards include:

❑ limit the number of people who are scheduled for work, so that the work available is apportioned in such a way as to allow all involved to earn a living wage;
❑ require rosters and work schedules to be drawn up as far as possible in advance to allow people to plan with certainty other parts of their lives;
❑ regulate the minimum call in time per session, the maximum call in times per session, and the breaks between session;
❑ set minimum and maximum hours that can be worked over a week, a month and a year;
❑ set rights to negotiate rostered time on and off, and rights to vary schedules once they are set (provided adequate notice or suitable, alternative labour is located);
❑ set clear appeal rights for those aggrieved by the design and/or operation of a schedule (these could be based on established grievance procedures in awards or agreements or by developing supplementary procedures designed especially for working time issues);
❑ generally, there needs to be basic rights to information, notice and to negotiate the design and functioning of work scheduling systems for all workers in a work group or workplace affected by a rostering system. Such general rights would provide a good safeguard on the operation of the other principles noted above.

In addition consideration needs to be given to reducing the length of the standard hours required to earn a living wage. Reduction in standard hours of work are an indication of how advanced a civilisation is. Progress on this issue has stagnated in Australia in recent years. It is essential that debate on this issue begins again. Such a debate also needs to consider raising base rates for the low paid to ensure they have adequate living standards. In addition, policies controlling overtime also need to be considered. These help ensure that reductions in standard hours bring about increased leisure and also maximise the possibilities of reducing unemployment (Buchanan and Bearfield 1997). In this context we note that Germany is debating an initiative for a standard working week of 32 hours, and France is experimenting with a wide range of working time reforms, including measures aimed at controlling unpaid overtime, especially amongst managerial and professional employees (OECD 1998, Ch. 5).

Employment security: more than a matter of working life policy alone

Without doubt the most important objective for policy on working life is to increase levels of employment security. In the 1990s the controversy surrounding increased unfair dismissal rights for employees has been the focal point of much of this debate. But what this debate has ignored is the fact that employment security is not something that can be simply legislated into existence or guaranteed by an industrial agreement. As Chapter 6 suggested, the problem is multi-dimensional and deep seated and must be addressed as a matter of macro-economic policy. As we argued earlier in this chapter, a full-employment policy and a revitalised manufacturing sector are essential for dealing with the problems of job insecurity. What Australia basically needs is a *new, socially inclusive social settlement* which puts an end to the emergence of two nations, the growing situation where society is split between those who have proper jobs and those who don't. As Elliot and Atkinson so eloquently put it:

All the employment regulations in the world cannot create a buoyant labour market in which employees can have the confidence to move jobs, to demand a better deal and—from time to time—down tools. Only an activist and expansionary economic policy can bring these conditions about, one combined with simplified tax and other paper work requirements on both employees and employers. True flexibility is our aim: one in which the employee enjoys the same ability to 'up sticks' as does the employer. No law, no verdict, is as liberating for the worker as the certain knowledge that an alternative job is waiting just down the road (1998, p. 287).

CONCLUSION

Life at work has been getting harder and less certain for many Australians. This is not inevitable in the longer term. The key issue is how to meet the growing challenges of increasing international competitiveness and maintaining decent living standards for all. Clearly the old policy mix inspired by the post-war settlement and based on the classical wage earner model is inadequate. But so too is the emerging neo-liberal alternative. An approach which goes beyond the limits of both is clearly needed. By themselves, industrial relations and labour market 'reforms' are not enough. However, in the context of a broader policy mix they can make an important contribution. The key issue in this regard is to build labour market and industrial relations policy around the equity aspects of work in Australia today. The new realities of work, and not the outdated assumptions of the past, must be our starting point. A more inclusive model of working life provides an appropriate basis: one built on the notions of people as 'workers', with pooling and portability arrangements where needed, with better integration between the industrial and social security frameworks, and with entitlements based on the concept of life cycle rights. Once we work out these kinds of ideas more fully, we then have a coherent basis for developing new responses to the problems concerning wages, hours of work and, to a lesser extent, employment insecurity. Unless changes are undertaken, we are likely to witness a further deterioration in the quality of jobs and people's relations at work. In the long run this also means a decline in productivity and efficiency.

We conclude by noting that growing numbers of Australians are being adversely affected by the rut within which policy is now stuck. Clearly, we must move on to a more positive policy trajectory which simultaneously promotes fairness and efficiency at work. For too long managers have believed in the fiction that all they do is 'just manage'. The result of this philosophy is that more and more people are 'just managing' to get by. It is time policy promoted a situation in which justice played a greater role in the way issues are managed at work. It is hoped this book makes a modest contribution to that outcome.

Notes

1   In Europe ultra nationalist forces in France and Germany have gained as much as 10–15 per cent of the vote at national and local elections. While racism forms a significant basis for their political platforms they also have a program committed to keeping all foreign threats at bay. In 1996 a groundswell of support for 'isolationist' foreign policy and protectionist industry policy was mobilised by Pat Buchanan, a Republican nominee for the presidential election of that year.

2   See for example Pauline Hanson's One Nation (1998) *Queensland State Election Small Business Position Statement*, http:/www.gwb.com.au/onenation/qldstate/polsmall.htm (accessed 29 July 1998) especially the section entitled: Status of Unions and Enterprise Bargaining.

> 11. One Nation policy is to support enterprise based unions, and encourage enterprise bargaining.
>
> 12. One Nation acknowledges the important role that unions have played in Australia. One Nation is concerned that employees are adequately represented when enterprise bargaining, and that state and federal governments establish minimum levels of wages and fundamental work conditions to protect Australian workers from the pressure which can be applied by employers, particularly when low cost labour is available from recent immigrants from countries with lower living standards than our own.

3   Note that the expression concerning the market being a good servant but a bad master is commonly attributed to Beveridge. See Eatwell (1982) and Froud (1997).

4   This expression was used in *Walker v Hussman Aust Pty Ltd* (1991) 40 IR 180 as cited in Nomchong 1998 p. 3.

5   Debate on the inadequacy of traditional notions of contract for underpinning the employment of labour has been intense amongst industrial lawyers for many decades. Some of the most recent contributions to debate have been considered in papers by Brooks 1993 and Creighton 1997.

References

ABS (Australian Bureau of Statistics) (1978–1998), *Labour Force Australia*, Cat. no. 6203.0, ABS, Canberra.

ABS (1990), *Award Coverage Australia*, Cat. no. 6315.0, ABS, Canberra.

ABS (1993a), *Training and Education Experience, Australia*, Cat. no. 6278.0, ABS, Canberra.

ABS (1993b), *Survey of Training and Education CURF*, Confidentialised Unit Record File.

ABS (1996a), *Labour Force Australia, 1978–1995*, Cat. no. 6204.0, ABS, Canberra.

ABS (1996b), *Trade Union Members, Australia*, Cat. no. 6325.0, ABS, Canberra.

ABS (1997a), *Australian National Accounts*, Cat. no. 5204.0, ABS, Canberra. .

ABS (1997b), *Working Arrangements*, Catalogue no. 6342.0, ABS, Canberra.

ABS (1997c), *Award Rates of Pay Indexes, Australia*, Cat. no. 6312.0, ABS, Canberra.

ABS (1997d), *SEUPDATE*, Edition 3, ABS, Canberra.

ABS (1997e), *Australian Women's Yearbook*, Cat. no. 4124.0, ABS, Canberra. .

ABS (1998a), *Australian Economic Indicators, February, 1998*, Cat. no. 1350.0, ABS, Canberra.

ABS (1998b), *Australian Social Trends*, Cat no 4102.0, ABS, Canberra. .

ABS (1998c), *Industrial Disputes*, Cat no. 6321.0, AGPS, Canberra.

ABS (1998d), *Persons in the Labour Force, Australia*, Cat no 6220.0, ABS, Canberra.

ABS (1998e), *Wage and Salary Earners, Australia*, Cat. no. 6248.0, ABS, Canberra.

ACAC (Australian Conciliation and Arbitration Commission), (1987), *National Wage Case, March 1987*. Print G6800.

ACIRRT (Australian Centre for Industrial Relations Research and Training) (1996), *ADAM Report, No. 8, March*.

ACIRRT (1997), *ADAM Report, No. 13, June*.

ACIRRT (1997) The Development of Quality Arrangements in Group Training. Report for NSW Department, of Training and Education Co-ordination, Unpublished.

ACIRRT (1998), *The Growth of Contractors in the Construction Industry: Implications for Tax Revenue*, ACIRRT Working Paper No. 54, ACIRRT, University of Sydney, Sydney.

ACOSS (Australian Council of Social Service) (1998), *ACOSS Agenda for Tax Reform*, ACOSS, Surry Hills, NSW.

ACTU (1991), *Congress Report*.

ACTU (1996), *1996 New Living Wage Case*, Speakers' Notes, July, pp 3–7.

ACTU (1997), *Stress at work—the 'sleeping giant' issue in Australian workplaces*, ACTU Media Release October 19.

ACTU and TDC Mission to Western Europe (1987), *Australia Reconstructed*, AGPS, Canberra.

ACTU, OH & S Unit (1997), *Report on the 1997 ACTU National Survey of Stress at Work: Stress at Work, Not What We Bargained For*, ACTU, Melbourne.

AIRC (Australian Industrial Relations Commission), (1988), *National Wage Case, August 1988. Print H4000*, AGPS, Canberra.

AIRC (1997), *Safety Net Review—Wages, April 1997*, The Commission, Melbourne.

AIRC (1998), *Safety Net Review—Wages, April 1998, Joint Governments' Submission*, Department of Workplace Relations and Small Business, Canberra.

AMWU (Australian Manufacturing Workers' Union), (1995), *Australia in Transition*, Melbourne.

AMWU (1996), *Part-time and Casual Employment: a Discussion Paper*.

AMWU (1997), *Rebuilding Australia: Industry Development For More Jobs*, AMWU, Granville, NSW.

Alexander, J. (1989), 'The Political Economy of Tax-Based Incomes Policy; Wealth Effects of Post-Keynesian TIP', *Journal of Economic Issues*, March, vol. XXIII, no. 1, pp. 135–146.

Apps, P. (1998), "Income Distribution, Redistribution and Incentives, *Wealth, Work, Well-being*, Occasional Paper 1/1998, Academy of the Social Sciences in Australia, Canberra.

Apps, P. (1992), 'The Failure of Financial Deregulation', *Quadrant*, November, pp. 53–56.

Armitage, C. (1996), 'Unis Tell Staff: Work on Weekends', *Australian*, September 18, 1996.

Australia. Parliament.Standing Committee on Employment, Education and Training (1995), *A Best Kept Secret: Report on the Role and Effectiveness of Group Training Companies*, Commonwealth of Australia, Canberra.

Australia. Department of Labour and National Service (1970), *The Training of Skilled Workers in Europe: Summary of Report of the Australian Tripartite Mission, 1968-69*, The Department, Melbourne.

The Australian (1994), 21 December, p. 6.

The Australian (1998), 9 June, p. 42.

Australian Business Chamber, (1997), *The High Road or the Low Road? Alternatives for Australia's Future*, A Report on Australia's Industrial Structure, Australian Business Foundation, North Sydney, NSW.

Australian Financial Review (1997), 'The Million Dollar Bosses', October 11–12, pp. 29.

Barrowclough, N. (1998), 'They get what?!', *Sydney Morning Herald*, Good Weekend, June 6, pp. 16–20.

Barry, A. Osborne, T. & Rose, N. (1996), (eds.), *Foucault and Political Reason*, University College Press, London.

Barry, P. (1993), *The Rise and Rise of Kerry Packer*, Bantam Book, Sydney.

Baumol, W.J., Blackman, S.E. & Wolff, E.N. (1989), *Productivity and American Leadership:The Long View,* MIT Press, Cambridge, Mass.

Beilharz, P. (1994), *Transforming Labor: Labour Tradition and the Labor Decade in Australia*, Cambridge University Press, Cambridge and Melbourne.

Belchamber, G. (1996), 'Disappearing middle or vanishing bottom? A comment on Gregory.', *The Economic Record*, September, vol. 72, no. 218, pp. 287–293.

Bell, J. (1996), *Preliminary Analysis of 116 Agreements Made Under the Victorian Employee Relations Act*, Mimeo, Australian National University, Canberra.

Benson, J. & Ieronimo, N. (1996), 'Outsourcing decisions: Evidence from Australian-Based Enterprises', *International Labour Review*, vol. 135, no. 1, pp. 59–73.

Biernacki, R. (1995), *The Fabrication of Labor: Germany & Britain 1640–1914*, University of California Press, Berkeley, CA.

Bittman, M. (1991) *Juggling Time: How Australian Families Use Time*, Office of Status of Women, Department of Prime Minister and Cabinet, Canberra.

Bittman, M. (ed.) (1997), *Poverty in Australia: Dimensions and Policies*, Reports and Proceedings No 135 May, Social Policy Research Centre, UNSW, Kensington, NSW.

Blake, Dawson, Waldron (1998), *Industrial Relations and Employment Briefs*, Blake, Dawson Waldron, Sydney. .

Bluestone, B. & Harrison, B. (1982), *The Deindustrialization of America: Plant Closings, Community Abondonment, and the Dismantling of Basic Industry*, Basic Books, New York.

Borland, J. (1996), .'Earnings Inequality in Australia: Changes and Causes', Centre for Economic Policy Research, ANU, Canberra. (Downloaded from Canadian International Labour Network, Working Papers Archive, http://labour.ciln.mcmaster.ca/papers).

Borland, J. & Norris, K. (1996) 'Equity', Chapter 6, *The Changing Australian Labour Market*, EPAC Commission Paper 11, K. Norris and M. Wooden (eds.), AGPS, Canberra.

Borland, J. Hirschberg, J. & Lye, J. (1996), *Earnings of Public Sector and Private Sector Employees in Australia: Is There a Difference?*, Research Paper No. 514, Department of Economics, University of Melbourne, Parkville, Victoria.

Bramble, T. & Fieldes, D. (1992), 'Post-Fordism: Historical Break or Utopian Fantasy?', *Journal of Industrial Relations*, vol. 34, no. 4, pp. 562–79.

Brenner, R. (1998), 'The Economics of Global Turbulence: A Special Report on the World Economy, 1950–98', *New Left Review*, no. 229, whole issue.

Briggs, C. (1994), *Trade Unions and Economic Restructuring: Strategic Unionism in the Clothing Industry*, ACIRRT Monograph No. 11, ACIRRT, University of Sydney, Sydney.

Brooks, A. (1993), 'The Contract of Employment and Workplace Agreements', Proceedings from a Conference, Sydney, 30th April, 1993, *A New Province for Legalism: Legal Issues and the Deregulation of Industrial Regulations*, Proceedings from a Conference, Sydney, 30th April, 1993. ACCIRT Monograph, No. 9, P.Ronfeldt & R. McCallum (eds.), ACIRRT, University of Sydney, Sydney.

Brosnan, P. (1996), 'The Dynamics of Change Between Standard and Non-Standard Employment', *Non Standard Employment in Australia and New Zealand*, Monograph 9, J. Teicher (ed.), National Key Centre in Industrial Relations, Monash University, Melbourne, pp. 23–42.

Brotherhood of Saint Laurence (1996), *Written Submission to the National Wage Case*, November, Brotherhood of Saint Laurence, Fitzroy, Vic.

Buchanan, J. & Bearfield, S. (1997), *Reforming Working Time: Alternatives to Unemployment, Casualisation and Extended Hours*, Brotherhood of St Laurence, Fitzroy, Vic.

Buchanan, J. & Campbell, D. (1992), *Retraining, Redeployment and Retrenchment Practices: A Review of Recent Overseas Literature*, Working Paper 22, ACIRRT, University of Sydney, Sydney.

Buchanan, J. & Watson, I. 'The Living Wage and the Working Poor', *Poverty in Australia: Dimensions and Policies*, Reports and Proceedings No 135, M. Bittman (ed.), Social Policy Research Centre, UNSW, Kensington, NSW.

Buchanan, J., Campbell, D., Callus, R. & Rimmer, M. (1992), *Facing Retrenchments: Strategies and Alternatives for Enterprises*, Office for Labour Market Adjustment, AGPS, Canberra.

Buffini, F. (1997), 'When making a sacrifice can lead to a tidy little package', *Australian Financial Review*, November 15–16.

Burgess, J. (1994), 'Restructuring the Australian Labour Force: From Full Employment to Where?', *Journal of Australian Political Economy*, no. 34, pp. 103–127.

Burgess, J. & Campbell, I. (1993), *Moving Towards A Deregulated Labour Market: Part-Time Work and the Recession in Australia*, ESC Working Paper No 11, Employment Studies Centre, University of Newcastle, Newcastle.

Burgess, J. & Campbell, I. (1998), 'Casual Employment in Australia: Growth, Characteristics, A Bridge or a Trap?', *The Economic and Labour Relations Review*, June, vol. 9, no. 1, pp. 31–54.

Business Council of Australia (BCA) (1989), *Enterprise Based Bargaining Units: A Better Way of Working: Report to the Business Council of Australia*, BCA, Melbourne.

Business Review Weekly (BRW) (1983), November12–18, pp. 24–82. .

Business Review Weekly (1998), 'Rich 200 in the Ranks', 25 May 1998, pp. 76.

Callus, R. & Buchanan, J. (1993), 'Efficiency & Equity at Work: The Need for Labour Market Regulation in Australia', *Journal of Industrial Relations*, vol. 35, no. 4, pp. 515–538.

Callus, R. Morehead, A. Cully, M. & Buchanan, J. (1991), *Industrial Relations at Work: The Australian Workplace Industrial Relations Survey (AWIRS 90)*, Commonwealth Department of Industrial Relations, AGPS, Canberra.

Callus, R., Kitay, J. & Sutcliffe, P. (1992), 'Industrial Relations at Small Business Workplaces', *Small Business Review*, AGPS, Canberra.

Campbell, D. & Rimmer, M. (1994), 'Managing Retrenchment: Award Standards or Enterprise Agreements?', *Australian Bulletin of Labour*, vol. 20, no. 1, pp. 45–65.

Campbell, I. (1996), 'Casual Employment, Labour Regulation and Australian Trade Unions', *Journal of Industrial Relations*, vol. 38, no. 4, December, pp.571–599.

Campbell, I. (1996) 'The Growth of Casual Employment in Australia: Towards an Explanation', *Non Standard Employment in Australia and New Zealand*, Monograph 9, J. Teicher (ed.), National Key Centre in Industrial Relations, Monash University, Melbourne.

Cappelli, P. et al. (1997), *Change at Work*, Oxford University Press, New York.

Carr, E. (1997), 'Do the Million Dollar Managers Deliver Value for Money?', *Australian Financial Review*, 11–12 Oct, pp. 29.

Castles, F.G. (1985), *The Working Class and Welfare*, Allen and Unwin, Sydney.

Clark, C., Geer, T. & Underhill, B. (1996), *The Changing of Australian Manufacturing*, Productivity Commission, Staff Information Paper, AGPS, Canberra.

Cleary, P. (1997a), 'How the Axe Fell on 3.3 Million', *Sydney Morning Herald*, October 20, p.1.

Cleary, P. (1997b), 'Manufacturing Hit Hardest', *Sydney Morning Herald*, October 22, p.6.

Collins, H. (1990), 'Independent Contractors and the Challenge of Vertical Integration to Employment Protection Laws', *Oxford Journal of Legal Studies*, vol. 10, no. 3, pp. 353–380.

Creighton, B. & Stewart, A. (1990), *Labour Law: An Introduction*, Federation Press, Sydney.

Creighton, B., (1997) 'Reforming the Contract of Employment', *Individual Contracts and Workplace Relations,* ACIRRT Working Paper No. 50, A. Frazer, R. McCallum & P. Ronfeldt (eds.), ACIRRT, University of Sydney, Sydney.

Cross, M. (ed.) (1985), *Managing Workforce Reduction*, Croom Helm, London.

Crossweller, A. (1997), 'Blue-collar White-out', *Australian*, December 13–14, p. 35.

Curtain, R. (1985), *The Labour Market Experiences of Workers Made Redundant from the Whitegoods Industry in Sydney: Results from a Longitudinal Survey,* Discussion Paper No 124, Centre for Economic Policy Research, ANU, Canberra.

Cutler, T., Williams, K. & Williams, J. (1986), *Keynes, Beveridge and Beyond*, Routledge and Kegan Paul, London.

Dabscheck, B., Griffin, G. & Teicher, J. (1992) (eds.), *Contemporary Australian Industrial Relations*, Longmans Cheshire, Melbourne.

Davis M, & Long S (1997), 'Wages Growth Averaging 4.6 per cent', *Australian Financial Review*, November 15–16.

Dawkins, P. (1997) 'The distribution of work in Australia', *Changing Labour Markets: Prospects for Productivity Growth*, Productivity Commission (ed.), Canberra.

Dawkins, P. *Towards a Negative Income Tax System.* A Report to the Full Employment Project Melbourne Institute of Applied Economic and Social Research, University of Melbourne, The Institute, Melbourne.

Dawkins, P. & Norris, K. (1990), 'Casual Employment in Australia', *Australian Bulletin of Labour*, vol. 16, no. 3, September, pp.156–173.

Dean, A. (1992), 'The Sunday Shift', *Sydney Morning Herald*, February 12, p.17.

Deery, S. Brooks, R. & Morris, A. (1985), 'Redundancy and Public Policy in Australia', *Australian Bulletin of Labour*, vol. 11, no. June, pp. 154–77.

Deery, S. Griffin, G. Brown, M. & Dowling, P. (1986), 'The Labour Market Experience of Redundant Workers: A Study of Plant Closure', *Australian Bulletin of Labour*, vol. 12, no. 3, June, pp. 173–194.

DEET (Department of Employment, Education and Training) (1988), *Skill Formation and Structural Adjustment. The Responsiveness of Industry Training*, Economic and Policy Division, Discussion Paper No 3, AGPS, Canberra.

DEET (1989a), *COSTAC Consultancy. Costs of Award Restructuring*, Industry Analysis Branch, Economics and Policy Division, Draft Conceptual Framework Working Papers, Typescripts, November.

DEET (1989b), *Separation from Skilled Occupation: An analysis of 1986 Census Data for selected major professions, para-professions and Trades*, Economic and Policy Analysis Division, Discussion Paper No 6, September, AGPS, Canberra.

DIR (Dept. Of Industrial Relations) (1986), *Industrial Democracy and Employee Participation*, AGPS, Canberra.

DIR (1992), *Best and Fairest: The Quiet Revolution in our Workplaces*, AGPS, Canberra.

DIR (1988), *Towards a New Metal and Engineering Award: The Report of the DIR, MTFU and MTIA Mission to UK, Sweden and West Germany*.

DIR (1996), *Annual Report 1995: Enterprise Bargaining in Australia*, AGPS, Canberra.

DIRETFE (Dept.of Industrial Relations, Employment & Further Education) (1989), *Report on the Usage and Effectiveness of the Log Books for Cooks*, Prepared by Rexton Consulting Services, DIRETFE, Sydney.

DITAC (Dept. of Industry, Technology & Commerce) (1987), *Australian Industry New Directions*, AGPS, Canberra.

DITAC & OECD (1988), *Industrial R&D, Investment and Structural Change in Australian Manufacturing, An International Comparison*, AGPS, Canberra.

DOLAC (1988), *A Discussion Paper on Competency Based Trade Training*, September.

Dusevic, T. (1997), 'The Lost Weekend', *Sydney Morning Herald. Good Weekend*, 5 April, pp. 13–17.

Dyster, B. & Meredith, D. (1990), *Australia in the International Economy in the Twentieth Century*, Cambridge University Press, Melbourne.

Eaton, M. & Stilwell, F. (1992), 'The Super Rich in Australia', *Journal of Australian Political Economy*, no. 30, December, pp. 141–47.

Eatwell, J. (1982), *What Ever Happened to Britain? The Economics of Decline*, Duckworth & British Broadcasting Corporation, Britain.

Economic Planning Advisory Council (1992), *Education in the 1990s: Competencies, Credentialism, Competitiveness*, Papers presented at an office of the EPAC seminar held in Canberra on July 7 1992, August, AGPS, Canberra.

Edwards, J. (1996), *Keating: The Inside Story*, Penguin, Ringwood, Vic.

Edwards, R. (1979), *Contested Terrain, The Transformation of the Workplace in the Twentieth Century*, Basic Books, New York.

Ehrensaft, P. & Armstrong, W. (1978), 'Dominion Capitalism: A First Statement', *Australian and New Zealand Journal of Sociology*, vol. 14, no. 3, October, pp. 352–363.

Elliott, L.E. & Atkinson, D. (1998), *The Age of Insecurity*, Verso, London & New York.

Ellis, S. (1997), 'A High Five: the Rich Let the Good Times Roll', *Australian Financial Review*, September 2, pp. 1, 11.

Employment and Skills Formation Council (1992), *The Australian Vocational Training System*, March, NBEET.

European Academy of the Urban Environment (1998), *New Industrial Arrangements in the Labour Market: Transitional Labour Markets as a New Full Employment Concept*, The Academy, Berlin.

Evatt Foundation (1996), *Contract on Australia: A Report for the AMWU on the 'New Contract of Employment' Developing in Australia*, September.

Ewer, P., Hampson, I., Lloyd, C., Rainford, J., Rix, S. & Smith, M. (1991), *Politics and the Accord*, Pluto Press, Sydney.

Ewing, K. (1996), *Working Life—A New Perspective on Labour Law*, Institute of Employment Rights & Lawrence & Wishart, London.

Fightback! Fairness and Jobs (1992), Liberal Party, Barton, ACT.

Field, L. (1990), *Skilling Australia: A Handbook for TAFE Trainers and TAFE Teachers*, Longmans Cheshire, Melbourne.

Ford, G.W. (1982), 'Human Resource Development in Australia and the Balance of Skills', *Journal of Industrial Relations*, vol. 24, no. 3, September, pp. 443–453.

Fox, C. (1974), *Beyond Contract: Work, Power and Trust Relations*, Faber, London.

Froud, J., Haslam, C., Johal, S. & Williams, K. (1997), ''From Social Settlement to Household Lottery', *Economy and Society*, vol. 26, no. 3, pp. 340–372, (note: page numbers in text refer to original manuscript, not journal article).

Froud, J., Haslam, C. Johal, S. & Williams, K. (1997), *Beyond Efficiency: Old History and new Numbers*, Mimeo, University of Manchester, Manchester.

Fuller, D., Oxley, S. & Hayton, G. (1988), *Training for Australian Industry: a Guide to Research Techniques for Assessing Industry Training Requirements*, DEET and TAFE National Centre, AGPS, Canberra.

Gahan, P. (1992) 'Forward to the Past?', *Contemporary Australian Industrial Relations*, B. Dabscheck, G. Griffin & J. Teicher (eds.), Longmans Cheshire, Melbourne.

Gibson, K. (1993), *Different Merry-go-rounds*, Centre for Women's Studies and Department of Geography, Monash University, Clayton, Victoria.

Gilmore, P. & Lansbury, R. (1978), *Ticket to Nowhere: Training and Work in Australia*, Penguin, Ringwood, Vic.

Gittins, R. (1998), 'Bargaining Shows Some Enterprise', *Sydney Morning Herald*, June 1, pp. 37.

Gollan, P., Pickersgill, R. & Sullivan, G. (1996), *The Future of Work: Likely Long Term Developments in the Future of Industrial Relations*, ACIRRT Working Paper No. 43, ACIRRT, University of Sydney, Sydney.

Gospel, H. (1993), *Whatever Happened to Apprenticeship Training?*, ACIRRT Working Paper No. 28, ACIRRT, University of Sydney, Sydney.

Gospel, H. (1995), 'The Survival of Apprenticeship Training : A British, American, Australian Comparison', *British Journal of Industrial Relations*, vol. 32, no. 4, pp. 505–522.

Gouverneur, J. (1983), *Contemporary Capitalism and Marxist Economics*, Martin Robertson, Oxford.

Grant, G., Elbow, P. & Ewan, T. (1979), *On Competence: A Critical Analysis of Competence-Based Reforms in Higher Education*, Jossey-Bass, San Francisco.

Green, A. (1990), *Education and State Formation: the rise of education systems in England, France and the USA*, Macmillan, London.

Green, A. (1995) 'The Role of the State and the Social Partners in VET', *World Yearbook of Education, 1995*, Kogan Page, London.

Green, R. (1993), *Industry Policy and Jobs*, Discussion Paper No. 299. Originally, paper presented to the DEET-CEPR Conference: Unemployment: Causes, Costs and Solutions 16–17 February 1993, ANU Centre for Economic Policy Research, Canberra.

Gregory, R. (1993), 'Aspects of Australian and U.S. Hiring Standards: the Disappointing Decades, 1970–1990', *Economic Record, March*, pp. 61–76.

'Hunter Valley Decision Overturned' (1998), *Australian Industrial Law News (CCH)*, no. 2, February, p.9.

Hall, W. (1996), 'Direction for Research', *Australian Training Review*, no. 20 Sept/Oct/Nov, p.10.

Hancock, K. & Isaac, J. (1992), 'Australian Experiments in Wage Policy', *British Journal of Industrial Relations*, vol. 30, no. 2, pp. 213–236.

Hancock, K. & Rawson, D. (1993), 'The Metamorphosis of Australian Industrial Relations', *British Journal of Industrial Relations*, vol. 31, no. 4, pp. 489–513.

Hancock, K. (1998), 'The Needs of the Low Paid', *Wealth, Work, Well- Being Occasional Paper 1/98*, Published by Academy of the Social Sciences in Australia, Canberra, pp. 1–26.

Harding, A. (1994), *Poverty and Inequality in September 1994*, Paper presented at the ACOSS National Congress, Challenging the Divide: Equity in the Age of Efficiency, October 27, Brisbane.

Harding, A. (1995) 'Equity, Redistribution and the Tax Transfer System', *Equity and Citizenship Under Keating*, Beyond the Headlines, no 2, June, M. Hogan & K. Dempsey (eds.), Public Affairs Research Centre, Sydney, Chapter 1.

Harding, A. (1995), *Rich and Poor: The Two Faces of Australia*, Menzies Research Centre Seminar, June 27, Canberra.

Harding, A. & Fischer, S. (1996), *A Portrait of Affluence: Expenditure Patterns and Other Characteristics of the Top 10 per cent of Australians*, Paper Presented at the 25th Conference of Economists, Canberra, 23–25 September.

Harding, A. (1997), *The Suffering Middle: Trends in Income Inequality in Australia 1992–1993–1994*, NATSEM Discussion Paper, National Centre for Social and Economic Modelling, Canberra.

Harley, B. (1994), 'Post-Fordist Theory, Labour Process and Felxibility and Autonomy in Australian Workplaces', *Labour and Industry*, vol. 6, no. 1, pp. 107–129.

Harris, C. (1996) 'Productivity at the plant and industry levels in Australia', *Sources of Productivity Growth*, D.G. Mayes (ed.), Cambridge University Press, Cambridge.

Harrison, B. (1994), *Lean and Mean: The Changing Landscape of Corporate Power in the Age of Flexibility*, Basic Books, New York.

Hassard, J. (1990) (ed.), *The Sociology of Time*, Macmillan Press, London.

Heiler, K. (1996), *Is Enterprise Bargaining Good for Your Heath?*, ACIRRT Monograph no 14, ACIRRT, University of Sydney, Sydney.

Heiler, K. (1997) 'What Has Happened to Hours of Work in Australia or Do We Need to Bring Back the Bundy Clock', *Divided Work, Divided Society*, RIHSS (ed.), Research Institute for Humanities and Social Sciences, University of Sydney, Sydney.

Henwood, D. (1997), *Wall Street: How it Works and For Whom*, Verso, London & New York.

Hirst, P.Q. & Thompson, G. (1996), *Globalization in Question: The International Economy and the Possibilities of Governance*, Polity Press, Cambridge, U.K.

Hogan, M. & Dempsey, K. (1995) (eds.), *Equity and Citizenship Under Keating*, Beyond the Headlines, no 2, June, Public Affairs Research Centre, Sydney.

Horin, A. (1997), 'All Work, Low Pay', *Sydney Morning Herald*, 27 December, p. 6s.

Industry Commission (1995), *Australian Manufacturing Industry and International Trade Data 1968–69 to 1992–93*, Information Paper, February.

Industry Task Force on Leadership and Management Skills (1995), *Enterprising Nation: Renewing Australia's Managers to Meet the Challenges of the Asia-Pacific Century*, Karpin Report, AGPS, Canberra.

Isaac, J.E. (1960), 'Training for Skill', *Personnel Practice Bulletin*, June, vol. 14, no. 2.

Isaac, J.E. (1990), *The Australian Industrial Relations System: A Flexible Institution*, Paper given to the ACLIR Conference, July 7, ACIRLS, University of Melbourne, Parkville, Vic.

Jobsback: The Federal Coalition's Industrial Relations Policy (1992), Authorised and Printed by John Hewson and Tim Fischer, Parliament House, Canberra.

James, P., Veit, W. & Wright, S. (1997) (eds.), *Work of the Future- Global Perspectives*, Allen & Unwin, St. Leonards, NSW.

Jencks, C. & Peterson, P.E. (1991) (eds.), *The Urban Underclass*, Brookings Institution, Washington.

Johnson, K.H. (1995), 'Productivity and Unemployment: Review of the Evidence', *The OECD Jobs Study: Investment, Productivity and Unemployment*, OECD, Paris.

Katz, M.B. (1989), *The Underdeserving Poor: From the War on Poverty to the War on Welfare*, Pantheon Books, New York.

Kelly, P. (1994), *The End of Certainty: the Story of the 1980s*, Revised edn., Allen & Unwin, St. Leonards, NSW.

Kenyon, P. (1993), 'Policy Forum on Long-Term Unemployment: Introduction ', *The Australian Economic Review*, No. 2, Apr/June, pp. 19–21.

Kern, H. & Schumann, M. (1987), 'Limits of the Division of Labour, New Production and Employment Concepts in West German Industry', *Economic and Industrial Democracy*, vol. 8, pp. 151–170.

Kilmartin, C. (1996), 'Are Australian Workplaces Family Friendly ', *Family Matters*, no. 44, Winter, pp. 36–37.

Knowles, M. (1960), *The Modern Practices of Adult Education: Androgogy vs Pedagogy*, Associated Press, New York.

Kyloh, R. (1989), 'Flexibility and Structural Adjustment Through Consensus: Some Lessons from Australia', *International Labour Review*, vol. 128, no. 1, pp. 103–123.

Latham, M. (1998), *Civilising Global Capital*, Allen & Unwin, St Leonards, NSW.

Lattimore, R. (1989), *Capital Formation in Australian Manufacturing, 1954–55 to 1987–88*, Bureau of Industry Economics, Canberra.

Lawrence, G. (1987), *Capitalism and the Countryside*, Pluto Press, Sydney.

Leijon, A. (1988), *The Swedish Labour Market*, H V Evatt Research Centre, Sydney.

Lipietz, A. (1997) 'Economic Restructuring: the new global hierarchy', *Work of the Future Global Perspectives*, P. James, W. Veit & S. Wright (eds.), Allen & Unwin, St. Leonards, NSW.

Littler, C. (1996), 'Downsizing: Disease or Cure?', *HR Monthly*, August, pp. 8–12.

Littler, C. (1997), 'Downsizing Distemper', *Sydney Morning Herald*, October 21.

Littler, C., Dunford, R., Bramble, T. & Hede, A. (1997) ' The Dynamics of Downsizing in Australia and New Zealand', *Asia Pacific Journal of Human Resources*, vol. 35, no. 1, pp. 65–79.

Lowenstein, W. (1997), *Weevils at Work: What's Happening to Work in Australia: An Oral Record*, Catalyst Press, Annandale, NSW.

Ludeke, J.T. (1996), *The Line in the Sand: The Long Road to Staff Employment in Comalco*, Wilkinson, Melbourne.

Macfarlane, I.J. (1996), 'The Economy and Wages', *Reserve Bank of Australia Bulletin*, Talk to the Metal Trades Industry Association's National Personnel and Industrial Relations Group Conference, Canberra, May 2, pp. 17–22.

Macintyre, S. (1985), *Winners and Losers: The Pursuit of Social Justice in Australian History*, Allen & Unwin, Sydney.

Maddock, R. & Stilwell, F. (1987) 'Boom and Recession', *Australians from 1939*, A. Curthoys et al. (ed.), Fairfax, Syme & Weldon, Broadway, NSW.

Mager, R.F. (1984), *Measuring Instructional Results: Or got a match?*, Pitman, California.

Marshman, B. (1996) *The Employment of Apprentices: The Barriers.*, Report prepared for ANTA, Marshman & Associates.

Martin, H.P. & Schumann, H. (1998), *The Global Trap: Globalization and the Assault on Prosperity and Democracy*, Translated by P. Camiller, Pluto Press, Leichhardt, NSW.

Mathews, J. (1989a), *Tools of Change—New Technology and the Democratisation of Work*, Pluto Press, Sydney.

Matthews, J. (1989b), *Age of Democracy: The Politics of Post-Fordism*, Oxford University Press, Melbourne.

Mathews, J. (1990), *Assessing the cost effectiveness of alternative modes of serving adults, especially those with low levels of education and skills*, Report to OECD Further Education and Training of the Labour Force Project, OECD, Paris.

Mayes, D.G. (ed.) (1996), *Sources of Productivity Growth*, Cambridge University Press, Cambridge.

McCallum, R., McCarry, G., Ronfeldt, P.(eds.), (1994), *Employment Security*, Federation Press, Annandale, NSW.

McCallum, R. & Ronfeldt, P. (1995) 'Our changing labour law', *Enterprise Bargaining: Trade Unions and the Law*, P. Ronfeldt & R. McCallum (eds.), Federation Press, Annandale, NSW, pp. 1–30.

McClelland, A. (1995), 'Growth and Inequality: A Welfare Perspective', *Growth*, July, no. 43, July, pp. 116–135.

McDonald, T. & Rimmer, M. (1988), 'Award Structure and the Second Tier', *Australian Bulletin of Labour*, vol. 14, no. 3, June, pp. 469–491.

McDonald, T. & Rimmer, M. (1989), 'Award Restructuring and Wages Policy', *Growth*, no. 37, September, pp. 111–134.

McGuire, P. (1993), *Changes in Earnings Dispersion in Australia, 1975–1992*, A paper presented at the 1993 Conference of Economists, Perth, September, unpublished.

Michalandos, M. (1997), *The Legal Environment of Rostering and Shiftwork*, paper presented to the IIR Conference Rostering and Shiftwork, October 27–28, Sydney.

Minister for Employment, Education andTraining (1988), *Industry Training in Australia: The Need for Change*, DEET, Canberra.

Minister for Employment, Education andTraining (1989), *Improving Australia's Training System*, April, DEET, Canberra.

Ministers for Employment, Education and Training & Employment Services and Youth Affairs (1987), *Skills for Australia*, AGPS, Canberra.

Mishel, L. Bernstein, J. & Schmitt, J. (1997), *The State Of Working in America*, M.E. Sharpe, Armonk, New York & London.

Moody, K. (1997), *Workers in a Lean World Unions in the International Economy*, Verso, London & New York.

Morehead, A., Steele, M., Alexander, M., Stephen, K. & Duffin, L. (1997), *Change at Work: The 1995 Australian Workplace Industrial Relations Survey (AWIRS 95)*, Longman, South Melbourne.

Morden, T.J. (1997), 'A Strategic Evaluation of Re-Engineering, Restructuring, Delayering and Downsizing Policies as Flawed Paradigm', *Management Decision*, vol. 35, nos. 3–4, March-April, pp.240–249.

MTIA (Metal Trades Industry Association), (1989), *Industry Training in Australia: The Need for Change*, Submission to the Employment and Skills Formation Council, Discussion Paper, April, Sydney.

MTIA (1997), *Make or Break. Seven Steps to Make Australia Rich Again.*, A Report for MTIA by EIU Australia, MTIA and Economist Intelligence Unit Australia, North Sydney, NSW.

Murphy, K. (1997), 'Cheers, Jeers, Fears for Decision', *Australian Financial Review*, April 23, p. 11.

NLCC (National Labour Consultative Council) (1987), *Labour Market Flexibility in the Australian Setting*, AGPS, Canberra.

NLCC (1988), *Wages Policy and Productivity Improvement*, AGPS, Canberra.

NSW Department of Further Education Training and Employment (1990), *Apprenticeship Separation Analysis: Report of an Investigation into the Reasons for NSW Apprentices Separating from their Trades*, DFET, Sydney.

NSW Department of Industrial Relations (DIR) Women's Equity Bureau (1997), *Pay Equity and the Undervaluation of Women's Skills in NSW. Report of the NSW Pay Equity Task Force*, NSW DIR Women's Equity Bureau, Darlinghurst.

NSW Dept of Industrial Relations, Employment Training and Further Education (DIRETFE) *Regional Employer Profiles*, Report of an investigation into Employer Training Capacity for 3 Automotive Trades in the Western Sydney Region.

NSW Government (1905), *Report of the Commissioners on Agricultural, Commercial, Industrial and other Forms of Technical Education*, NSW Government Printer, Sydney.

NSW Pay Equity Taskforce (1996), *A Woman's Worth: Pay Equity and the Undervaluation of Women's Skills in NSW*, Womens' Equity Bureau, NSW DIR, Darlinghurst, NSW.

NSW Teachers' Federation (1996), *Annual Report, 1996*, The Federation, Sydney.

National Board of Employment Education and Training (NBEET) (1992), *Disadvantaged job seekers: Casual, Part-time and Temporary Work*, AGPS, Canberra.

National Training Council (1987), *Multiskilling Techniques*, A Case Study, Canberra.

Neale, W.C. (1986), 'Tax-Based Income Policies: A Commentary for the Future', *Journal of Economic Issues*, December, vol. XX, no. 4, pp. 969–987.

Nicholas Clark & Associates (1986), *Standards-Based Training—A Discussion Paper*, commissioned by the (then) National Training Council.

Niland, J. (1989), 'Wages Flexibility and the NSW Green Paper on IR', *Growth*, no. 37, pp. 91–110.

Nomchong, K. (1998) 'In Defence of the Right to Fairness at Work: Rights For Employees and Non-Employees—The Role of Section 106 of the Industrial Relations Act 1996 (NSW)', *Industrial Relations Under the NSW System—Emerging Issues and Challenges*, ACIRRT Working Paper No. 53, ACIRRT, University of Sydney, Sydney.

Norris, K. & Wooden, M. (1996) (eds.), *The Changing Australian Labour Market*, EPAC Commission Paper 11, AGPS, Canberra.

Nowak, M. J. (1979), 'Internal Labour Markets and the Market for Highly Qualified Labour', *Journal of Industrial Relations*, vol. 21, no. 1, March, pp. 20–34.

Nyland, C. (1990) 'Capitalism and Work-time Thought', *The Sociology of Time*, J. Hassard (ed.), Macmillan Press, London.

O'Donnell, C. & Hall, P. (1988), *Getting Equal*, Allen & Unwin, Sydney.

O'Loughlin, T. & Watson, I. (1997), *Loyalty is a One Way Street: NESB Immigrants and Long-Term Unemployment*, ACIRRT, University of Sydney, Sydney.

OECD (Organisation for Economic Cooperation and Development) (1995), *The OECD Jobs Study: Investment, Productivity and Employment*, OECD, Paris.

OECD (1996), *Employment Outlook*, July, OECD, Paris.

OECD (1998), *Employment Outlook, June, 1998*, OECD, Paris.

Office of the Employment Advocate (1998), *Monthly Update,* March.

Pearce, A., Bertone, S. & Stephens, J. (1995), *Surviving Retrenchment: Experiences of NESB Immigrant Workers in the Western Region of Melbourne*, AGPS, Canberra.

Peetz, D. (1990), 'Declining Union Density ', *Journal of Industrial Relations*, vol/32, no. 2, June, pp. 197–223.

Peetz, D. (1997), 'Deunionisation and Union Establishment: the Impact of Workplace Change, HRM Strategies and Workplace Unionism', *Labour and Industry*, vol. 8, no. 1, August, pp. 21–36.

Petre, D. (1988), *Father Time: Making Time for Your Children*, Macmillan, Sydney.

Phillips, J.J. (1991), *Handbook of Training Evaluation and Measurement Methods*, 2nd edition, Gulf Publishing Company, Houston.

Pickersgill, R. (1994), *National Systemic Review of the AVTS*, unpublished typescript, DEET.

Pickersgill, R. (1995), *Evaluation of the AVTS Pilots in TAFE NSW*, ACIRRT Report, TAFE NSW.

Pickersgill, R. (1996), *Who is Using the Competency Standards for Assessment?*, ACIRRT Report for the Workplace Trainers and Assessors Competency Standards Body.

Pilat, D. Prasada Rao, D.S. & Shepherd, W.F. (1993), *Australia & United States Manufacturing : A Comparison of Real Output, Productivity Levels and Purchasing Power, 1970–1989*, Comparison of Output, Productivity and Purchasing Power in

Australia and Asia (COPPAA) series, no. 1, Centre for the Study of Australia-Asia Relations, Griffith University, Brisbane.

Piore, M. & Sabel, C. (1984), *The Second Industrial Divide*, Basic, New York.

Polanyi, K. (1957), *The Great Transformation: The Political and Economic Origins of Our Time*, Beacon Press, Boston.

Powell, S. (1995), 'The Age of Overwork', *Australian*, Review section, April 8 & 9.

Pragnell, B. & Ronfeldt, P. (1994) 'Redundancy Under Enterprise Bargaining and New Federal Laws', *Employment Security*, R. McCallum, G. McCarry & P. Ronfeldt (eds.), Federation Press, Sydney, pp. 115–137.

Pusey, M. (1991), *Economic Rationalism in Canberra: A Nation-Building State Changes Its Mind*, Cambridge University Press, Cambridge & Melbourne.

Quiggin, J. (1996), *Great Expectations: Microeconomic Reform and Australia*, Allen & Unwin, Sydney.

Quiggin, J. & Langmore, J. (1994), *Work For All: Full Employment in the Nineties*, Melbourne University Press, Carlton, Victoria.

Rainbird, H. (1990), *Training Matters, Union Perspectives on Industrial Restructuring and Training*, Blackwell, Oxford, UK; Cambridge, Mass.

RIHSS (forthcoming) (ed.), *Divided Work, Divided Society*, Research Institute for Humanities and Social Sciences, University of Sydney, Sydney.

Rimmer, M. & Zappala, G. (1988), 'Labour Market Flexibility and the Second Tier', *Australian Bulletin of Labour*, vol. 14, no. 4, September, pp. 564–591.

Rollen, B. (1988), *Skills for Prosperity*, H V Evatt Research Centre, Sydney.

Romeyn J. (1994), *Flexible working-time arrangements: Fixed-term and temporary employment*, Industrial Relations Research Series No 13, Department of Industrial Relations, Canberra.

Ronfeldt, P. & McCallum, R. (1995) (eds.), *Enterprise Bargaining: Trade Unions and the Law*, Federation Press, Sydney.

Rose, N. (1996) 'Governing advanced liberal democracies', *Foucault and Political Reason*, A. Barry, T. Osborne & N. Rose (eds.), University College Press, London.

Ross, I. (1997), 'Reasons for Decision of Vice-President Ross', *Safety Net Review—Wages, April, Australian Industrial Relations Commission*, Melbourne.

Ross, L.L. & Fitz-Gibbon, C.T. (1978), *Evaluator's Handbook*, Sage Publications, Beverly Hills.

Rubery, J. (1998), *Women and European Employment*, Routledge, London & New York.

Schedvin, C.B. (1987), 'The Australian Economy on the Hinge of History', *The Australian Economic Review*, 1st quarter.

Schmid, G. (1995), 'Is Full Employment Still Possible? Transitional Labour Markets As A New Strategy of Labour Market Policy', *Economic and Industrial Democracy*, vol. 16, no. 3.

Schmid, G., O'Reilly, J. & Schomann, K. (eds.) (1996), *International Handbook of Labour Market Policy and Evaluation*, Edward Edgar, Cheltenham, U.K.

Schor, J. (1992) *The Overworked American:the Unexpected Disappearance of Leisure*, Basic Books, New York.

Scott, A. (1991), *Fading Loyalties: The Australian Labor Party and the Working Class*, Pluto Press, Leichhardt, NSW.

Scott, D.J. (1992), 'A Review of Training and Development in Australia in 1991', *Asia Pacific Journal for Human Resources*, vol. 30, no. 2, Winter, pp. 25–29.

Selznick, P. (1969), *Law, Society and Industrial Justice*, Russell Sage Foundation, New York.

Sheehan, P. Pappas, N. Cheng, E. & et al., E. (1994), *The Rebirth of Australian Industry: Australian Trade in Elaborately Transformed Manufactures 1979–1993*, Centre for Strategic Economic Studies, Victoria, University of Technology, Melbourne.

Sheldrake, J. & Vickerstaff, S. (1987), *The History of Industrial Training in Britain*, Avebury, Aldershot, UK; Brookfield, USA.

Short, M. Romeyn, J.E. & Callus, R. (1994), *Reform and Bargaining at the Workplace and Enterprise: Evidence from Two Surveys*, Industrial Relations Research Series No. 12, Department of Industrial Relations, Canberra.

Short, M., Preston, A.E. & Peetz, D. (1993), *The Spread and Impact of Workplace Bargaining: Evidence from the Workplace Bargaining Project*, AGPS, Canberra.

Simpson, M. (1994), *An Analysis of the Characteristics and Growth of Easual employment in Australia, 1984–1992*, Discussion Paper 94/5, WA Labour Market Research Centre, Perth.

Smith, A. (1992), *Training and Development in Australia*, Butterworths, Sydney.

Social Justice Consultative Committee (1992), *Economic Restructuring and Job Loss*, SJCC, Melbourne.

Social Policy Research Centre (SPRC) (1998), *Development of Indicative Budget Standards for Australia,* SPRC, University of New South Wales, Kensington.

Spence, K. (1996), 'Stress! Burnout! Among Teachers', *Independent Education*, December, vol. 26, no. 4, pp. 3–6.

Spoehr, J. & Shanahan, M. (1994), *Alternatives to Retrenchment: Job Retention and Structural Adjustment in a Regional Economy*, Centre for Labour Studies, University of Adelaide, Adelaide.

Spurgeon, A. Harrington, J.M. & Cooper, C.L. (1997), 'Health and Safety Problems Associated with Working Long Hours: A Review of the Current Position', *Occupational and Environmental Medicine*, vol. 54, no. 6, pp. 367–375.

Streeck, W. (1989), 'Skills and the limits of neo-liberalism: the enterprise of the future as a place of learning', *Work, Employment and Society*, vol. 3, no. 1, pp. 89-104.

Study Group on Structural Adjustment (1979), *Report, 1979 / Study Group on Structural Adjustment*, AGPS, Canberra.

Sweet, M. (1996), 'High Fliers Glide to a Calmer Place', *Sydney Morning Herald*, January 4, 1996.

Swenson, P. (1991), 'Bringing Capital Back In, Or Social Democracy Reconsidered: Employer Power, Cross-Class Alliances and Centralization of Industrial Relations in Denmark and Sweden', *World Politics*, no. 43, pp. 513–544.

Sydney Morning Herald (1996), 'The Potential Killer that Lurks in your Mind', 3 January, p. 1.

Taylor, F.W. (1915), *The Principles of Scientific Management*, Harper & Brothers, New York.

Taylor, F.W. (1919), *Two Papers on Scientific Management. A Piece Rate System and Notes on Belting*, George Routledge & Sons, London.

Taylor, V. & Yerbury, D. (1985) 'Australia', *Managing Workforce Reduction*, M. Cross (ed.), Croom Helm, London.

Teicher, J. (1996) (ed.), *Non Standard Employment in Australia and New Zealand*, NKCIR Monograph 9, National Key Centre in Industrial Relations, Monash University, Melbourne.

Textile, Clothing and Footwear Union of Australia (1995), *The Hidden Cost of Fashion: The Report of the National Artwork Information Campaign*, TCFU, Sydney.

Textile, Clothing and Footwear Union of Australia (1996), *S113 Application to Vary An Award, Clothing Trades Award 1982*, Cat no. 33902 of 1996, A Living Wage Case Submission.

Thompson, R. 'Competency Based Training: An Industry Learning Experience', *Asia Pacific HRM*, vol. 27, no. 3, August, pp. 86–91.

Time, 23 March 1998, pp. 54–57.

Training Costs Review Committee (1990), *Training Costs of Award Restructuring. Report of the Training Costs Review Committee*, vol 1, The Report, AGPS, Canberra.

Training Costs Review Committee (1990), *Training Costs of Award Restructuring. Report of the Training Costs Review Committee*, vol 2, Supporting Papers, AGPS, Canberra.

Turner, M. (1983), *Stuck! Unemployed people talk to Michele Turner*, Penguin, Ringwood, Vic.

VEETAC (Vocational Education, Employment and Training Advisory Committee) (1992), Assessment of Performance Under Competency-Based Training: Administration of Competency-Based Training, VEETAC, Darlinghurst, NSW.

Vamplew W.E. (1987) (ed.), 'Australians, Historical Statistics', *Australians, A Historical Library,* Fairfax, Syme & Weldon, Broadway, NSW, vol. 10.

Vandenheuvel, A. & Wooden, M. (1995) *Self-Employed Contractors in Australia: What Are the Facts*, NILS Working Paper no. 136, National Institute of Labour Studies, Adelaide.

Von Otter, C. (1995), 'Employment Pools: A Common Resource Approach to the Labour Market', *Economic and Industrial Democracy*, vol. 16, no. 2, pp. 301–313.

Webber, M. & Campbell, I. (1996), *Labour Market Outcomes Among Retrenched Workers in Australia: A Review*, Working Paper 44, NKCIR, Melbourne.

Webber, M.J. & Rigby, D.L. (1996), *The Golden Age Illusion: Rethinking Postwar Capitalism*, The Guilford Press, New York.

Williams, K., Haslam, C., Johal, S.E. & Williams, J. (1994), *Cars: Analysis, History, Cases*, Bergahn Books, Providence, R.I.

Williams, K. Haslam, C. Williams, J. Johal, S. Adcroft, A. & Willis, R. (1995), 'The Crisis of Cost Recovery and the Waste of the Industrialised Nations', *Competition and Change*, vol. 1, pp. 67–93.

Willis, E.E. (1988), *Technology and the Labour Process: Australasian Case Studies*, Allen & Unwin, Sydney.

Wilson, W.J. (1991) 'Public Policy Research and "The Truly Disadvantaged"', *The Urban Underclass*, C. Jencks & P.E. Peterson (eds.), Brookings Institution, Washington.

Windsor, K. (1991), *Skill Counts: How to Conduct Gender- Bias Free Skills Audits*, AGPS, Canberra.

Withers, G. (1982), 'The Concerned Politician's Guide to Countering Inflation and Unemployment', *Australian Bulletin of Labour*, vol. 9, no. 1, December, pp. 55–68.

Witts, P. (1998), 'Banks Rule, Okay?', *Weekend Australian*, Cover IT Section, May 23–24, pp. 4 5.

Wolff, E.N. (1987), *Growth, Accumulation and Unproductive Activity*, Cambridge University Press, Cambridge & New York.

Wooden, M. (1988), 'The Impact of Redundancy on Subsequent Labour Market Experience', *Journal of Industrial Relations*, vol. 30, no. 1, March, pp. 3–31.

Wooden, M. & Sloan, J. (1987), 'Plant Shutdown: A Case Study in Managed Change', *Australian Bulletin of Labour*, vol. 14, no. 1, December, pp. 358–381.

World Yearbook of Education, 1995 (1995), Kogan Page, London.

Wright, E.O. (1978), *Class, Crisis and the State*, Verso, London.

Index

Accord, the 6–7, 57
    emergence of 21–22
agreements, *see* enterprise bargaining, non-
    union agreements
arbitration system
    New Right and the 25
Asian labour 14
Australian Industrial Relations Commission
    25–26
    decentralisation and the 63
    enterprise bargaining 40
    restricted powers 42
Australian Workplace Agreements 26, 42, 76
    working time arrangements and 114
'award stripping' 65
award system 13, 15, 65

basic wage 15, 17, 173
    see also 'living wage'

'casino capitalism' 27
Chifley, Ben 14, 17
collective bargaining 41
cost-cutting 4–6, 8
    working arrangements and 112, 122

decentralisation 37–41
    non-union agreements 49–51
    the AIRC and 63
    trade unions and 57–61
    wages system 75–76

'dependent contractor' 84
Depression, the 12, 14
deregulation
    and the AIRC 25–6
    financial system 21, 27
    Labor Party and 26
downsizing 6, 11, 52–54
    workplace insecurity and 147–50

economy
    history 12
    key problems 11
employee
    portability and entitlements 169–71
    status 167–68
employment
    casual/temporary 138–41
    decline and growth 130–31
    full 15, 17, 162
    jobs satisfaction 118–19
    part-time 136–39
    replacing and retaining jobs 133
    security 175–76
    see also job insecurity, retrenchment,
        unemployment
enterprise bargaining 6–7, 22, 41–3
    Enterprise Bargaining Principle 40
    Enterprise Flexibility Agreements 41
    family-friendly measures 123–25
    focus 51
    hours of work and 112–13
    Labor and 25
    linking wages to work arrangements 51
    non-union agreements 49–51, 61
    regulation 52
    Restructuring and Efficiency Principle 37
    Structural Efficiency Principle 38–40
    wage increase dispersion 79–80
enterprise bargaining agreements 44–6
    assessing 48–49
    components 46
    wage rises and 47, 51
extended operating hours 119–21

family-friendly workplace measures 123–25

globalisation 8, 10, 31
    industry policy 163
    policy dilemma 157–60
    policy fairness 164
    tax reform 164

'gold-collar' workers 3
'golden age', the 15
guaranteed minimum income 174

H. R. Nicholls Society 24
Harvester judgment 13
Hawke, Bob on micro-economic reform 36

income inequality 2, 12
    gender and 74–75
    government intervention 69–70
    occupational dispersions 81–84
industrial relations
    decentralisation 37–41
    rule-making 51–52
'Industrial Relations Club' 25
industry competition 16
international competition 31

job insecurity 126–7, 147, 154
    workplace change and 153–54
    see also employment, unemployment,
      retrenchment

Karpin Report 30
Keating, Paul
    and the mining industry 24
    on industrial relations 40–1
    on wealth 19
Kelley, Paul 12, 21–2
Kelty, Bill 58
Keynesian economics 15, 18–19, 21–22

Labor Party
    deregulation 26
    enterprise bargaining 40
    legacy 162
    values in the 1980s 21
    wage fixing 25–26
labour
    as a commodity 15
    productivity 16–17, 31–32
labour market
    'losers' 3
    'winners' 3
    bottom end 69
    change 2, 136–39
    character formation 13–15
    full-time 1
    in the 1980s 19–20
    mobility 133
    part-time 3
    policy recommendations 169–71

policy-making 160–64
post-war regulation 13–14
protection 14, 86–87
segmentation 86–90
standards 173–74
top end 67–69
transformed 17
transitional 169–71
'leisure society' 101
Liberal–National Party workplace reform 26
'living wage' 64–65, 95, 175
low-paying jobs 90
    childcare workers 99–100
    deregulated market and 93
    Europe 93–94
    individual implications 94–95
    social costs 95–99
    standard of living 100
    United Kingdom 91–92
    United States 90
    working poor 90
macro-economic policy-making 161–65
management
    changing the workplace 54–57
    enterprise bargaining and 48–49
    power 6–7
    power consolidation 33
    prerogative and AWAs 26
    workplace flexibility 112, 119, 122
manufacturing 11–12
    farmers and 23
    full-time jobs 66
    malaise in the 1970s and 1980s 27–28
    research and development 30
    transition 28–29
    unemployment and 129, 131
McEwen, 'Black Jack' 23
micro-economic reform
    ACTU and 37
    agenda 32
    Bob Hawke and 36
    emergence of 19–20
    Labor Party and 22
mining and investment 27–28
monetarism 16, 161

neo-liberalism 8–9, 15
    globalisation and 157–58
neo-liberal project 11, 20, 76
    and wage determination 100
    outcomes 156–57
'New Protectionism' 14, 158
non-union agreements 49–51, 61

occupational income dispersions 81–83
Office of Employment Advocate 42
One Nation Party, protectionism 158
outsourcing 142–45
   across industries 146
over-award payments 85–85
overtime 104–5
   culture 111–12
   see also work intensity, working time
      arrangements
overwork *see* work intensity

policy-making
   fairness 164
   full-employment 162, 175
   globalisation and 157–60
   industry 163
   macro-economic 161–65
   needs 176
   state intervention and 18
   tax reform 163–64
   wages 173
poverty 17–18, 94
   see also low-paying jobs
productivity 16–17
   decline 17, 31–32
   pursuit of 32

Restructuring and Efficiency Principle 37–38
retrenchment 132–33
rural producers and manufacturers 23

salaried staff 7
self-employment 84–85, 110
   see also outsourcing
social protection 34, 125
'social settlement' 10–11
   dismantling 15–16
   new 175
   post-war 12–15, 17
stagflation 19
stress 3, 107–8
   of retrenchment 132–33
Structural Efficiency Principle 38–40

technological change 68
trade unions
   at the workplace 61–62
   membership decline 57–61
   'New Right' and 25

unemployment 127–29
   addressing 161–63

casualties 129–30
long-term 132–33
manufacturing and 129, 131
poverty and 17
real rate of 128
white-collar 132
unions
   the Accord and 6
   labour market change and 7

wages
   award only 77
   classification scheme 84–86
   decentralised system 75–77
   determination 47, 64, 75
   enterprise bargaining 47
   fixing 25, 83
   in the recessions 72–73
   increase dispersion 79–80
   linked to work arrangements 51
   tax system regulating 173–74
   see also income inequality, low-paying
     jobs
wealth distribution 65
   'disappearing middle' 66, 90
   bottom end 69
   top end 67–69, 75
welfare state 14
White Australia policy 14
Whitlam, G. 20
Willis, Ralph 22
women in the labour force 19
work intensity 5–6, 32, 175
   by industry 107–9
   overwork 106, 115–18
   stress 3, 107–8
workers
   decision-making process 54–57
   redefined 142–45
working hours 4–5, 32
working poor 90
working time arrangements 44
   assessing 115–18
   bargaining 112–14
   by occupation 103–5
   career building and 109–10
   culture 119–21
   flexibility 122–23
   recommended policy 174–75
   standard 101, 119–22
   weekends and 110, 121

workplace
    decision-making 54–57
    family-friendly 123–25
    flexibility 112, 119
    individualising 33
    pressures 3–4
    reform 8, 19
    regulation framework 169–71
    restructuring 150–53
    stress 3, 107–8
    union representation 61–62
workplace change 1–6, 52–54, 119, 136–39
    causes of 11
    productivity and 16
    results of 156–57
Workplace Relations Act 26, 41–42